The Bellwomen

The Bellwomen

The Story of the Landmark AT&T Sex Discrimination Case

Marjorie A. Stockford

Rutgers University Press

New Brunswick, New Jersey, and London

Library of Congress Cataloging-in-Publication Data

Stockford, Marjorie A., 1957–

    The bellwomen : the story of the landmark AT&T sex discrimination case / Marjorie A. Stockford.
        p.   cm.

Includes bibliographical references and index.

    ISBN 0-8135-3428-3 (hardcover : alk. paper)

    1. American Telephone and Telegraph Company—Trials, litigation, etc.   2. Sex discrimination
against women—Law and legislation—United States.   3. Sex discrimination in employment—Law
and legislation—United States.   I. Title.

    KF2849.A4S76   2004

    344.7301′4133—dc22

                                                                                2003019800

A British Cataloging-in-Publication record is available for this book from the British Library.

Design by Karolina Harris

Manufactured in the United States of America

For
Becky, Eva, Meriwether,
and
Kanha

Contents

Preface

The Bellwomen is based in large part on interviews with dozens of individuals who were directly or peripherally involved in, or who benefited from, the landmark 1973 employment discrimination settlement between the American Telephone and Telegraph Company (AT&T) and the U.S. government. In the text, all direct quotes from these interviews or from documents or transcripts related to the case are in quotation marks. All quotes that were recounted to me in recent interviews from conversations held thirty years ago are in italics.

The story of the case unfolds in chronological order, from November 1970 to January 1973. Interspersed in this sequential narrative are profiles of three women—Peggy Falterman, Gwen Thomas, and Margaret Hoppe—who eventually benefited from the case's resolution.

Cast of Key Characters

The Government

Equal Employment Opportunity Commission (EEOC)

Bill Brown, chairperson

Susan Ross, attorney, General Counsel's Office

Judy Potter, lead attorney, AT&T case

Jack Pemberton, acting general counsel

Charlie Wilson, director, Office of Conciliations

Bill Oldaker, assistant to the chair

Phyllis Wallace, witness coordinator

- **EEOC's AT&T Task Force**

David Copus, attorney and task force chair

Larry Gartner, attorney

Randy Speck, investigator

Bill Wallace, researcher

Katherine Mazzaferri, law student

Marjie Fagan, secretary

- **Key EEOC Witnesses**

Sandra and Daryl Bem, psychology professors, Stanford University

Judith Long Laws, assistant professor, sociology/psychology,
    Cornell University

Bernard Anderson, associate professor, industry, Wharton School,
    University of Pennsylvania

Lorena Weeks, Southern Bell employee

Helen Roig, South Central Bell employee

Gay Semel, New York Telephone operator

Federal Communications Commission (FCC)

Frederick Denniston, hearings examiner

Jim Juntilla, hearings attorney

Ruth Baker, hearings attorney

Jenny Longo, hearings attorney
George Sape, attorney

General Services Administration (GSA)
Ed Mitchell, director, Civil Rights Office
Arthur Sampson, administrator

Department of Labor
Bill Kilberg, associate solicitor, labor relations and civil rights, Office
    of Federal Contract Compliance (OFCC)
Phil Davis, director, OFCC
Dick Schubert, solicitor
Carin Clauss, associate solicitor, fair labor standards, and director,
    Equal Pay Act
Karl Heckman, attorney, Equal Pay Act

Department of Justice
David Rose, attorney

White House
Richard Nixon, president
Len Garment, special consultant

U.S. District Court, Pennsylvania
Judge Leon Higginbotham

The Corporation
American Telephone and Telegraph (AT&T)
H. I. (Hi) Romnes, chairman of the board and chief executive officer,
    January 1967–April 1972
John deButts, vice chairman, February 1967–April 1972; chairman
    of the board and chief executive officer, April 1972–February 1979
Bob Lilley, executive vice president, January 1970–April 1972;
    president, April 1972–March 1976
Alvin von Auw, executive vice president and assistant to the
    chairman
Horace Moulton, general counsel during 1970 and most of 1972

Mark Garlinghouse, general counsel beginning late 1972

Rex Reed, vice president, labor relations

George Ashley, attorney, regulatory (FCC) matters

Hal Levy, attorney, regulatory (FCC) matters

William Mercer, vice president, personnel, during 1970 and until
    December 1971

Dave Easlick, vice president, personnel, from December 1971 into
    1973

John Kingsbury, assistant vice president, personnel

Don Liebers, director, employment

Dan Davis, director, Equal Employment Opportunity Office

Lee Satterfield, attorney, government relations

Clark Redick, attorney, labor law

Charlie Ryan, general attorney, labor law

Bell Operating Company (BOC) Attorneys

Walt Maneker, New York Telephone

William Diedrich, Pacific Telephone and Telegraph

Outside Counsel

Tom Powers, Steptoe and Johnson

Jane Lang, Steptoe and Johnson

James Hutchinson, Steptoe and Johnson

Key AT&T Witnesses

Robert Ferguson, assistant vice president, Traffic Department

Joe Hunt, assistant vice president, Plant Department

Therese Pick, employment benefits secretary

Robert Guion, professor of psychology, Bowling Green State University

Frank Coss, advertising executive

Leona Tyler, professor emeritus, psychology, University of Oregon

The Unions

International Brotherhood of Electrical Workers (IBEW)

Elihu Leifer, attorney

Communications Workers of America (CWA)

Joseph Beirne, president

Richard Hackler, assistant to the president

The Advocates

National Organization for Women (NOW)

Wilma Scott Heide, president

Ann Scott, vice president, legislative affairs

Whitney Adams, chair, FCC Task Force

Center for United Labor Action (CULA)

Mary Pinotti

Gavrielle Gemma

Kathy Dennis

Luella Smith

Other

Dave Cashdan, attorney for civil rights groups

The Media

Eileen Shanahan, *New York Times*

Jack Anderson, *Washington Post*

The Beneficiaries

Peggy Falterman, Southern/South Central Bell

Gwen Thomas, New England Telephone

Margaret Hoppe, AT&T Long Lines

Abbreviations

ACLU	American Civil Liberties Union
AT&T	American Telephone and Telegraph
BFOQ	bona fide occupational qualification
BOC	Bell Operating Company
BSQT	Bell System Qualification Test
C&P	Chesapeake and Potomac Telephone
CRLA	California Rural Legal Assistance
CULA	Center for United Labor Action
CWA	Communications Workers of America
DOL	Department of Labor
EEOC	Equal Employment Opportunity Commission
FCC	Federal Communications Commission
GSA	General Services Administration
IBEW	International Brotherhood of Electrical Workers
MALDEF	Mexican American Legal Defense and Educational Fund
MARC	Metropolitan Applied Research Center
MDP	Management Development Program
MIT	Massachusetts Institute of Technology
NAACP	National Association for the Advancement of Colored People
NET	New England Telephone and Telegraph
NOW	National Organization for Women
OFCC	Office of Federal Contract Compliance
PEPCO	Potomac Electric Power Company
PSC	Public Service Commission
PT&T	Pacific Telephone and Telegraph
SDS	Students for a Democratic Society
SMSA	Standard Metropolitan Statistical Area

The Bellwomen

Introduction

One day not so long ago, women became a common part of the American workforce. When this transformation happened is subject to debate. Perhaps it occurred in 1985, when for the first time more than 50 percent of adult American women held paying jobs.[1] Or it may have taken place in 1990, when Doubleday published *The Female Advantage,* which celebrated women's business skills instead of encouraging women to emulate men, the approach taken by many earlier advice books. Or possibly the year of transformation was 1992, when the number of female owners of U.S. businesses crossed the five-million mark, meaning they led more than one-third of all small firms.[2]

The signs of this change were unmistakable. Thirty-something women leading marketing meetings or flying business class to London no longer appeared unusual. A female construction worker, wearing a hard hat and driving a bulldozer, didn't evoke surprise. A woman paying the bill after a lunch with male co-workers seemed almost normal. She fit in, this woman at work—in a bus driver's seat, at a political rally, with a reporter's notebook in hand, behind a corporate conference table. She had become integral, at least in appearance, to an American workplace.

Not that these late-twentieth-century women are pioneers. American women had worked outside their homes since the country's birth, particularly poorer women, needing to find whatever paid job they could. Middle-class women joined them during World War II when there weren't enough men at home to staff the factories. All along, there were exceptional women of every economic class who bucked their husbands and communities to become doctors, police officers, or whatever type of worker they chose.

Today's working women, however, still aren't triumphant. They haven't achieved equality with men in either pay or responsibility. Women's salaries in 2000 languished at just over 75 percent of those of their male counter-parts,[3] and in 2002 there were only eleven female CEOs of U.S. Fortune 1000 corporations.[4] In addition, corporations haven't yet implemented policies enabling parents to hold their jobs easily and ensure their children's care si-multaneously, a deficiency that disproportionately hurts women's incomes and careers.

But these working women *have* achieved something. When they reached a critical mass, it changed the way we—Americans, both men and women—saw a woman's role in society. No longer just supportive wives, moms, or house cleaners, women had become wage earners whose salaries were needed, in many families, to meet the monthly bills. Moreover, they proved themselves to be legitimate independent participants in the U.S. economy. Most important, they had been accepted. Politicians began to pander to them; advertisers targeted them as consumers with their own money, not just their husbands' checkbooks; the country's financial stability came to de-pend on them. When there were too many women at work to ignore, woman herself took on an additional dimension.

This shift seemed to happen suddenly, as if one day women were every-where, but like any major social change, it actually occurred slowly, spurred on by several influences including the second wave of feminism of the 1960s. Women read *The Feminine Mystique* and rejected the world it portrayed, wanting more than the boredom and mundane life of a housewife. House-wives and career girls attended consciousness-raising groups and strategized how to improve their marriages and get decent jobs. Feminist leaders formed the National Organization for Women to advocate for women's rights, in-cluding their right to work at levels equal to those of men.

Legislation, the muscle essential to force male-dominated and -led com-panies to change their policies, was also needed. In response to civil rights leaders' advocacy in the mid-1960s, President Lyndon Johnson introduced legislation that prohibited discrimination based on race. Then a clever con-gresswoman, Martha Griffiths, one of only twelve in the House, tagged a prohibition against sex discrimination onto the bill. It passed in 1964 as the Civil Rights Act, which outlawed discrimination against minorities and women, including in the workplace.

However, legislation is useful only when someone puts it into action. In late 1970, that someone, a young government lawyer named David Copus, came along. As he was male, white, and privileged and had never suffered discrimination himself, he was an unlikely candidate to fight for women's rights, and the team of committed colleagues who would join him would prove no more appropriate for the job. Yet the innovative idea Copus conceived and the hard work he and his co-workers put in over the next twenty-six months would force the country's largest company, AT&T, to give its female employees equal access to all company jobs, beginning an avalanche that would eventually spread through the American workplace. By the time the case was resolved in January 1973, women had begun filling jobs at salaries they never could have hoped to attain before, and separate roles at work, for both women and men, had been eliminated. American culture and the American workplace had been changed forever.

Beneficiary Profile:
Peggy Falterman

When Peggy Falterman graduated from the technical drafting program at her local community college in late 1966, she couldn't find a job. She visited the only architectural firm in her hometown, Thibodaux, Louisiana, after graduation, and the partners generously reviewed her portfolio, telling her *You do nice work* but that they had no openings. As disappointed as she was, she had to try something else. She was eighteen years old, six months out of high school, with strict parents who were anxious for her to find a job, quickly, close to home.

Fortunately, her neighbor's sister, who worked for the phone company in Houma, Louisiana, about twenty miles from Falterman's house, had another suggestion. Houma, nearly twice the size of Thibodaux with thriving oil and seafood industries, offered far more job opportunities than its smaller Cajun cousin. At that time, the Traffic Department in Southern Bell's Houma office was hiring telephone operators, a position the company typically filled with candidates just like Falterman—young white women from the community. The acquaintance even put in a good word for Falterman with the office's manager, a big boost to her application, since knowing someone who worked at the phone company was one of the straightest routes to getting hired. Before long, Falterman was running through a battery of tests in Southern Bell's personnel office in Houma, which evaluated her dexterity to run an operator's cordboard and her intellectual aptitude to respond to callers' queries. She worried she might not pass because some of the questions seemed "weird," like "which weighs more—a barrel of apples or oranges?"[1] She was pleasantly surprised when the personnel supervisor called with a job offer in late December and a start date of January 12, 1967.

Falterman, tall, pretty, and slight with brown hair that fell to her waist, had been determined to "stand on my own two feet and take care of myself" since she was a young child. Her parents had sent her to Catholic school and severely limited her dating as a teenager. As a result, she longed to spread her wings—to travel beyond Thibodaux, to New Orleans and maybe someday even around the world. When she compared her father, who left the house every morning at dawn to start his Sunshine Biscuit sales route, with her mother, who stayed behind to cook and clean for a handful of kids, Falterman knew she needed to follow in her dad's footsteps and "go out and be in the working world." Probably she would later marry and have a family, but for now she wanted to ensure that she could take care of herself just in case she had to someday.

Living in a small town with few good job opportunities close by, Falterman's family and friends were impressed when they heard about her new position. Employment at the phone company meant benefits and, most of all, security; "once you got hired, you'd be there for life" is the envious slogan Falterman remembers hearing often. At the time, though, the job's weekly paycheck and the independence it implied meant more to her. She could pay off the Chevy coupe her father had begrudgingly put a down payment on and start saving for her future adventures beyond Thibodaux.

But once she started the job, she didn't actually like it very much. Responding to the same queries for telephone numbers, from the same people it seemed, every day, hour after hour, Falterman found that the work got unbearably monotonous incredibly fast. She couldn't complain about the office physically considering that the air-conditioning was on almost all the time, but the working environment made it oppressive. The crew of all-female supervisors treated their charges like soldiers: they had to dress alike (in a skirt that fell below the knee during an era when young women's closets housed only miniskirts), arrive exactly on time, and enter the operators' room en masse at the shift's start. Once Falterman and her colleagues were at their consoles, the supervisors paced behind them to be sure they sat up straight, stared directly ahead, and never spoke a single word to the operators sitting on their left and right, though each was only six inches away. In addition, many of Falterman's co-workers had to work split shifts—a few hours in the morning, then a few hours more in the evening of the same day—a fate she escaped because of her long commute.

The worst treatment Falterman faced related to something beyond the job. Each operator had to raise her hand if she needed to use the bathroom, as if she were in grade school, with permission granted only if someone could fill her spot. One Sunday, after a late night out with friends, Falterman came to work feeling a little ill. When no one came to relieve her after several minutes with her hand up, she unplugged her operator's console, announced to her supervisor that she was about to be sick, and ran to the bathroom. The supervisor followed in close pursuit, leaving Falterman alone only when she witnessed for herself that Falterman was telling the truth. No wonder Ernestine, the nasal-challenged telephone operator on TV's *Laugh-In*, was so nasty to her callers.

When Falterman arrived at work each day, anywhere she looked she saw white women and no one else. The men who oversaw her supervisor and the other supervisors in the office rarely appeared on the operators' floor, and in this era the company almost never hired black women, even at this lowest of all entry-level jobs. And there were, of course, no male operators because, as everyone knew, it was a woman's job.

One day, after Falterman had been working for Southern Bell for about a year, her supervisor unexpectedly called her to her desk. *You're such a nice polite girl,* she said, *but you look like you're really not interested in doing this work.*

Falterman wasn't sure where the supervisor was headed but figured she might as well answer honestly. *You're right,* she responded. *I don't like the work at all.*

Well, what do you want to do?

I took a drafting course when I finished high school. I really would like to do something more like that. She didn't expect anything would come of it because she didn't think any supervisor in the office cared about her employees.

To Falterman's surprise, however, her supervisor volunteered to help. In retrospect, Falterman surmises that because the woman was older and had survived several surgeries, she had developed a sympathetic side her peers lacked. Falterman may not have been aware of another possibility: doing what was feasible to keep a company employee satisfied in her job, even an underperforming operator, was the Bell System way. Whatever the supervisor's motive, she told Falterman, *I have a friend in engineering,* referring to one of the other Southern Bell departments in Houma. *I'll call him and see if he has any openings.*

A month later, the supervisor reported back to Falterman with the perfect opportunity—a job as a drafting clerk in the Houma Engineering Department. The office's manager chose Falterman soon after she bid on the job, and she quietly and gratefully exited her operator's hell.

Two years passed before Falterman again became bored with her job, now with South Central Bell, which had split from Southern Bell in the summer of 1968. At first, she had liked being a drafting clerk, redrawing the sketches of cables so that outside technicians would know where to install them. Plus, with no supervisor breathing down her neck and the ability to wear her bell-bottom jeans to work, the environment was far more comfortable. But with budget crunches, her work had now deteriorated to simply correcting errors on drawings made by someone else. Again the ensuing ennui she exhibited worked in her favor. Now rated unsatisfactory and fearful of being fired, she was again pleasantly surprised when her supervisor's boss—her second-level manager in Bell System terminology—offered her a job as a facilities appraisal clerk, whereby she would travel from central office to central office around the state, testing lines to make sure they weren't noisy. She jumped at the chance, having loved the job when she filled in temporarily six months before while the incumbent was out sick. There was just one caveat, the manager said when he offered Falterman the job permanently one Friday—she had to report for work in New Orleans, sixty miles away, the following Monday morning. With a sister who had an apartment there and her drafting clerk's job already in jeopardy, Falterman agreed without hesitation. Although her father made it clear he wasn't happy that his just-turned-twenty-one-year-old, still single daughter was leaving home, she didn't care. She headed off to the big city.

As expected, Falterman couldn't have been happier in her new assignment, particularly enjoying the travel, which, even if it didn't take her around the world, at least had gotten her out of Thibodaux. She drove a company car, stayed in nice hotels, ate meals paid for by the company, and flew home, if necessary, for the weekend. She may have started in the worst job imaginable, but now Ma Bell couldn't have been taking better care of her.

Or so she thought. Her travels around Louisiana were starting to open her eyes about other jobs under the Bell System umbrella, with her curiosity sparked about one in particular. In each location, she observed framemen who climbed physical frames to connect wires creating each individual telephone circuit that transported phone conversations or data transmissions. It looked like fun to her, "doing something with your hands, a job where you could see what you were [accomplishing]." Once or twice, she asked the men in the offices she visited, *How can I get that job?*

But the response was always the same. *Oh, women don't get those jobs.*

That didn't seem fair to Falterman because she knew she could do it and couldn't see what difference her gender made. Plus, she had recently checked the salary list in the union book, which showed, in black and white, that she could earn up to 50 percent more working on the frame. As much as she loved her job, as fun as it was to travel and meet new people and eat nice meals out, it was slowly becoming clear that she was stuck where she was. But she needed a job, she worked for a great company, and, most important, she knew there was nothing she—a low-level, nonmanagement employee—could do to change her predicament. She swallowed her frustration, kept her bags packed, and focused on enjoying her peripatetic life as much as she could.

1

The Idea

November 1970

David Copus had seen one type of complaint in his job as an Equal Employment Opportunity Commission (EEOC) lawyer so many times, he had nearly memorized it. An unwed African American mother living in Georgia or Mississippi couldn't get a job in her local phone company office. Sometimes, the complaints had a twist—a few came from white women who already worked for the American Telephone and Telegraph (AT&T) division in their state but couldn't get promoted out of a telephone operator's or clerk's job. Some even came from black women who lived north of the Mason-Dixon line and had managed to get hired by Ma Bell, AT&T's nickname, but couldn't rise to a better-paying job there either. All together, there were so many that Copus's brain was getting as cluttered as his desk.

The complaints came almost exclusively from women, a fact Copus would later prioritize, but now, since black women had filed most of the charges, they became his focus. He didn't actually sympathize with them. They lived in a world entirely separate from his, an island with no bridge to his experiences. He had known a few blacks, mostly maids working for his or his friends' families, while growing up in Texas, and he'd had classes with some at Northwestern University. There were even a couple at Harvard Law School but none he considered a friend. Of course, as a white liberal twenty-nine-year-old in 1970, he believed in their cause. He'd attended civil rights rallies at Harvard and signed up for the 1965 Selma-to-Montgomery march. But he'd never gone without food or wondered if he would lose the roof over his head simply because his race or gender disqualified him from work.

These complaining women were abstract to him, merely a symbol of the injustice he hated.

Yet they still got under Copus's skin. The year before, in January 1969, looking for a place to put his beliefs into action, he'd taken a job as a civil rights lawyer in the federal government's EEOC. Even with his new title, though, he found he couldn't help the women very much. The agency, established to enforce the employment provisions of the 1964 Civil Rights Act, had no legal authority to take an employer to court, leaving its lawyers the limited tools of negotiation, pressure, and, finally, referral. By the time a complaint reached Copus's desk, the first two had failed. He then had to review each case one last time to determine if it merited forwarding to the Justice Department, which did have authority to pursue legal action. To his disappointment, fewer than ten complaints made his cut during his first two years in the job because, as he recalls today, "The [EEOC] investigators weren't lawyers and had no training in human resources, labor relations or statistical analysis," ensuring their investigations would be deficient.[1] Fortunately, he did have one other responsibility: writing amicus curiae—friend of the court—briefs in support of appellate court cases that a minority or woman had already filed, lost, and appealed. But even in these he remained in the background. He hardly felt like an instrument of civil rights.

In 1970, with a shiny sparkle in his eye, a jeans and T-shirt wardrobe, and an abundance of long dark hair, David Copus looked like he might step out of his EEOC office at any minute, hop on an oversized chopper, and join the "easy riders" Peter Fonda and Dennis Hopper on their trip to Mardi Gras. All that hair was certainly his defining physical attribute—dark brown, unkempt, falling to his shoulders, plus a beard, mustache, sideburns, and eyebrows with a life nearly their own. His oversized black-framed glasses appeared simply a fashion accessory to complete his shrouded look.

True to his generation, Copus paid little attention to traditional fashions for the office, wearing his jeans with sandals to work on most days, but he did keep a dark blue velvet suit in his closet for important occasions. Some of his former colleagues remember their shock at seeing him in court or at a high-level meeting in all his soft royal wonder. He was aware the suit was inappropriate but wore it anyway because "It was an in-your-face attitude. . . . If I had to wear a suit, I wasn't going to wear the standard suit. I wanted to wear something they would remember me by."[2]

Being remembered would never prove a problem during Copus's career at the EEOC. He left an impression on everyone—his bosses and co-workers at the agency, his colleagues in other government departments, his adversaries across the courtroom—although their views were far from uniform.

He functioned as a human Rorschach test—a person's opinion of Copus told more about his or her own personality than Copus's. The equally confident saw him as creative, while the shy found him intimidating to work with; the highest achievers called him brilliant, whereas the fighters for fairness believed he was an egotist. But almost all the memories shared one characteristic. People recalled his easygoing nature and light touch, which, even if often well calculated, helped him get what he wanted.

Copus's carefree outlook developed during his childhood. Although his parents weren't well educated—his father had finished only eighth grade, while his mother had completed high school—and had been poor in their own youth, they built a successful orange grove operation in California after they married. When David was about to start fifth grade, they moved to Texas, parlaying their agricultural success into real estate and oil fields. Since they weren't interested in politics, they played little part in developing Copus's commitment to civil rights, but they built his taste for the easy life, giving him whatever he wanted: an electric typewriter at his first mention of typing lessons; a trip across the country, in one direction or the other, each summer; a new car every two years.

After graduating from high school, Copus headed to Northwestern University, a rich, conservative campus nestled in a midwestern suburb north of Chicago. Although he had achieved honors at his Texas high school, he chose to study Northwestern's "gut" major, political science, while enjoying the burgeoning sexual revolution. When he was a senior, his favorite professor suggested he apply for a Rockefeller Foundation Scholarship to Harvard Divinity School. Copus's first reaction was *Divinity school? You've got to be kidding me,* considering he was "as agnostic and secular as any teenager is today."[3] But on a lark, he applied and won the scholarship.

He took so much ribbing from his friends, however, who saw him as "the guy on the make, drinking beer, taking all the easy courses," that he applied to Harvard Law School "purely as a defense mechanism" and got accepted there, too.[4] When forced to decide, he chose law over divinity school for one simple reason. It was the Vietnam era, when the absence of a family to support or a degree to pursue sent every able-bodied young man to an active theater of war. To get the longest deferment possible, he would pass on the two-year divinity school program and go to law school for three.

Copus's first year at Harvard was so unimpressive that it nearly ran his easy life offtrack. On a first-semester practice exam, he scored in the bottom 10 percent, shocking to a young man used to straight A's. In law school he would actually have to study. But he still had fun with his string of girlfriends and drinking buddies. Like every self-respecting student who entered law school in 1963, just after the March on Washington and the year before the Civil Rights Act passed, he supported the civil rights cause. In that activist environment, a painful memory from fifth grade surfaced. One day, his favorite teacher had advised his class of boys about automobile aesthetics, telling them, *Don't nigger up your car*. Even back then, Copus recalls, "that expression stunned me," but it wasn't until twelve years later at Harvard, surrounded by the struggle for blacks' rights, that he could interpret it clearly, as a "living anecdote of the depth of prejudice," which he didn't share.[5]

But in spite of this revelation, Copus could be called an activist only in thought, as he put most of his nonacademic energies into planning his summer vacations. Still bankrolled by his parents, he traveled through the Middle East, Asia, and North Africa instead of working. With a letter of introduction from a law school professor, he even met the Indian president, socialized with local movie stars, and lived for a time with the American ambassador. He almost felt like a celebrity himself.

Even law school graduation didn't impede his good times. He joined the Peace Corps and got an assignment back in India, successfully keeping himself out of Vietnam for two more years. He should have been miserable, living in a mud hut without electricity, hauling drinking water a quarter mile a day, but not Copus. Soon after he returned to India, he captured the heart of a U.S. diplomat's young daughter and now, in his spare time, "was living the embassy life, which was quite posh," including commissary privileges and regular invitations to black-tie parties.[6] With all these advantages, he'd become a bit brash and cocky, but he also remained idealistic and carefree. To him, the world seemed full of opportunity and entertainment, a smorgasbord for the taking.

David Copus may have been less earnest than most of his Harvard classmates, but he still wanted to "do good" when he started work, the apparent motive of his generation. They seemed alike, the young white college-educated men of that era—upper middle class, intelligent, optimistic, and financially secure. All of Copus's Harvard Law friends had taken government jobs or were representing the poor; "I didn't know anybody who had gone to work for a law firm or company," he recalls today.[7] These young men weren't drawn to high-paying jobs because they didn't need the money and didn't agree with big business's politics, but their pull to public service seemed more complicated. Many remembered the call President John F. Kennedy made in his 1961 inaugural speech—"Ask not what your country can do for you, ask what you can do for your country"—and took public sector jobs to make a difference. Others had guilt for escaping combat duty in Vietnam or sought penitence for surviving the early days of sex, drugs, and rock and roll, while some just wanted to fit in with their friends already working in government and nonprofit jobs. No matter the reasons, by late 1968 the young men of Copus's age and class were crowding the federal government's Washington offices and its agencies worldwide.

There weren't many women of any race hunting for professional jobs in Washington, D.C., at that time. Colleges had been producing their share of female graduates—42 percent of all U.S. college graduates in 1968 were female[8]—but they were still most likely to become nurses, teachers, or secretaries, supportive and caring positions that required hard work and offered little pay. Of course, there were a few women, more ambitious, motivated, or self-assured than their peers, who had become lawyers and found professional government jobs. Several found their way to the EEOC. But in general, women's access to professional America was still in the future.

Just back from the Peace Corps in the summer of 1968, Copus had decided he would look for a job in only one place—the Foreign Service. He would return to India or go to an equally alluring locale, where he could still serve his country but would live in the comfortable manner to which he had become accustomed. He scheduled the Foreign Service exam for a couple of weeks after he returned to the States and passed it on the first try.

Finally, however, his luck had run out. He received his assignment—an agricultural project in South Vietnam—which would have been tough to accept even a year or two before but now wasn't even an option. Nine months earlier, in January 1968, the debacle of the Tet Offensive in South Vietnam had demonstrated the futility of the United States' position in the war. Copus couldn't take a job there, even in a nonmilitary role. An ideal candidate, with agricultural experience in a third-world country, he got two more offers for positions in South Vietnam. He refused them, too, because, as he says today, "the antiwar fever here was so strong, it was not something I was going to do."[9] In one swift blow, the next phase of his worry-free life disappeared in the name of his beliefs. At the age of twenty-six, either wisely or naively—he's still not sure—he gave up the career, and lifestyle, he had wanted.

For perhaps the first time in his life, David Copus had to be serious. By 1968, with the draft to be invoked only in a national emergency, he no longer feared going to Vietnam, but nothing else was going right. He'd turned down his dream job, he had no income of his own, and his parents had finally cut off his credit cards. He needed a job, and he saw only one alternative—a government position in Washington, D.C. A law school friend who had recently made the interview rounds produced a list of government departments with a liberal mission and lawyers on their payroll: Lyndon

Johnson's Office of Economic Opportunity, the Justice Department, and the EEOC. The EEOC was last on the list, but Copus liked its profile of legal work helping minorities who had been discriminated against in their jobs. Plus its bureaucracy moved the fastest. Copus put on one of his only ties and drove to the agency's headquarters to deliver his résumé in person; Daniel Steiner, the general counsel, agreed to meet with him immediately. Later Copus remembered he was a little nervous about an on-the-spot interview, but he shouldn't have been. Steiner, a Harvard Law School alumnus, hired any graduate of his alma mater he could find. Copus had his job "doing good."

Copus started work in January 1969 just prior to Richard Nixon's first inauguration. Over the next eighteen months, he was remarkably successful in maintaining his idealism in the face of a country gone to hell and a job proving to be in vain. Nationwide, the optimism of the early 1960s had, by the end of the decade, given way to sadness and cynicism after the 1968 assassinations of Martin Luther King Jr. and Robert Kennedy and the growing awareness of the folly of American involvement in Vietnam. But Copus had been far away for most of this time, "living out [his] idealism" in India, which managed to survive the trip home.[10] He had to accept that his employer, the EEOC, had been nicknamed the "toothless tiger" because its most effective tool, cajoling an accused company into changing its employment practices, invariably failed, and he *was* frustrated over the stacks of complaints against the Bell System. But with perhaps a bit of youthful hubris, he still believed he could make a difference for victims of discrimination.

As a result, he worked hard, writing his amicus curiae briefs for appellate court cases and reviewing the agency's backlog of unresolved investigators' complaints. The women who occupied his mind had filed hundreds of these complaints, which were against AT&T, the company that monopolized U.S. phone service for most of the century. It didn't surprise Copus that Ma Bell was accused so often, since at that time, years before its 1984 antitrust dissolution, AT&T was America's largest employer, with more than three-quarters of a million people on its payroll.[11] The similarity of the AT&T cases struck him, though, particularly the fact most were filed by African Americans. A couple of women in his office, who went by the term "feminist," argued that the women's unfair treatment was due just as much to their gender as to their race. Copus looked at the women he knew, both his dates and his co-workers; they had money, were well educated, and seemed just like his friends and himself. He didn't think they, or any female for that matter, deserved sympathy simply because of their gender. Moreover, with black unemployment twice that of whites in the mid-1960s and even employed blacks earning only a little more than half of whites' salaries,[12] Copus's focus on the black females complaining about AT&T made sense.

On Wednesday morning, November 18, 1970, thanks to a brilliant brainstorm, he figured out how to help them. Around 5 A.M., having spent the night at a girlfriend's apartment in downtown Washington, he rolled out of bed and headed for the front door to grab the morning's *Washington Post*. Walking back inside the apartment, he glanced over the headlines. They made him stop short. Splashed across the business section's front page was the announcement "AT&T Seeks Higher Long Distance Rates." Instantly, he thought, Shit, let's get them.

It was a simple idea—stop Ma Bell from raising its phone rates until the company, in turn, stopped discriminating against its employees. From the instant it flashed through his mind, Copus loved the idea. It had a sense of justice, a quid pro quo with teeth. He knew that attacking AT&T's earnings would be the sharpest cut because, in that era, AT&T could essentially charge whatever it wanted. More than a decade before AT&T relinquished its monopoly status, in a time devoid of competition and price wars, cell phones and Internet voice, Ma Bell was it. When you called your friend or business colleague, you used Ma Bell's services and paid its rates, you rented its phones, spoke with its operators, talked over its lines. The only regulator the company faced was the U.S. government's Federal Communications Commission (FCC), which heard few complaints from American consumers. In general, the public was satisfied with good-quality phone service at, if not cheap, at least reasonable rates. As a result, the FCC rarely questioned AT&T's pricing policies. An EEOC attack on them would be guaranteed to get the company's attention.

Copus's idea was elegant in its simplicity. Not only would it get AT&T's attention quickly because it would hit the company in the pocketbook, but it would also attract the media. Any federal agency taking on the country's largest company over how much it charged consumers was bound to be news. And with the attention of Washington and national media, the public would see that the EEOC had clout after all. The agency's profile could only increase. And Copus's approach would help people. If these black women were justified in their complaints, going after Ma Bell en masse could bring them, and thousands of others like them—men and women, blacks and whites—jobs and salaries they had been unjustly denied in the past.

Like most lightbulb ideas, Copus's was sparked by bits of knowledge long planted in his mind. For one thing, he knew that the FCC empathized with the EEOC's mission to fight employment discrimination. The FCC was split into two divisions that focused on related but different industries: the Broadcast Bureau, which oversaw radio and television stations and networks around the country, and the Common Carrier Bureau, which monitored the United States' phone companies, meaning, essentially, AT&T. (The Common Carrier Bureau also oversaw the few independent companies that coexisted with the Bell System's monopoly.)

The FCC's primary responsibility was regulation, which meant keeping the more than two dozen divisions of AT&T in legal line. These included twenty-three Bell Operating Companies (BOCs), which had their own well-known monikers such as New England Telephone and Telegraph (NET) and Northwestern Bell and provided local telephone service to homes and businesses nationwide. Their workers installed phones and climbed telephone poles to connect and disconnect wires. Although each division was only a small part of AT&T, many were the largest company in their home state. AT&T's long-distance division, known as Long Lines, enabled the long-distance phone connections between the operating companies. It supplied the circuitry and equipment that allowed a college student in Chicago to talk to his mother in Dallas by simply dialing a ten-digit number. In addition, AT&T owned a manufacturing company, Western Electric, that produced the telephones and switching equipment for American homes and offices, and a research and development department, Bell Labs, that developed innovations to make phone communications faster, easier, and more efficient. The FCC's rules and regulations covered them all.

Most FCC regulations addressed the meat-and-potatoes concerns of any federal oversight agency such as what services their licensees could provide, what rates they could charge, and where they could operate. But Copus knew that the agency also had regulations prohibiting employment discrimination on the part of any company it monitored. During the previous year, Nick Johnson, a liberal commissioner of the FCC who was also concerned about employment discrimination, had charged one of his staff members, George Sape, with developing antidiscrimination regulations; Sape then drafted them with Bill Oldaker, a lawyer and special assistant to the EEOC chairperson. After the regulations went into effect on August 5, 1970, any telephone company could be denied its license if it discriminated against its employees, a fact not lost on Copus that November morning. (The FCC's Broadcast Bureau had previously passed similar regulations; as a result, TV and radio companies were already under the same legal pressure.)

Copus had had another, more direct experience that influenced his thinking. In 1969, Bill Brown, the EEOC's chair, agreed to provide pro bono support to Washington, D.C.'s Urban League chapter in its efforts to fight employment discrimination. The league had become concerned about the treatment of the black employees at the Potomac Electric Power Company (PEPCO), Washington, D.C.'s government-regulated electric company, and was brainstorming on how to improve it. Finally its executives decided that a bottom-line attack would be best. PEPCO had been up for a rate increase, which would elevate electricity prices for all D.C. residents. Why not petition D.C.'s Public Service Commission (PSC) to deny the rate increase until discrimination against the utility's black employees stopped? Brown looked for a smart, aggressive lawyer to dig up statistics for the league's petition and chose David Copus. Copus's work ultimately led to naught: although the U.S. District Court, District of Columbia, found that PEPCO's employment practices were a legitimate issue for its regulator, the PSC, to consider, the complaint was thrown out for procedural reasons. However, this concept, now legitimized by a court of law, had been stored in Copus's brain.

Frustrated by the impotence of the agency he worked for, aware of the FCC regulations against employment discrimination, and inspired by his pro bono work on the PEPCO project, Copus came up with the idea of a lifetime. Now he needed to convince others, most important his boss, of its power.

Few people offered a starker contrast to David Copus than his ultimate boss, Bill Brown, who had been appointed to the EEOC chairmanship by President Johnson a year and a half earlier. A tall, slender African American man who meted out smiles judiciously, he carried the proud bearing of someone frequently underestimated. Impeccably dressed in a suit and tie on any workday and exuding calm and patience, he clashed dramatically with Copus's casual clothes, youthful exuberance, and frustration with bureaucracy. Despite his refined demeanor, however, Brown shared Copus's fervent commitment to fighting employment discrimination, and, with far more power, he could pursue it even more aggressively.

Brown had never worried about appearances, so he ignored Copus's attire and hairstyle but felt he often had to rein in his enthusiasm. Brown had gotten to know Copus easily because there were only about a hundred employees in the EEOC Washington headquarters office; plus Copus was a drinking buddy of Brown's assistant, Bill Oldaker. Brown thought enough of Copus's abilities to assign him a key role in the EEOC's public hearings held in Houston earlier that summer and to send him to the Washington, D.C., Urban League to help in its intervention with PEPCO. Today Brown remembers Copus as "exceedingly bright, tenacious and very hard working" but also "impetuous" and needing "some restraints."[13] He saw Copus for who he was: a privileged young man whose surfeit of ideas wasn't yet balanced by professional experience. As a result, Brown proceeded with caution whenever Copus was involved.

Brown's antennae were on full alert on November 18, 1970, when Oldaker brought Copus into his office, but in this case Brown liked what he heard. At the very minimum, as he saw it, Copus was describing a way to reduce substantially the workload of the small, resource-strapped EEOC. Since AT&T complaints made up 6–7 percent of the agency's total, a strategy that could wipe them out in one action had to be considered. More important, Oldaker's enthusiasm on that Wednesday morning swayed him. Brown surrounded himself with smart, thoughtful, and thorough aides who were the antithesis of "yes" men or women. He may have believed that Copus's judgment was often impaired, but he trusted Oldaker's implicitly. He agreed to take at least one step forward.

Brown was fully aware of the political consequences of a broad-sided attack on America's largest employer, but, in general, he wasn't interested in politics. He'd come to Washington from Philadelphia, where he'd been a low-profile but effective deputy district attorney. He had only one goal for his new job—to turn the EEOC into an organization that made real strides in seeking equal opportunity for American workers. He'd heard the gossip. He knew that many of his government colleagues believed he'd gotten his job because he represented a rare combination in the pre–Clarence Thomas days, a black Republican, a combination crucial for a bipartisan agency fighting for minorities' rights. In addition, he'd ruffled feathers in the administration more than once over discrimination cases he had pursued. He paid little attention to the criticism, however, since his focus was on effecting change, not appearing successful. And in Copus's idea, he saw the possibility for real change—an effective weapon to increase the EEOC's profile, get AT&T's and the country's attention in the name of civil rights, and clear up his agency's backlog of cases. He wanted to give it a try.

That hardly meant Copus had been given the green light to begin writing the intervening petition to the FCC. Brown saw several steps that came first. Most important, he needed to know whether the EEOC had enough legitimate information against AT&T to justify an intervention. As much potential as he saw in Copus's idea, he understood what he was taking on. AT&T was a corporate icon, arguably the most respected company in America at that time. Moreover, with more than $2.3 billion in net income in 1970, it seemed to have endless resources.[14] If the minuscule, nearly powerless EEOC went after it without overwhelming evidence, Brown knew his agency would become a laughingstock, significantly impeding his ability to make future strides for aggrieved employees. Brown also wanted to know the legality of Copus's proposed intervention. The FCC regulations against employment discrimination were in place, but he wasn't certain that an outside agency, even within the federal government, could invoke them.

Under Brown's orders, the EEOC's Research Department went after the issue of evidence, and Copus pursued the idea's legality. The researchers collected data from the EEOC investigative offices around the country, counting more than fifteen hundred complaints against the Bell System and ascertaining their progress toward resolution. Their results convinced Brown he had enough ammunition against AT&T to justify stepping into the FCC's proceeding. In the meantime, Copus dug into every statute he could find, even if it was only remotely related to inter–federal agency intervention. He called friends at the FCC, he bounced ideas off his fellow EEOC lawyers, but he turned up nothing. "We saw no precedent for it, no prohibition against it, no procedure defining how to do it," Copus remembers. "Apparently it hadn't been heard of." [15] As long as it wasn't prohibited, that was good enough for Brown.

With his doubts relieved, Brown had one more job. As apolitical as he was, he still knew he needed his fellow commissioners' support before approaching the FCC. The EEOC had been designed as a bipartisan independent agency made up of five commissioners including the chair. Commissioners were appointed by the sitting president whenever a commissioner's slot opened, and they were confirmed by the Senate for staggered five-year terms. In the winter of 1970/1971, Republican representatives outnumbered Democrats three to two. Strong, preferably unanimous, support from his four colleagues would provide Brown at least some political cover from the critics who were bound to attack the EEOC for going after the American icon AT&T. Brown worried mostly about Colson Lewis, a Republican commissioner whose African American heritage belied his conservative approach to fighting discrimination. Brown had to prepare a solid sales job so that no commissioner could even consider disagreeing.

Since Brown felt sure his colleagues would share his initial doubts, he brought in his full team for the commissioners' presentation. Copus; Jack Pemberton, the EEOC's acting general counsel; and several Research Department representatives helped make the pitch in support of the report the commissioners had already reviewed. As Brown expected, they had a litany of questions, generally the same as his: *Can we justify taking on the country's largest company? At what risk are we putting our agency and ourselves if we don't succeed?* Brown downplayed the fact that Copus had found nothing authorizing the EEOC to take this action, instead directing the commissioners toward a "should we?" or "shouldn't we?" decision. The discussion lasted longer than most commissioners' reviews, but in the end Brown achieved his goal. As he and Copus recall, all four of Brown's colleagues supported the idea, even if some weren't enthusiastic about it. Brown and Copus had gotten their green light.

Over the next few days, Brown shared Copus's idea with a few of his top managers. At least one of them thought it should be blessed by Brown's government colleagues. *Check with the White House, check with Labor, check with Justice,* they said. Brown resisted, not so much because he worried that President Nixon's Republican administration would give him a hard time but because he wanted to maintain the independence of his agency. "We're not going to call anybody," he remembers saying, "because what do you do if they say no? Don't do it?"[16] He could take the political heat. His researchers had shown that the action was justified, Copus had proved it wasn't illegal, the commissioners had given their assent. So they were going to do it. They were going after AT&T.

2

The Petition

Late Fall 1970

If approved, AT&T's rate increase request would become effective January 19, 1971, less than two months after David Copus brought his "brilliant" idea to Bill Brown, giving the EEOC little time to turn it into action. AT&T was requesting 6 percent more in long-distance revenue, which would add nearly $400 million annually to its receipts,[1] a figure Brown and Copus knew Ma Bell wouldn't let slip away easily. Brown set Copus off on the project he'd been waiting to start: developing the petition for the FCC—the EEOC's written argument documenting AT&T's discrimination against its female and minority employees. Copus immediately recruited Susan Ross and Larry Gartner, two of his colleagues in the General Counsel's Office, to help him.

In 1970, Susan Ross represented a rare breed within the EEOC—an actual living and breathing feminist. With her brown hair worn loose and an ability to laugh at herself, she hardly fit the militant image of women's libbers often depicted in newspapers and magazines. Her conversion to feminism in the early 1960s came from neither facing discrimination herself nor migrating from civil rights marches to women's rights rallies. She had had the same privileged background as Copus: she also attended an elite liberal arts college in Illinois—in her case, Knox College—and went on to a prestigious law school, New York University, making her a poster girl for Copus's belief that women didn't suffer from discrimination. But she had learned what he hadn't. Inspired by a college summer spent in France in the early 1960s, she read Simone de Beauvoir's *The Second Sex,* which "had been an incredible eye-opener."[2] It helped her see the inequities women faced, even women with economic advantages like herself and her friends. Then came

The Feminine Mystique, Betty Friedan's unveiling of the depressing and often desperate lives of educated American women with no intellectual or
productive outlets, particularly middle-class married mothers. Through these
books, Ross learned about the subtle but fierce oppression she wanted to
fight.

Her activism may have had intellectual origins, but it was based in a prac-
ticality often unmatched by her college peers who had spent their time protesting. At Knox, she helped wage a campaign to get rid of women's hours—
that is, curfews for women only—and at New York University she created
the first women's issues course. When she arrived at the EEOC in September 1970, a few months after her law school graduation, she was determined
to continue her crusade for women's rights.

Unfortunately for Ross, a couple of the white male lawyers in the EEOC's
General Counsel's Office didn't particularly welcome her passions. On her
first day, in a time-honored and most likely familiar tradition of that generation of men, one of them teased her, using a classic argument against equality. Questioning the legal foundation of her feminist perspective, he asked
her how she would propose dealing with a construction firm that planted
only one porta-potty at its job site. He contended that the company was
legally covered by an exception to Title VII of the 1964 Civil Rights Act that
went by a fancy title: bona fide occupational qualification, or BFOQ. The
BFOQ exception stated that a business could hire only one gender for any
job that, by its fundamental nature, was limited to that gender or for which
the changes needed to accommodate another gender would be outside a
company's "normal operation." One example at that time was limiting some
telephone craft jobs to men because women supposedly couldn't lift the
necessary equipment. Ross's questioner argued that since urinating was a requirement of getting through a workday, if women couldn't use the same
singular potty as the men, the construction firm would have to pay for a separate women's potty, an expense its "normal operation" wouldn't otherwise
require. Ross quickly realized that her co-worker was just playing devil's advocate, and later he even became a close friend. But as she recalls now with
a laugh, it was "a little tough on the first day."[3]

Ross might have hoped that the women already on staff at the EEOC
would have embraced her beliefs more openly, but that didn't prove true.
During her first months at the EEOC, she remembers one young female
lawyer who was friendlier with the men in the office saying to her, *Oh,
you're a feminist?,* in a harsh, unsupportive tone. Ross found only one
other woman in the office who identified herself with the fight for women's
equality, Sunny Pressman, who was at least a decade older than she. But

Pressman focused on education—giving speeches and writing articles—not pressing women's cases in court. Before Ross arrived, there was only one activist lawyer working on women's behalf on the EEOC's general counsel staff, Dave Zugschwerdt, whose reputation as an iconoclast made his fight for women's rights logical. Ross was happy to have a hardworking colleague, sympathetic to her concerns, even if he was a man.

Ross's reception at the EEOC would hardly have surprised the leaders of the country's preeminent feminist organization, the National Organization for Women (NOW), which was privately disdainful of the agency. Some of their frustration stemmed from the EEOC's inability to take complaints to court, which, although not the agency's fault, made it unpopular with many activist groups. NOW leaders had more personal reasons for their unhappiness, too: the EEOC had given them minimal help on the *Weeks v. Southern Bell* case, which reached the Supreme Court and would soon figure prominently in the EEOC's battle with AT&T; in addition, a NOW executive witnessed a panel discussion in which the agency's executive director, who reported to Bill Brown, allowed "the subject of equal employment opportunity in employment for women [to be] alternately ignored, dismissed as unimportant or ridiculed."[4] Perhaps most important, NOW leaders believed that the EEOC didn't even carry out its own mission. They observed so few women in high-level EEOC jobs that they demanded a statistical breakdown of the EEOC staff, the same type of data the agency used to build its own cases against companies it accused of discriminating. Ann Scott, NOW's legislative director, clarified the relationship between the two organizations in a fall 1971 memo to a colleague. "I'm so goddamn disgusted with the EEOC at this point," she wrote. "I feel we should maybe just ignore them and file our own . . . suits through the Department of Justice."[5] For the EEOC's part, NOW, a feminist organization only three years old, was hardly in its lawyers' consciousness. Theoretically the two groups were working toward the same goal, but they had little respect for each other.

When Copus borrowed Susan Ross and Larry Gartner from the EEOC's General Counsel's Office to help him on the FCC petition, he had found two lawyers with entirely dissimilar motivations. Whereas Susan Ross's intellect drove her straight to activism, Larry Gartner's impelled him in the exact opposite direction. Gartner was a bit less radical than most of his male peers at the EEOC: his brown hair landed on his neck, not his shoulders; he had a mustache but not a beard; he occasionally even wore a suit to work. That slightly more conservative bent had been evident since his college days at Berkeley in the late 1960s. While his classmates were out fighting the fight on the activist left, he stayed inside, writing articles for the student newspaper, the *Daily Cal,* maintaining his perspective as an observer, albeit a liberal one. After graduation, he went on to law school at Harvard, hanging tightly to that objective observer's perspective. From the start of his legal career, he believed that the most effective lawyer was the one without a mission, the one trying to get to the right answer no matter what his or her personal beliefs were. He arrived at the EEOC during the summer between his second and third years at Harvard when the agency hired him to write appellate briefs. He liked the other lawyers, the small office, and the excitement of Washington, so the following year he accepted a full-time job and began work around the same time Ross started.

Copus may not have known of the differences in motivation between Ross and Gartner, but he chose them for the same reasons. They were brand-new lawyers at the EEOC and therefore eager, idealistic, and longing to put their imprint on something; an interagency petition that they would play a key role in writing would fit that bill. They also had reputations as two of the brightest young lawyers in the department, and since they weren't too busy with anything else, they could help Copus on short notice. The three of them went to work.

Among the cacophony of criticism EEOC lawyers would hear over the next several months, one accusation would feel particularly inappropriate to Bill Brown. AT&T executives were angry that a complaint about their personnel policies was being brought before an agency, the FCC, which they perceived to have no role in federal employment policy regulations. To them, this intervention smacked of just a clever way to hit their company in the pocketbook. Brown, however, believed that discrimination, in fact, *did* cost money. As he says today, "Discrimination of any type means you're eliminating a very significant portion of the population—women, particularly, and minorities" from being considered for jobs.[6] The corporate executives who discriminated seemed to assume that only white men had talent and, therefore, should be the only ones put on the payroll or promoted. Brown understood that there was just as much talent among the women and minorities, but these policies would keep them in lower-level positions. By not choosing the best candidates, the executives would be getting people who would be less effective in their jobs: not as quick at installing telephones or as clever in designing an advertising campaign or as capable of motivating a team.

The problem would get worse for any company entering a competitive environment. In 1970, AT&T's executives didn't have this worry because the U.S. unemployment rate was climbing and their company's reputation and monopoly status practically guaranteed them the applicants they needed whenever they had jobs to fill. But if their world ever changed, as Brown points out today, they would "be competing to bring people on board." By relegating females, blacks, Hispanics, and other minorities to low-level, undesirable jobs, the company's ability to serve its customers well and maintain its market share would be compromised. These discriminatory employment policies would no longer seem just costly, they would be irresponsible.

Brown also notes another economic consequence of discrimination: "When you have a large corporation whose women and minorities feel they're not being treated fairly, they aren't nearly as productive." For example, if female telephone operators and black installers believed they would never get a promotion, they would be unlikely to do their best work for the company, behavior that would equate to actual dollars off the company's bottom line.

Brown felt certain that these factors justified the EEOC's intervention with the FCC, but he realized he still faced an uphill battle. AT&T's executives would be critical at best, and Brown's own boss, President Richard Nixon, was likely to disagree with his approach. In his 1968 election campaign, Nixon had used images of ghetto uprisings in his television ads and had appealed to white southern voters with the statement "our schools are for education—not integration."[7] And in the two years he'd been in office, Nixon had sent both subtle and direct signals that blacks weren't his priority: he appointed Warren Burger, a conservative judge known not to "meddle" in social issues, to the Supreme Court and came out against extending the 1965 Voting Rights Act, which had reduced the barriers blacks faced in voting. This track record predicted that he wasn't likely to welcome aggressive action, even by his own civil rights agency, to help minorities. In addition, Brown's analysis of the cost of discrimination was complex, a factor that rarely helped in politics. Even in 1970, ideas that couldn't be distilled down to one or two sentences weren't likely to gain a lot of traction.

AT&T executives, for their part, had thought little about any aspect of discrimination, but they were well equipped to face the EEOC in the battle it had initiated. Over the years, they had built and nurtured a close relationship with the FCC, so close that sometimes the commission appeared to be more an adviser to the company than a monitor of it. When a maverick FCC chair instigated an effort in 1963 to control AT&T's rates, resulting in a 1967 recommendation to cut its interstate revenues by $120 million, the company simply refused, and the FCC backed off.[8] It seemed unlikely that the commission would be any less amenable to AT&T's wishes just three years later. Finally, AT&T had vast financial resources in comparison with the EEOC, whose annual budget was less than $20 million.[9] Those resources could quickly translate into aggressive positive publicity for AT&T, extolling its excellent treatment of its employees, whether factual or not, and criticizing its new adversary in the federal government.

Brown understood the power of publicity. In fact, he had already invested a lot of his own limited government resources in raising his agency's profile. He had enlisted celebrities to appear in radio and television ads about the EEOC—Ray Charles, Bill Cosby, and Ricardo Montalban had made them—and was developing a film, *Voice of La Raza,* to be narrated by Anthony Quinn that addressed the discrimination problems of America's ten million Spanish-speaking Americans. Brown wanted every American employee to know what the EEOC was and how it could fight discrimination. Just as important, he wanted American corporations to know about his agency and fear its potential power.

But Brown also knew, if he was counting only on publicity to "win" the AT&T case, he would lose. An attack on AT&T would initially make big and impressive news for the EEOC, as the David-versus-Goliath nature of the pursuit would prove irresistible to the big-city journalists on the East Coast. However, that coverage would undoubtedly be short term and soon overshadowed once AT&T starting using those tremendous resources in its back pocket. The publicity would be useful to the EEOC only if it could come up with solid evidence, clearly and unequivocally demonstrating AT&T's discrimination against various groups of its employees.

Beyond evidence, the EEOC needed luck. The FCC would have to step outside two of its most comfortable roles—close colleague of AT&T and regulator of technical telecommunications issues only—into a new one: investigator of employment practices. Only then would Brown and the EEOC get their opportunity to present their case. Without strong, legitimized proof of AT&T's discrimination and that chance, the EEOC had already lost.

Brown controlled only the gathering of data against Ma Bell, which he was confident Copus, Gartner, and Ross could handle, but he had no influence over the FCC's reaction to the EEOC's petition. All he could do was hope the FCC's leadership would make the right decision and open the door, giving the EEOC a chance to make a difference for the thousands of women and minorities who worked for AT&T.

Bill Brown's faith in his EEOC team had been well founded. From the time Copus heard that all EEOC commissioners were on board, he and his team had immersed themselves in numbers and stories to build the most powerful petition possible. They were aiming for blatant charges and high drama. They weren't going to waste their one shot at an American corporate icon.

Ironically, their richest source of information emanated from reports the Bell System companies themselves had provided. Soon after the EEOC was formed, Stephen Shulman, its second chair, in search of any tool to prove discrimination, instituted the Employee Information Report EEO-1 (commonly known as the EEO-1 report), which the agency required annually from American employers with more than one hundred employees or government contracts of more than $10,000. The report, a two-page form of eighteen questions, quickly became an irritant to human resource managers and corporate executives nationwide because of one question: *Provide the number of employees in each job classification, identified by sex and race.* The form's categories for employees—*Negro, Oriental, American Indian or Spanish Surnamed American*—read as a shock today, when African American, Asian, Native American, and Hispanic are the equivalent but more "politically correct" terms. The majority race, Caucasians, didn't even have to be counted at that time.

The statistics these reports depicted looked bad for AT&T. In 1968, in the nineteen largest BOCs, women filled 96.9 percent of the office and clerical positions and only 2.9 percent of the more skilled craft jobs. Women were also paid less. In 1969, telephone operators, who were nearly 100 percent female, averaged $95 per week, about one-half the average weekly earnings of line construction workers, who were overwhelmingly male. Blacks fared no better. In 1968, blacks held less than 2 percent of high-paying craft jobs in those same nineteen Bell companies and only 1.2 percent of high-paying white-collar jobs like managers or salesmen.

The lawyers also had access to the thousands of complaints against Ma Bell that Copus and other EEOC lawyers had been reviewing for the past five years. They dug out the most clear-cut and dramatic stories across the BOCs: a woman had been denied a high-paying technician's job because she couldn't lift twenty-five pounds; another woman had earned lower wages than her male counterpart for the exact same work; women weren't allowed to apply for jobs designated as "men only." The lawyers included the story of the unwed black mothers who had been flat-out denied employment in Southern and South Central Bell—the women on whom Copus had originally focused—and they mentioned several women who said that Bell System recruiters told them they wouldn't be hired for technicians' jobs because they simply "weren't suited for them." Because no formal recruitment process had been used to come to that conclusion, the approach obviously had no legal standing.

In addition, the EEOC team found evidence of discriminatory "word-of-mouth" recruiting practices. Male technicians at various BOCs had been recommending their male buddies for high-paying jobs, never thinking to mention the positions to their wives or sisters. The recommendations weren't the company's fault, but the recruiting strategy, when used by Bell System managers exclusively to fill good, high-paying jobs, was illegal. Under this approach, a candidate would have to fill out a job application and a form or two, but that was the entire hiring process he faced. No one else, black or Hispanic or female, or white and male for that matter, would even be considered. The EEOC team added its description to the petition.

The team's research extended beyond the information already collected in the EEOC's files. One study by Bernard Anderson, an African American professor at the Wharton School of the University of Pennsylvania, proved particularly useful. Anderson had written several books about the prevalence of African Americans, or Negroes in that day, in various industries; one, *The Negro in the Public Utility Industries,* had been published just a few months earlier. Although AT&T's corporate policy had admonished its operating companies not to participate in Anderson's study, he gathered enough statistics from public records and the participation of one independent-minded Bell division to damn the whole company for its discriminatory policies leaving blacks in low-level and low-paying jobs.

Copus viewed this book as particularly valuable because it strengthened the EEOC's racial case against AT&T, but, fortunately for the female AT&T employees stuck in low-paid jobs, Susan Ross was on Copus's team. While Copus prioritized race, Ross focused on gender. In researching the petition, it had struck her that the vast majority of complaints against Ma Bell had been filed by women, both black *and* white, and the statistics and anecdotes she and her two colleagues were uncovering trumpeted that the company's women, of all colors, were the most mistreated. Women were telephone operators, the company's worst job; women couldn't get past the second level of management; women couldn't get certain jobs because they couldn't lift enough or didn't know the right person or the job had been designated "men only." Ross could see that women were the chief losers at AT&T. She would make sure the petition stated that clearly.

In the next three weeks, Copus, Gartner, and Ross completed the petition, which specifically targeted AT&T's twenty-three local BOCs and its Long Lines division. A sixty-page tome, it defined government hyperbole in its accusations, demands, and documentation of laws broken. Its opening

statement became its most notorious. The EEOC accused AT&T of "pervasive, system-wide and blatantly unlawful discrimination in employment
against women, blacks, Spanish-surnamed Americans, and other minorities." [10] Ross had secured women in the first spot on the list. For AT&T's egregious behavior, the EEOC asked the FCC to "suspend the operation of
AT&T's proposed rate increase, conduct a hearing and declare the proposed
increase illegal until AT&T's operating companies have ceased their unlawful discrimination against women, blacks, Spanish-speaking Americans and
other minorities." [11]

To justify the EEOC indictment, the team had thrown everything it could
into the petition. Copus, Gartner, and Ross accused AT&T of violating every
law or regulation against any form of discrimination they could find on
American legal books. This included the obvious federal statutes—Title VII
of the Civil Rights Act of 1964, the Equal Pay Act of 1963, and Executive Order 11246, signed in 1965 and amended by EO 11375 in 1967—along with
two less likely federal laws and a litany of state and local fair employment
practices. They further claimed that AT&T was violating the Fifth Amendment. They arrived at this convoluted contention by first concluding that
AT&T was subject to constitutional oversight because it was government-
regulated. Next, they leaped to the assumption that fair employment along
with its associated income is a property right. As a result, they stated that
the Fifth Amendment's commitment that "no person . . . shall be deprived
of life, liberty or property, without due process of law" meant that no AT&T
employee should be denied fair employment. It's doubtful the authors of the
Fifth Amendment had this interpretation in mind, but Copus and his colleagues didn't care. They just wanted to be certain they'd covered every possible offense.

The EEOC lawyers reinforced their petition with almost as many pages of
background information, including even more anecdotes from settled and
pending discrimination cases along with statistics gleaned through analysis
of AT&T's EEO-1 reports. They also tacked on a copy of Bernard Anderson's
345-page book, emphasizing Copus's racial focus. If nothing else, AT&T
would understand that the details of its past treatment of female and minority employees, not much of it laudatory, would become public if an agreement couldn't be reached.

In the midst of the voluminous data they presented, the EEOC lawyers
found a way to get AT&T's executives on the record about their responsibilities to their employees, with a notable focus on their treatment of blacks.
The three lawyers had spent time reading old AT&T annual reports and
public meeting minutes and had dug out some relevant quotes from the

company's leadership. The petition noted that seven years earlier, in 1963, Frederick Kappel, then AT&T's board chairman, had said, "The question of how Negro and White people shall live, go to school and work as fellow citizens demands good solutions in every part of the nation. . . . We [the Bell System] have more people at work than any other organization except the government. So the matter of how we handle ourselves has more than ordinary significance."[12] Then, in 1970, W. W. Straley, an AT&T vice president, added his perspective. "Thus we attempt to articulate our belief that, for whatever reasons—and I would include among them our size, our ubiquity and the dependency of increasing numbers of people upon our communications network—we have a *social responsibility,* and that is inextricably associated with our operating responsibility."[13] Copus's team spun those comments directly back at AT&T. The EEOC petition noted the many ways in which AT&T hadn't been meeting its "social responsibilities" to provide blacks and women with the opportunity to compete for jobs with and work beside their white male "fellow citizens," which clearly violated U.S. antidiscrimination laws. While AT&T's own statistics, written up on hundreds of EEO-1 reports, documented its culpability in discrimination against its employees, its executives' self-important words had added a layer of embarrassment. Ma Bell had gotten into this predicament all by itself.

On December 10, 1970, an EEOC messenger delivered the AT&T petition to the office of the FCC registrar. It was logged in and sent on to the next part of the FCC's bureaucracy, the Rates Office in the Common Carrier Bureau. After logging the documents in again, Rates would be responsible for determining how the complaint would be treated and would set up hearings, if deemed necessary.

As the EEOC's petition traveled through the halls of the FCC, the only notice it got was its size. There was little surprise that an intervention request related to employment discrimination had been filed. Commissioner Johnson's antidiscrimination regulations had been well publicized throughout the FCC when they were put in place the previous year, so an attack on a licensee's employment practices was expected sooner or later. But the EEOC petition's heft stood out. As Jim Juntilla, an FCC lawyer who became involved in the case, remembers, we "never had a case of this scope before."[14]

But nothing more could happen until AT&T's management had had a chance to look it over and respond. A copy was made and immediately sent to the twenty-sixth floor of 195 Broadway in New York City, where the AT&T executives spent their days. The Rates Office filed the original and waited to hear from Ma Bell.

3

The Reaction

December 1970

Don Liebers had taken the day off. It was Friday, December 11, 1970, just two weeks before Christmas. With their children at school, Liebers and his wife were stealing a day away to go antiquing and escape their hectic routine. He'd just been promoted, ten days earlier, to become AT&T's director of employment and already had a full plate.

The phone rang while Liebers was upstairs shaving. He picked it up to hear one of his new co-workers ask, *Did you see the front page of the New York Times?* Knowing a call at home on a day off was never good, he hung up, headed quickly downstairs, grabbed the newspaper from the front porch, and read, "U.S. Agency, Charging Job Bias, Opposes Rate Rise for AT&T." In that one glance, just like Copus's three weeks earlier, Liebers, at only thirty-seven, understood he had a significant challenge before him.

A tall, husky man with a long face and kind eyes, Liebers perfectly fit the image of a gentle giant. By 1970, he had accomplished a rare feat in the Bell System, reaching fifth-level management before the age of forty. He was well equipped for his new job, with experience at Michigan Bell in its top college recruiting position, and he had several attributes often seen in high-level Bell executives: a tremendous capacity for work, a reputation as "Mr. Nice Guy," and a constant emphasis on searching for the middle ground to solve a problem. He also rose quickly because he was known for flexibility. As he says today, "I was always willing to try something new,"[1] like the psychedelic recruiting poster he produced in 1967 that looked more like a Grateful Dead album cover than an enticement to join a corporate monolith. It drew interest and job candidates, which pushed his career forward a little faster.

Remembering the anxious echo of his colleague's voice on the phone, Liebers quickly read the *Times* article's first paragraph, which stated the charge against AT&T of "pervasive, system-wide and blatantly unlawful discrimination in the employment of women, blacks, and Spanish-surnamed Americans," Copus's quote from the FCC petition. Liebers was both shocked and troubled to see it in print. He had to admit that there was an element of truth to the accusation. As he says today, "There were a lot of very good women's jobs in the telephone industry . . . but women were limited relative to how high they could go" and "the culture was you had women's jobs and men's jobs."[2] But, given the era, Liebers didn't think AT&T was doing that badly. As a matter of fact, he adds, "on the relative scale of hiring women and minorities and utilizing them well, . . . AT&T and its companies were probably doing as well or better than any other company."[3] It was by far the country's largest employer of women, including tens of thousands of telephone operators, and hundreds of other women had been promoted into supervisory jobs, overseeing those operators or customer service representatives. Since he knew that other U.S. companies didn't allow women to hold any managerial title, Liebers felt that the government's decision to single out AT&T was unfair, even if the charge itself was somewhat justified.

By the time he arrived at his office on the twenty-sixth floor of a southern Manhattan high-rise, the atmosphere had turned frenetic. Hi (shortened from Haakon Ingolf) Romnes, the company's CEO, had had a much stronger reaction to the news than Liebers. He was angry. A Wisconsin native of Norwegian descent, he combined movie star good looks with a soft-spoken manner, although he was anything but soft-spoken that Friday morning. The company's immediate response, which he was in the midst of organizing, would resonate with outrage. He called a press conference for later that day and agreed to an exclusive interview with a *New York Times* reporter. The company would meet the government's attack with an equally aggressive response.

Addressing a public relations crisis wasn't an infrequent task for Romnes and his number two, John deButts, AT&T's vice chairman. With his square face, small glasses, and slicked-back hair, deButts looked the part of the engineer he was, but, like Romnes, he viewed issues through the customer's eyes. AT&T's product reached into 85 percent of U.S. homes,[4] and its name was known by almost every American; therefore, although generally well respected, AT&T was an obvious target for customer complaints and reporters' critiques. Its executives rarely changed policies based on these criticisms, but they still had to devote time to a response. In just the past few years, the executive team had dealt with a spate of obscene phone calls that, although not Bell System employees' fault, were annoying to their customers. Along with some of those same customers, the executives had also suffered through two years of major service failures in New York City. And in 1970, they were already in a battle with the FCC over the company's appropriate rate of return, unrelated to the EEOC's charge against them.

But Romnes and deButts took this latest charge harder. The EEOC was attacking AT&T for a problem its executives didn't believe they had. In fact, they were proud of their employment record, having taken direct action to hire disadvantaged workers. In 1962 AT&T had joined John F. Kennedy's Plans for Progress, which the president had formed the previous year, and most of the Bell divisions had followed suit over the next few years. A voluntary program, Plans for Progress asked companies nationwide to make a special effort to bring those who had been excluded from good jobs—primarily blacks—onto companies' payrolls. Romnes took a leadership role, lending managers to the organization to help recruit other companies and serving himself as honorary chair of the 1965 Plans for Progress National Conference. The company's involvement continued when Plans for Progress merged with the National Alliance for Businessmen's JOBS program in 1968, and AT&T committed to hiring more than fifteen thousand "hard-core unemployed" over the next three years.

In addition, AT&T's employment statistics were impressive. According to Romnes's statement to the press that morning, 12.4 percent of all Bell System employees were minorities at a time when the U.S. minority population was almost exactly the same at 12.5 percent[5] and the general U.S. workforce was only 11 percent minority.[6] And since 1963, total employment in the Bell System had increased 37.5 percent at the same time minority employment had jumped 265 percent.[7]

AT&T had even gone beyond joining philanthropic hiring programs and employing significant numbers of minorities. Seeing its responsibility to employees and shareholders on almost the same par, the company treated its employees well. This philosophy sounds atypical today, an era when large companies downsize employees based on the latest quarter's financial results and workers hop from corporation to dot-com start-up to independent contract to guarantee the biggest paycheck. However, in the early 1970s, many companies considered their long-term employees one of their most valuable assets. At AT&T, Theodore Vail, an early and influential company president, had originated the belief that a corporate focus on profits should be balanced with a commitment to serving customers, and later Bell System leaders expanded that public service philosophy to emphasize treating their employees well, exemplified in their quotes about "social responsibility" that Copus and his colleagues included in the EEOC's petition.

For years, AT&T had watched over its employees in different ways, which continued under Romnes's reign. For most AT&T top executives, including Romnes and deButts, there was a standard, insular career path. They received an engineering or other technical undergraduate degree, went into an entry-level position in a Bell division soon after college or military service, and worked their way through a variety of Bell System jobs, typically beginning by climbing telephone poles or wiring circuits, passing through at least one operations job, and continuing through executive leadership in two or more divisions. As long as they continued to produce results that their bosses expected, these young men were treated exceedingly well, given frequent promotions, and guaranteed lifetime employment. This strategy proved symbiotic: with job security and good compensation, the high-potential employees were happy to stay with AT&T, and the company was developing a well-trained, homogeneous workforce.

AT&T also cared for its lower-level employees. The treatment they received was less generous and more condescending than the care the company's high-potential managers enjoyed, but company executives valued these less-skilled workers just as much. Although any employee without a college degree, and not white and male, would almost never advance beyond the two lowest levels of management, she still had a lifetime Bell System job with excellent benefits. Some female and minority employees who felt pinned down at the company's bottom rungs didn't agree that they were being treated fairly, but many others, grateful for regular and known work, felt satisfied.

The indignation Romnes and deButts felt over the EEOC's charge had origins beyond their belief that they were doing well by their employees. The men who ran AT&T in this era were monopolists on a grand scale. They worked for a company whose monopoly of the U.S. phone industry was fully government-sanctioned and whose assets were larger than the gross national product of all but twenty countries.[8] In addition, since their career paths had followed the insular route required to reach Bell System top management, very few had worked in another company, meaning most had no experience in a competitive environment. They had neither need nor desire to look outside their company to identify better management practices.

Things worked a certain way at AT&T: women were telephone operators, men telephone installers, and women and blacks were never promoted beyond second-level management. Under those policies, the company was earning money, so why should they be changed?

Romnes, deButts, and their executive colleagues were aware that complaints had been filed with the EEOC against Bell System employment policies since the agency was formed in 1965. Moreover, the company's poor record of hiring and promoting blacks had been documented in Bernard Anderson's book, *The Negro in the Public Utility Industries,* even if most Bell divisions had refused to participate in Anderson's study. But since the company's executives had the self-assurance of decades gazing only inward, they easily justified their policies in the face of the criticism. Women can't lift the reels of cable and ladders a telephone installer must carry every day, so how can they ever qualify for that job? Telephone operators' stations are set within inches of one another, so how can we hire men without instigating an unmanageable workplace? In the limited world of AT&T's top brass, these explanations made perfect sense.

Another factor may have played into the executives' reaction on that December Friday. In 1970, AT&T's twenty-sixth floor could have been mistaken for a staging area for soon-to-be retirees, with Romnes sixty-three years old, deButts fifty-five, and their executive colleagues in the same range. Although they were far better educated, they came from the same generation as the intolerant Archie Bunker from TV's *All in the Family,* not that of his liberal college student son-in-law whom he called Meathead. And since none were black or female, they had no personal experience of discrimination. As a result, they had no way to relate to the EEOC's criticism. It was just one more pressure, about issues they had previously noticed only in news accounts of rallies and sit-ins, that was now invading their workplace.

Finally, the AT&T executives were mad because they weren't being treated in the manner to which they were accustomed. In their monopolistic culture, you talked, you asked, you suggested, you discussed. You didn't just launch an assault. "The fact that we were attacked rather than approached about any perceived problems in this area was why the management reacted so strongly," George Ashley, an AT&T general attorney in 1970, says today.[9] Apparently, it should have been obvious the company would willingly acquiesce to this government request as long as it came in a calm, professional package.

A pocket of Bell System employees actually had been aware that this type of attack might occur. AT&T's general attorneys, who reported directly to

Horace Moulton, the company's general counsel, noticed months before that the FCC had started to meddle in the employment policies of some TV and radio stations it licensed. They discussed the activity among themselves, shared the information with Moulton, and filled their personnel colleagues in. Even though they felt little imminent threat because AT&T was monitored by the FCC's other half, the Common Carrier Bureau, they were aware that it could affect them some day. As George Ashley says now, "If the FCC was going to get involved with broadcast licensees in personnel stuff, it could be very possible they'd do it with us."[10]

It's unknown if this awareness ever reached the twenty-sixth floor, but if so, the top executives shared the lawyers' generally unconcerned attitude. AT&T's leaders saw the broadcast networks as far more vulnerable, under pressure to include African Americans in TV shows and commercials and facing the FCC's scrutiny annually during their required license renewals. On the other hand, the FCC merely required the Bell System to provide top-quality service to its customers. Since the numbers of blacks or Spanish-speaking Americans AT&T managers hired would have no influence on the company's ability to do that, the executives weren't worried. In addition, the FCC Broadcast Bureau's attacks on its licensees to date had been race-based. The fact that AT&T was doing well by blacks, as well as anyone in that time, offered additional assurances that the Bell System wouldn't be targeted.

Some of AT&T's personnel employees also heard about the EEOC's pro-posed attack more directly before it was launched. On November 24, 1970, less than a week after Copus's brainstorm, John Kingsbury, AT&T's assistant vice president of personnel, and one of his staffers had lunch with Bill Brown in Washington, D.C., to discuss Bell System employment tests. Brown wanted to make sure that all BOCs were using standardized tests that didn't unfairly disqualify minority job candidates, but he also had other things on his mind. During the lunch, in his calm, professional manner, Brown men-tioned that the EEOC was planning to intervene in AT&T's rate case, hop-ing this would encourage AT&T executives to think about their present poli-cies and motivate them to change. Kingsbury, a mild-mannered, slight man a generation older than the young EEOC lawyers who would soon become his opponents, took the news calmly himself. *Oh, that's interesting,* he re-plied. Perhaps he didn't believe Brown, perhaps he thought AT&T's record on race would make such an intervention irrelevant, perhaps he had no clue of the magnitude of the upcoming EEOC charges, perhaps he looked at the EEOC as a tiny gnat capable of doing little harm to AT&T, or perhaps he saw this issue as beyond the paper-pushing purview of his job. In any case, whatever communication he passed on to his bosses from Bill Brown did nothing to prepare them for the EEOC's assault. They were outraged, and they were going to make sure the world knew it.

The press conference Romnes had called for that December afternoon brought out reporters from the *Wall Street Journal,* the *New York Times,* and the *Washington Post.* Romnes, as planned, allowed his anger to come out. He called the EEOC's action "outrageous" and expressed his concern that the government was hindering, not helping, progress by attacking a good corporate citizen like AT&T. The cause of equal opportunity "can only be harmed if organizations sincerely committed to expanding minority employment and with a record of progress like our own can be singled out for public attack by a presumably responsible Government agency," he stated.[11] Romnes had no problem directly insulting the EEOC.

After the press conference, Romnes and two members of his executive team—Bob Lilley, AT&T's executive vice president, and Bill Mercer, vice president of personnel—sat for the interview with the *New York Times.* They presented statistics from Romnes's earlier press statement to demonstrate their success at achieving equal opportunity: 12.4 percent of all Bell System employees were minorities, and 33.5 percent of all Bell managers were women, they claimed. And they vehemently denied that any of their divisions maintained separate jobs for blacks and whites. They did make one concession to the government, wisely admitting they weren't satisfied with only 2.9 percent minorities in management jobs. They then quickly suggested that failure would turn around once black employees gained more experience in their jobs and therefore were ready for promotion.[12] Fortunately for them, the reporter never asked about their own responsibility in making that happen.

The next day, the *Times* printed just one article, covering both the press conference and the interview, and buried it on page 16, while, at the same time, the EEOC's attack against the company got front-page coverage for a second day in an article about a racial discrimination suit the Justice Department had brought against U.S. Steel.[13] The company's benevolent image had been at least smudged, and the executives' hard work of defending themselves and their business had hardly begun.

No matter their anger, AT&T executives had to put together a response to the petition and get ready for any further work required. To coordinate the effort, Romnes chose Mercer, a company vice president and its top personnel employee. Mercer, who resembled Romnes in appearance with his finely chiseled face, swept-back graying hair, and polite demeanor, was a traditional AT&T leader. He had worked at executive levels in two BOCs—

NET and Indiana Bell—and in Western Electric; he also belonged to Romnes's cabinet, an advisory group of top AT&T managers who helped make most corporate decisions. He knew the company—the working conditions, many of the executives and their beliefs, and the types of business problems they faced every day.

Mercer also had more personnel expertise than anyone else in the upper echelon of AT&T. Although he had moved through Bell System departments like his peers, he had spent more than half his career in human resources—recruitment, labor negotiations, standard setting. The choice was also symbolic. By having his top personnel executive lead the task force, Romnes was signaling that AT&T and its executives weren't just tossing the project to the lawyers. They were going to defend their position as a first-class employer.

Mercer's best qualification to lead the company's anti-EEOC team was his experience in equal employment rights, which in 1970 made him unique. Lyndon Johnson had appointed him in 1968 as one of two men on the thirteen-member U.S. Task Force on Women's Rights and Responsibilities. The group was exclusively charged with reviewing the status of women in American society and pushing for legislation that could advance their opportunities. As the head of personnel for the country's largest employer of women, Mercer was a logical choice to participate. The task force met about a dozen times over the course of a year and produced one result—a forty-page pamphlet demanding that corporate and college doors open wider for American women. It was an unimpressive effort by today's standards, but at least a document legitimizing women's legal interests had been put on the government record.

Like most corporate executives in 1970, Romnes and his executive colleagues were far from equal employment experts, their Plans for Progress and JOBS experience notwithstanding. No matter how angry they were that AT&T had been singled out, they had to accept that the company was facing a legal challenge, founded on legitimate U.S. government laws. Even though they were sure AT&T was doing as well as any American company by its employees, they had to consider that that wouldn't be enough. Hopefully, Mercer's firsthand experience on the government's equal employment task force would help.

This hope proved correct. Mercer's task force assignment did make him better equipped than any of his colleagues to deal with the government, but it had another effect, too, less beneficial to AT&T. During his task force tenure, he spent long afternoons and some evenings with his eleven female colleagues. (The other male member, Vassar's president, rarely attended their meetings.) These women were lawyers and judges, graduate students and union officials, all "top grade . . . outstanding individuals."[14] He hadn't actually felt very comfortable around them. He remembers going out to dinner one night and sensing "people looking at me," the only man with eleven women. But it wasn't just the social awkwardness. Their views made him anxious, too. They would go on, literally for hours, talking about the rights and opportunities they believed American women deserved. But by the last meeting, he had to admit that, at some level, their ideas had sunk in. As he says now, "I certainly came away from it with a far greater appreciation of what women's concerns were and what they felt they could do." He hadn't become a feminist, but he'd opened his mind enough to see the issues from a woman's perspective. He would bring those feelings into his work as the leader of AT&T's team.

Immediately Mercer went to work on the AT&T response to the EEOC attack, assigning his assistant vice president of personnel, John Kingsbury, to develop its first draft. Knowing Kingsbury had a quiet but thorough approach to his work, Mercer had recruited him to join the corporate personnel staff in New York. Although Kingsbury's political antennae missed signals occasionally, with Bill Brown's lunchtime warning of the EEOC attack slipping by him just three weeks earlier, he *was* smart, knew the issues, and could present them clearly on paper. Plus, equal employment opportunity fell under his job description. Kingsbury also enlisted Liebers, who, with his work ethic and eagerness to impress in his new job, had all the needed characteristics.

The personnel staff shared responsibility for writing the response with AT&T's Legal Department. Company statements invariably underwent routine legal review, even if the lawyers involved had little knowledge of the subject matter covered. Although AT&T's legal staff included no equal employment opportunity experts, it still had capable lawyers to join this effort. Since the EEOC's petition had been filed with the FCC, George Ashley, the company's top regulatory lawyer, got involved immediately. Ashley brought in his right-hand man, Hal Levy, another FCC regulatory expert, and Horace Moulton, AT&T's vice president and general counsel, sitting atop the company's legal pyramid, would also review any document released by the company's twenty-sixth floor.

There was a strong similarity among the AT&T executives working on the EEOC complaint. They brought to mind the contestants in a beauty pageant, except, of course, for their gender. Carefully dressed in nearly identical costumes of dark suits, white shirts, and dull ties, with polite smiles on every face and exuding an undeniable earnestness, they were white men who had advanced by accommodating themselves to a workplace that valued conscientiousness, loyalty, and assimilation. And they weren't alone. In every Bell System office around the company, another set of these managers, albeit at lower levels, could be found.

They seemed alike partially because most had worked only in the monopolistic culture of Ma Bell. As a result, they took a careful, conservative approach to their jobs and brought no new ideas from outside AT&T into their workplace. In addition, the company's "generalist" management philosophy created more similarity among its staff. Bell System managers were required to move, typically every couple of years, to Atlanta or San Francisco or wherever the next promotion was. Company literature made the official reason clear: frequent job changes built excellent general managers who had learned the business from the vantage point of different cities and departments. But this policy also made every manager's experience nearly the same, deepening the monochromatic appearance of the company's workforce.

Over the years, writers have called these men "a bit dull and tamed to a corporate yoke," influenced by "a numbing uniformity in attitude, appearance and action." [15] This image could easily be interpreted as an employee body without abilities or accomplishments, but that wouldn't be accurate. Almost to a man, they were bright and purposeful, completely invested in AT&T's success. Their dedication and determination were far more valuable than innovation or individualism in the bureaucratic monopoly of AT&T.

The AT&T executives developing the company's response took an approach different from the EEOC's. They went small, preparing a five-page report and supporting it with statistics they considered impressive. Perhaps thinking a personal approach might enhance the document, Mercer also had his managers look through company files so that he could provide his own testimony about AT&T's employment record. At the same time, the lawyers wanted to be sure AT&T was legally protected from any hint of wrongdoing.

The resulting report appeared an unpolished compromise between the personnel and legal teams. Meandering from point to point, offering a mix of arguments, it read more like notes taken during the initial conversations between Romnes, deButts, Mercer, and Ashley than a declarative statement from a well-respected corporation. The report started with a complete denial of these "intemperate and irresponsible charges" and then launched directly into a case for the rate increase, justifying from every angle why the company shouldn't lose those dollars: the FCC wasn't the appropriate agency to review discrimination charges, U.S. phone service would suffer if the company failed to get its rate hike, and, most ironically, an even higher rate increase might be needed to pay for any affirmative action program the government might demand, an argument exactly opposite the opinion the EEOC's Bill Brown had espoused.[16]

Mercer's testimony, the second part of the report, documented recent court cases that lauded Bell's commitment to affirmative action and explained that the company's retirement plan actually favored women over men. He also spoke proudly of the company's good works for minorities and women: leadership in the government-sponsored JOBS program for the "hard core" unemployed who were predominantly black, strong support for the telephone operator's job that "provides interesting and satisfying work" for 150,000 female taxpayers, and the achievement of nearly 58,000 women managers, which represented 13 percent of all female Bell System employees. (It's not clear why the company chose to use this statistic rather than the earlier 33.5 percent women out of the total management workforce quoted in Romnes's *New York Times* interview. Simply based on numbers, the initial figure appeared more impressive.) While these were all points the EEOC would refute over the next two years, in their initial response to the agency's charges, AT&T's executives had presented a company profile they were proud of.

In an attempt to buy some credibility, Mercer admitted that AT&T had made a few mistakes in its employment policies. He acknowledged the company had segregated jobs by sex at one time—for example, the switch*man* and the frame*man*—but those distinctions, he claimed, had been almost completely eliminated. Only jobs with a legal BFOQ based on gender, meaning they required a capability men had and women didn't, were still sex-segregated. For example, the Bell System had no female cable splicers because management believed the job required a strength no woman possessed. Then, right in the midst of his testimony, Mercer announced an immediate policy change. "We still believe the [lineman and cable splicer] jobs require certain physical capabilities not usually found in females," he wrote. "However, if a qualified female should apply for such a job, she will be given an equal employment opportunity."[17] The government would see that AT&T was ready and willing to change.

In the end, though, Mercer's job was to defend AT&T. He claimed that "word-of-mouth" recruiting was cost-effective in a tight labor market and reiterated, in conclusion, the company's total refutation of the petition's charge of "pervasive, system-wide and blatantly unlawful discrimination. . . . We submit that our record of accomplishment affirmatively shows such a charge to be untrue and irresponsible."

The personnel executives and lawyers had done their best to make AT&T's case, given the time frame and the facts. They sent their package back to the FCC on Friday, December 18, 1970, even though they doubted this would dig them out of their hole. As Mercer says now, "I just felt that once that suit had been filed, the FCC would find it difficult to say no, and we would [have to defend ourselves.]"[18] But for now, all they could do was wait for the FCC to respond.

4

The Beginning

Winter/Spring 1971

While EEOC and AT&T staffers enjoyed holiday celebrations as 1970 ended, the stone the EEOC had tossed into the corporate ocean continued to produce circles of waves. Before the end of the year, newspapers in Scranton, Pennsylvania; Minneapolis; and several other smaller cities and towns had printed articles about the EEOC's petition against AT&T. Some writers supported the government while others sided with the company, but no matter the slant, the publicity added to the negative climate AT&T faced.

In the meantime, EEOC supporters were rallying to its cause. Between mid-December and mid-January, letters of support for the agency's pursuit of the Bell System arrived in the FCC's mailbox from the National Association for the Advancement of Colored People (NAACP), NOW, the NOW Legal Defense Fund, and the American GI Forum. Even Curtis Wagner, an Army lawyer in the conservative Office of the Judge Advocate General, weighed in against the rate increase request.

However, neither the volume of letters supporting the EEOC's effort nor the number of news items about it affected what would happen next. A government bureaucracy pinned down by its own prescriptive rules, the FCC was required to act on any properly processed filing that was based on its regulations—in this case, against employment discrimination. As the former FCC lawyer George Sape says today, "It could have been the Ku Klux Klan that had filed this filing—it wouldn't have mattered. The Commission wasn't going to throw it out because all the procedures had been fulfilled and it was, at least on the appearance, filed under the Commission's own rule."[1]

AT&T's top brass wanted to influence the approach the FCC took. The rate increase the EEOC was trying to stop was vital to the company's strategic plans, and top executives feared that the case addressing that request would be dismissed entirely or postponed until the EEOC's complaint got resolved, probably after months or even years. However, if the FCC gave the employment issue its own forum, perhaps the discussion of higher rates for AT&T could still proceed, just on a separate track. As a result, George Ashley's bosses, the company's top regulatory lawyers, suggested that approach to the FCC, hoping to recoup at least some of their expected revenue jump.

The FCC bought the company's pitch. Spacing its decision over nine days, it first announced on January 12, 1971, that it would approve an immediate jump of 4 percent (instead of 6 percent) in AT&T's long-distance rates and would arrange for expedited hearings on the larger amount. Then on January 21, 1971, it ordered separate public hearings about AT&T's employment practices.

When the AT&T executives filed for the lower rate increase the next day, another stream of letters arrived at the FCC, this time in protest. Bill Brown and the EEOC themselves weighed in along with the NAACP, NOW, the NOW Legal Defense Fund, the American Civil Liberties Union (ACLU), and California Rural Legal Assistance (CRLA) and the Mexican American Legal Defense and Educational Fund (MALDEF), both of which represented Hispanics. Even Ralph Nader, already America's most powerful consumer advocate based on his 1965 automobile industry exposé *Unsafe at Any Speed,* wrote a letter. But all the complaints went for naught. The FCC allowed AT&T the smaller increase, guaranteeing the company $175 million in additional long-distance revenues.

The executives on AT&T's twenty-sixth floor acquiesced to this series of decisions. Just five weeks earlier, they had been attacked by the EEOC for their poor employment record and threatened with no long-distance increase at all. Now at least the FCC had assured them a majority chunk of that revenue jump, without the pain of public hearings. In addition, although they were still mad about the EEOC assault, they had secured a forum to address it where they thought they'd look the best.

The mood at the EEOC on that January Thursday was markedly different. It was now the government's turn for surprise, even shock. After filing their petition against the Bell System, the most Brown and Copus had actually hoped for was the chance to present evidence in the FCC hearings about AT&T's rate increase request. Even that opportunity had felt like an uphill battle to Brown, but now he and his young legal team would see their charges against the country's largest company placed front and center in a hearings procedure before a major federal commission. For the agency known as a "toothless tiger," this outcome was far better than anything they could have imagined, "a staggering result," as Copus says today.[2] Brown also understood that AT&T's request for separate hearings would work only to his agency's advantage. "It was much better for us that [the FCC] separated out the portion we were concerned with," Brown recalls now, "because it allowed us to put the spotlight on a very narrow issue—whether or not AT&T discriminated against women and minorities."[3]

At the EEOC, however, jubilation had to share the stage with trepidation, particularly for David Copus. Being assigned their own FCC docket number, #19143, and given notice that hearings would start soon, the EEOC lawyers now had to litigate a lawsuit, which meant digging up evidence, preparing witnesses, presenting testimony, cross-examining, and objecting and maneuvering around a courtroom, something with which few, if any, lawyers in the EEOC's General Counsel's Office had experience. Copus certainly had none. Once past his initial surprise, he remembers he had just one question: "What do we do now?"[4]

Copus and his EEOC colleagues weren't the only players in this drama suffering from inexperience. A close examination of the roster of key participants revealed that not one could be considered truly prepared for the job ahead. First came Frederick Denniston, the FCC hearings examiner just assigned who would sit as judge and jury for the proceeding. For any FCC hearing, a hearings examiner—later known, more accurately, as an administrative law judge—was selected from a pool of FCC lawyers to preside over the hearings room, just as a judge would oversee a courtroom trial. However, the hearings examiner never had a jury's help. At the end of the proceedings, he alone would decide the case, whether to allow a telephone company rate increase request or, in this situation, order a change in a major licensee's employment practices. Before he made his final ruling, the examiner *would* get advice from FCC lawyers who, participating as a party equal to the case's plaintiff and defendant, represented the public during the hearings. But the final and legally binding judgment lay solely in the hearings examiner's hands.

This structure placed a lot of responsibility on Fred Denniston. A white-haired gentleman close to retirement, he had built a reputation as being competent and fair in his years on the FCC bench. He had also become an expert on the hearings process and was known for his ability to evaluate objectively the evidence presented, earning the sobriquet of "classic" hearings examiner from FCC insiders. The EEOC staffers, however, were less impressed, seeing him as a kindly grandfather who knew nothing about the issue at hand: employment discrimination. As Randy Speck, who would work on the EEOC's AT&T Task Force, remembers, "[Denniston] was your standard run-of-the-mill hearings examiner who had done communications issues exclusively. I don't think he had any background at all that would have been relevant."[5] This, of course, made sense, since regulating employment discrimination was new and the FCC's regulations against it were even newer. In fact, Denniston was as good a choice as the FCC had. No other examiner had more experience on the issue at that time, and at least Denniston knew the process. Starting that winter of 1971, he would just have to learn, quickly, about equal employment law.

George Ashley and Hal Levy, the lawyers AT&T chose to head the company's defense during the FCC hearings, needed to take the same crash course in employment discrimination law as Denniston would. Simply by looking at the company's lead lawyers, you could guess their hometowns. Ashley, who was of average build and in his forties, had the wholesome, content look of someone who grew up in the midwestern state of Missouri; Levy, several years younger, appeared every bit the New Yorker with his helmet of dark hair and intense gaze. Like Denniston, they also came to the hearings with tremendous expertise in their field and reputations as being smart and capable. But as Ashley admits today, "I wasn't a labor specialist . . . and Levy wasn't a specialist in employment work."[6] Perhaps the company's executives should have assigned some of their labor experts, but those lawyers' experience lay primarily in dealing with unions, not aggrieved female or black employees. Because few EEOC complaints made it to the Justice Department's desk, never mind into court, the company had little reason to employ equal employment lawyers. In any case, those lawsuits would have been primarily against BOCs, like Southern Bell, in which AT&T corporate lawyers would have played little role. As a result, AT&T assigned two lawyers who, in their daily jobs, were "responsible for any issues before the FCC."[7] Like Denniston, they knew the hearings process even if they had no experience in defending their company against this type of charge.

This lack of equal employment law expertise within AT&T and the FCC represented a fact of the times, not an error by either's management. By the spring of 1971, Title VII of the Civil Rights Act, which prohibited discrimination against women and minorities in the workplace and had established the EEOC, had been in effect for less than six years. A body of law in the field hadn't yet been built, never mind a stable of expert lawyers. At the same time, relevant laws and court decisions were regularly popping up: On March 8, 1971, the Supreme Court decided *Griggs v. Duke Power,* upholding the illegality of "disparate impact," in which an employment policy leads to discrimination, whether intentionally or not, and in December President Nixon's Labor Department would implement Revised Order #4, which required federal contractors to set goals and timetables for hiring women. In such a new field, the Bell System and its evaluator, the FCC, had produced the best candidates they had to work on this groundbreaking case.

Of the three groups with key roles in the case, the EEOC alone could claim employment law expertise, although it was not very deep. Copus and Larry Gartner, who had been named as the EEOC's other litigator, had each passed the bar just a year or two earlier, an achievement that proved they understood the law intellectually but offered no prediction about their ability to practice it. At least they were steeped in the issues. They had studied Title VII and Executive Order #11246 and the Equal Pay Act, they had researched the statistics, they had written the briefs. They knew nearly as much as anyone in the United States knew about equal employment law in that day.

However, they too would bring impairments into the FCC hearings room, their lack of litigation experience the most significant one. As a former deputy district attorney, Bill Brown knew this was a problem from the start. As he points out today, "David certainly was not a solid litigator," and Gartner, with even less legal experience, wasn't either.[8] Yet stepping into the hearings room himself fit into neither Brown's job description as EEOC chair nor his busy calendar. For the time being, he would live with Copus and Gartner behind the prosecution's table and hope their intelligence and motivation would overcome their utter lack of experience.

This two-man EEOC team was missing one other attribute typically important in a successful legal effort: they lacked the true conviction of their case. Although neither had been true activists for civil rights—Copus being too easygoing, Gartner too cerebral—they both believed in blacks' cause and continued to see this case solely through a racial lens. To date, they had paid little attention to the gender discrimination Susan Ross had emphasized in their petition to the FCC, and, looking for a more exciting project, she had moved on to fight against pregnancy discrimination laws. She wasn't around to whisper, or shout if necessary, in these two young men's ears that the sex discrimination aspect of this case was the most powerful.

Although this across-the-board inexperience was sure to hamper the efficient legal pursuit of the case, it bestowed a bit of poetic justice on the proceedings. Three groups of lawyers were about to step off a precipice. They would litigate or evaluate a historic case about a brand-new legal issue, and none had anywhere near the appropriate experience and knowledge to carry it off. With the backing of their executive management and top government commissioners, they would simply do their best.

The initial schedule for these FCC hearings was extremely optimistic, with a start date just two months in the future, on March 29, 1971. As a result, Copus and Gartner needed to get to work quickly on their first responsibility, and even they knew what it was. During their first year of law school, they learned about "discovery," the process by which a lawyer gathers the information to develop his or her argument; it can encompass questions to answer, documents to produce, or interviews to carry out. Copus and Gartner chose the easiest focus: the paper trail a company as large as AT&T had to have created.

Anxious to get started, Copus began negotiating for these documents even before the first prehearings conference, which was scheduled for February 22, 1971. On February 11, Copus met with Hal Levy of AT&T and Dave Cashdan, a lawyer jointly representing interested civil rights groups including the NAACP, NOW, MALDEF, and CRLA, giving Levy the EEOC's first request for fifty-three groups of papers. He was looking for anything at all related to the Bell System's recruiting, hiring, and promotion policies, from recruitment brochures to job application forms to memos on job transfer policies. He also described the statistical report of Bell System employment the EEOC needed, showing "sex and ethnic composition as of December 31, 1970, by EEO-1 job categories, job titles and departments" for thirty cities around the country.[9] Just those requests seemed like a lot to the Bell lawyers, but Copus was far from finished, requesting seventy-four more groups of documents the following Friday.

Copus thought these meetings went well, believing he and Levy were developing a cordial relationship and sensing only "minor differences" between them over the discovery ground rules.[10] AT&T, on the other hand, couldn't have seen things more differently, which Hal Levy made clear at that first prehearings session on February 22. Although the AT&T lawyers never had a problem working with Copus, they were already becoming concerned about the EEOC's approach: the differences between the company and the EEOC were more than minor; the EEOC was sending AT&T on an "unprecedentedly burdensome fishing expedition" because the agency had already developed its case; the EEOC's requests were untenable because they would take more than six months to address and would produce thousands of pieces of paper as evidence. AT&T was "not encouraged that any continued informal discussions would be fruitful," Levy concluded.[11]

In some sense, that's what this case was about: paper. In 1971, when companies and their employees had no desktop computers that automatically archived work, or e-mail accounts that recorded every note written, or voice mail that stored detailed phone messages, business was done via paper. A giant corporation like AT&T with its two dozen plus divisions produced a massive amount: letters, memos, policies, reports, forms, all produced on sturdy white paper, recording corporate procedures and practices, filed in the offices and back rooms and basements of thousands of Bell System buildings around the country. These were the items the EEOC would need to build its case, whether they filled one file cabinet or an entire building, and after Levy finished his initial speech, Copus said as much: "If we are to conduct an examination of [the Bell System's] employment practices, it will require a substantial amount of information from the company"; the documents would "indeed be voluminous."

Denniston wanted to address one other issue Levy had mentioned— whether the EEOC had already built its case against the company. Although Copus, Gartner, and Ross had produced the original petition in short order, it did lay out a detailed position, including statistics, against the Bell System's employment practices, which might have appeared sufficient to confront the company in these hearings. But since that petition was written based on information only from past EEOC complaints or those found in the public record, Copus explained it had touched, "in [the EEOC's] view, only the tip of the iceberg." The EEOC lawyers needed more information, Copus said, to confirm discrimination's existence in the Bell System, identify where and how it occurred, and devise an appropriate remedy. "Where discrimination exists, it requires pinpoint accuracy in removing it, much like surgery in removing the cancer." Wildly mixing his metaphors, Copus justified the EEOC's demands.

By the day's end, the parties were teetering on the edge of an impasse, since even Copus had lost confidence in further discovery discussions. But Denniston, acting more as mediator than judge, pushed all parties to continue talking. As a result, on March 5, the parties reported that a discovery schedule was finally taking shape. The EEOC had narrowed its requests down to 107 sets of questions and seventy total categories of documents, and they also committed to respond to nearly all AT&T's requests. Even though he expressed concern that these agreements were documented only in scribbled notes, Denniston appeared pleased with the progress.

On some items, the parties promised immediate action. Copus agreed to produce the requests from AT&T by March 29, and AT&T stated it could provide its study of employment demographics by June 1. However, Copus refused the biggest commitment both Denniston and Ashley wanted:

commencement of their case by the scheduled hearings start date of March 29. Denniston had been feeling pressure to move the case forward in concert with the related rate increase hearings, and Ashley believed a delay would enhance the EEOC's ability to turn these administrative hearings into a courtroom-style investigation into AT&T's guilt. But with Ashley predicting a four- to five-month lead time to collect all the documents the EEOC had requested from every BOC, Copus stood his ground. "We wouldn't want to leap off before we were prepared to do a thorough job," he said. Denniston, much to his disappointment, postponed the hearings commencement date indefinitely.

Although Copus had requested thousands of documents from the Bell System, the statistical study of the company's employment patterns was the most critical to the EEOC. Copus had learned the importance of statistics when he got involved with public hearings Bill Brown had arranged in Houston the previous summer. Brown had enticed local companies to testify voluntarily about their employment practices and demographics simply by sending each an invitation engraved on federal government stationery. After the hearings were complete, Brown had sent Copus to Houston to learn how investigations worked by observing those resulting from these hearings. But, true to form, Copus went beyond his mission. He quickly discovered the operation in what he calls "a complete shambles,"[12] with EEOC investigators interviewing each charging party individually over every minor ax they had to grind. The futility of that effort convinced him that discrimination could be proved far more easily by examining a company's overall employment demographics, instead of "looking at each little grain of sand on the beach to see how big the beach was."[13] Copus recommended this approach to Brown, who then assigned him to Houston for the rest of the summer to head a task force building the statistical case against the companies that had testified.

Nine months later, in the spring of 1971, Copus was mentally designing the EEOC's attack on AT&T based on the same numerically based model, which had led him to request the company's employment study as part of discovery. To process that data and to review the reams of documents, he needed help. He approached Bill Brown, who agreed, empowering him with the rare authority to build his own team for the AT&T case. Brown designated a task force, assigned Copus as its chair, and told him, as Copus remembers, *you can have anyone in the agency working with you, anyone you feel you'll need to make this case happen.* Brown gave him some advice, strongly suggesting he include an EEOC researcher on the team, and formally requested the necessary job reassignments, but Copus handpicked the individuals who would take up his cause.

Larry Gartner was his first and most obvious choice. Having helped write the petition against AT&T and participated in the prehearings conferences, Gartner knew nearly as much about the case as Copus. His involvement was a relief in some ways. Most of the other lawyers in the EEOC General Counsel's Office were tied up on other things—Susan Ross on pregnancy discrimination and several others fighting for the EEOC's legal enforcement authority—and not so enticed by Copus's attack on AT&T. Copus was lucky to have lassoed a lawyer of Gartner's brains and reason.

Copus did take Brown's advice and recruited an EEOC researcher named Bill Wallace, whom he'd met in Houston the previous summer. When he arrived in Texas in June 1970, Wallace was twenty-five, long out of his adolescence, married and separated already, with most of a Ph.D. complete. Although he'd always been the classically shy "nerd," he didn't look the part. Thin, with a mustache, beard, and hair long enough to braid, he resembled John Lennon in his waning days with The Beatles. He did have nerd credentials: high intelligence, an interest in physics and philosophy, an awkwardness with women, although during his Houston hearings assignments, he got a chance to leave some of that behind. Soon after arriving, he befriended the Houston project's secretary, who at younger than twenty had all the savoir-faire he lacked. Evenings Wallace would hang out in his hotel room and get high with her and her boyfriend, a Californian with movie star looks, his own car, and no apparent responsibilities. Each morning after, he would drag himself into the EEOC office against their protestations. Somehow he managed to keep his job but devoted most of his ten weeks in Texas to growing up.

Copus, a few years older than Wallace and a tiny bit more mature, never ran into Wallace outside the office in Houston, but they did meet at work. Copus needed help with his assignment to build statistical cases against the Houston companies to prove discrimination. For one company, the percentage of blacks on its payroll was much lower than the EEOC target, but Copus needed to know if that difference was statistically significant, meaning the EEOC could file its charges. A friend suggested that Wallace was good with figures, so Copus sought him out.

Although Wallace's reputation as a former physics major at the Massachusetts Institute of Technology (MIT) had given him the title "the guy to go to for numbers," in reality, he knew little about statistics. When Copus arrived with his question, Wallace, a little embarrassed, had no clue how to determine statistical significance, but he could tell Copus was in a hurry. And there was something about Copus—a sense of authority and certainty, an aura of importance—that made Wallace, who was nearly Copus's equal in the EEOC hierarchy, put aside his other work and try to find the answer. With Copus leaning over his shoulder, Wallace called Bill Enneis, an EEOC researcher who *had* completed his Ph.D.; he talked Wallace through the computation. *You have to do a chi-square test. Now put your first figure in the upper left hand corner and your next figure . . . ,* and he went on. As Wallace copied each number, he could feel Copus's breath on his neck and discomfort beginning to flood his spine. This wasn't how he liked to do things, on the quick, patching an answer together, depending on someone else's knowledge, not his own. But at least it would get Copus out of his office. When he got off the phone, he told Copus, *OK, it's statistically significant.* Oblivious to Wallace's concerns, Copus responded with a smile. He had gotten what he needed.

A few months later, when Copus and Wallace were back in Washington and Copus was building his AT&T Task Force, he naturally went after Wallace for the project. He didn't know anyone else in the Research Department well, and, as far as he was concerned, that one encounter in Texas had shown that Wallace knew statistics or at least how to learn them. Plus, Wallace had worked fast and come up with the right answer. He was exactly the kind of person Copus wanted on his team.

In contrast, Wallace felt ambivalent about joining Copus's mission. He was hardly a statistical expert and had no confidence he'd always produce the right answer, a Copus priority. In addition, Copus "worked workaholic hours and wanted you to do the same," which made Wallace uneasy.[14] Wallace didn't mind hard work; he just wasn't sure he could handle Copus's scrutiny or match his pace.

On the other hand, as a twenty-five-year-old who, on good days, fancied himself an intellectual, Wallace also felt flattered. Copus had looked around the commission and said, *Here's a guy who knows his stuff, I need him on this project.* That was hard to refuse. Whether he actually had a choice or not he's still not sure, but in any case, he agreed to work with Copus.

To complete his team, Copus signed up one more professional, Randy Speck, another young white guy he had met in Houston. Speck, who had the requisite mustache, beard, and long hair of his generation, wore a wide smile and carried a soft heart. With a political science undergraduate degree and a master's in international relations, he was neither a lawyer nor a researcher in the early 1970s. He had been hired by the federal government in September 1969 as a management intern and had rotated through various government jobs by the following summer, when he landed in Houston to work on the EEOC project. While living out of a hotel, digging up data to prove the Houston companies' culpability in discrimination, Speck came across David Copus. In just one adventure, he became an ardent fan.

As part of his job in Houston, Speck had been interviewing minority employees from the involved Houston companies to uncover the individual, ax-grinding anecdotes Copus believed so ineffective. In one of those interviews, an African American employee of Houston's power company told Speck that the company maintained racially segregated locker rooms in the "underground," the area where electric cables were buried. Speck had toured it once with a company vice president and found nothing, but when he told Copus about it, Copus couldn't resist the challenge of trying again. Dressed in an all white suit—apparently the only other one in his closet—on a ferociously hot day, Copus, with Speck at his side, arrived at the underground facility's gate. Copus flashed his EEOC ID card, announced to the guard, *We're with the government, we're on official business,* and barged right past. Using a hand-drawn map Speck had gotten from his contact, they walked straight to the "black" locker room. An older African American employee they came across was happy to confirm the segregation claim.

Speck couldn't help but be a little amazed by Copus's enthusiasm and audacity that day, characteristics he observed repeatedly as he got to know Copus that summer. Whereas Bill Wallace viewed Copus with ambivalence, Speck saw him purely, as a "very charismatic, incredibly bright, very creative" figure.[15] So when Copus, who, for his part, had observed Speck's abilities and hard work in Houston, asked him to sign up for the AT&T Task Force, Speck didn't hesitate.

Needing administrative support, too, Copus asked Marjie Fagan, a middle-aged African American secretary, to join his team. Known as both down to earth and outspoken, she could provide these four young white men a reality check when needed. Although she appeared less emotionally invested in the case than her fellow task force members, she was good at her job, and, perhaps more important, her race and gender gave the team a tiny drop of legitimacy to fight for its cause.

Copus and his team of professionals were hardly the optimal poster boys for a discrimination case that, in the end, would dramatically expand women's and minorities' rights. Their appearances had changed little since their job hunts of one or two years ago: they were obviously still young and white, and, in their jeans and open-collared shirts, they still looked like unemployed hippies. But although they made lousy symbols, they had all the qualities to do the job. Bill Brown's tolerance of their appearance allowed an informal and energetic culture to thrive throughout the EEOC and certainly within this new task force. They may have resembled a group of young actors who had just come from a rehearsal of the musical *Hair,* but, in truth, they were bright, motivated young people, hard at work.

Over the next few weeks, the grumbling between AT&T and the EEOC continued. Although the teams briefly agreed on discovery requests at a late March 1971 meeting, they were bickering again by early April. As a result, the timeline dragged on. At the April 8 prehearings conference, Denniston allowed AT&T another week to document its latest disagreement with the EEOC and until July 1, instead of June 1, to hand over its statistical employment study. The actual hearings wouldn't be starting soon.

In the midst of the snail's pace, Denniston tried to maintain a sense of humor. When Copus expressed concern that Denniston had missed some discussions, Denniston replied, "I suspect I am fortunate in that, Mr. Copus," and he coined a nickname for the EEOC's efforts to cut down on its document requests: a trip to the "reducing salon." [16] But mostly he kept pushing, admonishing the parties that all remaining problems "had better be resolved promptly." [17]

Denniston was grateful for one announcement Copus made during the March 5, 1971, prehearings conference. With free time while AT&T collected its documents, the EEOC lawyers had decided to prepare a "prehearings memorandum." As Copus described, it would serve as "a brief for the Examiner's use during these hearings which will indicate our theories of discrimination . . . [and] set the hearing in perspective." [18] Denniston, happy to learn anything that might improve his effectiveness, responded, "This is excellent." [19]

The thirty-three-page memorandum, published on April 15 and now documented as a request from Denniston, hardly mentioned the Bell System by name but clearly laid out the coming charges against the company, specifically related to two concepts in equal employment law. The first, disparate impact, a type of employment discrimination the Supreme Court had just upheld as illegal in *Griggs v. Duke Power,* resulted from policies affecting different groups unequally and unjustly, whether a company planned that outcome or not. For example, a policy requiring successful applicants for a job to be at least 5 feet 8 inches tall would significantly limit the number of women qualified, even if gender was never mentioned in the policy. The second, institutional discrimination, a far more familiar term today, sprang from practices in existence so long and so ingrained in a company's fabric that they are seen as part of the accepted culture, even if they produce discriminatory results. Always directing female job applicants to operator jobs and males to installer positions without a clear justification would be one obvious example. The memo also discussed how to prove these types of discrimination, what employment policies and practices could lead to them, and ways to eliminate them. Copus and his task force had produced a fine educational document for the hearings examiner and an excellent blueprint for the case they were about to produce.

Naturally, AT&T was less than thrilled. By early June, Ashley, Levy, and an AT&T general attorney, Charlie Ryan, published their own highly critical forty-page response. Their primary complaint was the EEOC's decision to reverse the tenets of the American legal system, requiring the company to prove its "innocence" instead of the federal government submitting adequate evidence to justify its charges of discrimination. But the company's response included at least one sexist statement—"statistical comparisons totally ignore the significant differences in occupational interests and physical ability between the sexes"—which proved part of the EEOC's point.[20] In any case, the AT&T lawyers added this report to the case's pile of papers and headed back to their corporate office to collect more.

Beneficiary Profile:
Gwen Thomas

On most weekday afternoons, Gwen Thomas headed directly from her classes at Dorchester High to her new job as a 411 directory assistance operator in NET's Roxbury office. She had started in December 1966, three months later than she had hoped, having applied for a phone company job the summer before at a recruitment fair her high school had sponsored. When she had heard nothing by late fall, one Friday she stopped at the NET office near her home, where the recruiter, wasting no time, immediately put her through a series of tests, similar to the ones Peggy Falterman, the future Southern Bell employee, was suffering through, almost simultaneously, in Houma, Louisiana. Thomas, too, thought she might fail, especially after she struggled to list the five ways to spell "Smith," but her intuition proved wrong. On Monday, she heard she'd passed the test with flying colors. She reported to her new office two weeks later and started a nearly full-time schedule—3 to 7 P.M. almost every day and split shifts on the weekends: 8 A.M. until noon, then leaving the office for a few hours before returning for the 5–9 stretch.

Thomas, an African American woman who was of average weight and height and wore her thick, black, middle-parted hair off her face, hated the job almost from her first day, but she couldn't quit. Her mother, who put an enormous emphasis on hard work, told her "working for the phone company is the best job in the world," so she stayed.[1] As the responsible eldest child, she probably would have listened to her mother in any case, but any leanings toward disobedience had died the day, in 1958, a fire destroyed her family's home and killed her father. He had moved his family to Roxbury from Atlanta three years earlier, hoping to start his own business and provide a better life for his wife and children. He'd been on his way, already opening and operating a successful auto-body shop in the three years before his death.

With the support that business had provided now gone and seven children to feed with another one on the way, Thomas's mother was under pressure to survive, never mind advance her children's opportunities. She quickly proved she was no one to underestimate. When she returned to Atlanta to bury her husband, her own family expected her to abandon her northern dreams and stay, but she ignored them and took the train straight back to Boston after the funeral. Her sisters and brothers each volunteered to help by taking one or two of her kids into their homes, but she declined their offers, keeping her family intact. Neighbors probably expected she'd sign up for welfare, but in the eighteen years she would need to raise eight children, she remained a stay-at-home mother, making ends meet through her social security and disability checks along with an occasional donation from the church. Facing daunting financial pressures, living in an increasingly risky urban community, and hobbled by a chronic heart condition, she still managed to bring up eight kids who went to college and stayed out of jail. By example, fortitude, and a dollop of good luck, she taught them "the most important thing in life is a person's character. The rest will fall in place," and it stuck.[2]

Since education was at least as important to her mother as hard work, Thomas started courses at Northeastern University during the fall after her high school graduation. She took night classes, but with the odd schedule of a telephone operator, she found it hard to fit them around her hours on the job. The schedule wasn't the worst thing about the job, though. She hated the boredom, the lack of bathroom privileges, and the oppressive way she was treated, all the things Peggy Falterman also despised as a Southern Bell operator. Although NET executives had recently revoked the policy of firing an operator when she got married, the office environment still felt Orwellian: operators sat in long rows, as close together as chairs at a dining room table, with partitions to eye level on three sides, which ensured that an operator could see the heads of the women next to and in front of her but could never make eye contact. Supervisors often listened in on calls to chastise an operator for her diction or personal chats. Male technicians were frequently called in to repair the operators' antiquated equipment, working under the operators' desks while they, in their required skirts, were forced to continue taking calls.

The bathroom rules were similar to those Falterman lived under at Southern Bell, although NET's had an additional unpleasant aspect. In Thomas's office, the supervisors maintained a cardboard, two-dimensional dog house with eight slots that housed the names of the operators who could leave their consoles to go to the bathroom at any one time. Thomas also remembers being escorted to the "quiet room" when she had menstrual cramps, where the matron handed her a "greenie," a little green pill that knocked her out. Forty-five minutes later, when her lunch break was up, the matron would wake her up and send her back to her operator's console. Although Thomas never heard the results of the chemical analysis done when an operator smuggled a greenie out of the office, it was clear a doctor should have been prescribing them, not a Bell System employee. As Thomas says today, "In that era, we tolerated it because of job survival, needing the wages. You sit back today and you laugh."[3]

She doesn't laugh today about the guidance one boss gave her, though. In June 1967, when NET announced a final opportunity for employees to purchase company stock through payroll deduction, Thomas considered having the $5.50 withheld from her paycheck each week. But being "young, naive, and gullible"[4] and feeling she needed advice, she turned to her chief operator, a white woman, who recommended against it. *You don't need that, you need to save your own money,* the supervisor told her, a recommendation that, regretfully, Thomas took, costing her thousands and thousands of dollars over her long Bell System career. Today Thomas suspects that the treatment was more sexist than racist and perhaps not even that woman's fault. In that era, few women were thinking about saving money and buying stock. This chief operator was probably giving the same advice to everyone, advice she was most likely following herself. But for Thomas, the financial loss still stings.

From the time she started with NET, Thomas was well aware of what type of person was allowed to fill which job. Like Peggy Falterman at Southern Bell, Thomas worked only with women, both operators and supervisors. Racial diversity was limited in NET's Traffic Department, too: the managers had hired Thomas and a few other black women as operators, a reflection of the office's increasingly minority neighborhood, but they had filled only one supervisory job out of thirty with an African American. The Plant Department, where Thomas transferred as a dispatch clerk in early 1968, on the other hand, was more definitively split. The technicians were white men, the clerks black women with only one exception. Now in a less oppressive environment with a more flexible schedule and more interesting work—dispatching technicians to install phones—Thomas liked this job much better. Her supervisor even sent her for training in communications and organizational skills, an opportunity offered no one in the Traffic Department. The technicians did call her racist nicknames at will, but it didn't bother her much because, as she says today, "I was strong enough to express I didn't like what someone said to me."[5] She didn't take offense to the otherwise kindly man who called her Sunshine, but she made it clear Sambo was not a term of endearment and "bitch" just couldn't be used at all, "not around me."[6]

She worked hard in her new job while continuing to take college classes and paid little attention to the office struggles over race and gender, an attitude that paid off. With no union-sanctioned transfer plan in place, a year later, in 1969, Thomas's supervisor offered her a job as a station assigner, a low-level semiskilled craft position, an unheard-of offer for a black female. At the time, the EEOC was racking up employment discrimination complaints against the Bell System from women and blacks, but it was still a year away from filing its FCC petition against the company. Today Thomas believes she got this improbable opportunity because she was young, motivated, and capable while her co-workers, who had been in their jobs for much longer, were too set in their ways. Moreover, her boss, a kind former priest, worried more about the job getting done than the skin color of the person doing it. Finally, Thomas was a cheap hire. By advancing her instead of hiring a white male, the company could pay a far lower salary for the same work.

When Thomas got the news of her promotion, she responded with a self-deprecating *Why me? What an honor,* while her officemates had a much less low-key response. Although most of her female peers were supportive, even those who, based on seniority, should have been promoted ahead of her, the men were infuriated when they heard the news, demanding *What are you doing here?* when she showed up in their corner of the office on her first day. They had enjoyed working with her as a subordinate, but now that she, a younger black female, had been recognized for her hard work and was beginning to encroach on their territory, they were mad. Since their primary complaint was that she had moved up ahead of her white older female colleagues, her supervisor resolved the conflict by promoting one of them the following week. But Thomas hardly noticed. She was at her new desk, working at her new job—determining the appropriate wires to use for any specific circuit—and doing the best job she could.

5

The Paper

Spring/Summer 1971

By mid-April, George Ashley's protestations over the EEOC's document requests were sounding more like whining than lawyerly argument, but the company's recalcitrance in producing the paper was understandable. Few American corporations could have easily responded to requests for present and past collective bargaining agreements, job descriptions for all positions in thirty locations, and all memos written in the past seven years about equal employment and job advertising policies. Just those three responses, which would satisfy less than one-twentieth of the agency's total requests, could fill a few two-inch binders. AT&T's challenge was exacerbated because each EEOC request targeted all twenty-four Bell divisions involved in the case. Although these organizations took policy direction from and answered for financial performance to their parent company, AT&T, they had remarkable autonomy within Ma Bell's monopolistic design. They had their own job descriptions and union contracts and had produced their own personnel policy memos.

AT&T executives' concern stemmed from both the size of the stack the EEOC's requests would create and the time they'd need to track down all those pages. Since no central depository in any Bell company housed employment applications and classified advertisements and newspaper articles about personnel activities, each document the EEOC wanted would have to be found individually. Even then, it couldn't be sent to the EEOC until it had been reviewed by AT&T's corporate office.

Don Liebers, who had been assigned by his boss, John Kingsbury, as the personnel point man for AT&T on the case, obviously couldn't review

all the documents by himself. By March 5, 1971, while Ashley was continuing to argue with Copus at prehearings conferences about the specific documents the company would provide, Liebers had already begun to design
a process to find, analyze, collate, and hand over each of these pieces of
paper.

Teaming up with the manager responsible for coordinating AT&T's testimony preparation, Liebers recruited forty-five personnel managers from
BOCs around the country to come to New York for three- to six-month assignments. The temporary employees under Liebers's control would be responsible for reviewing every document that came in, ensuring it was relevant to the EEOC's requests, collating it with the equivalent papers from the
other twenty-three companies, and packaging it for delivery to the EEOC.

Beginning in mid-May 1971, Liebers's team spent their days at an old telephone company building in southern Manhattan, going through the reams
of sheets arriving from Southwestern Bell or Mountain Bell or Bell of Pennsylvania. And they quickly came flooding in. As Bill Mercer describes today,
"AT&T dictated what we expected of the [BOCs]." [1] If corporate headquarters wanted all this paper, the Bell divisions would send it right there.

Surprisingly, few grumbles were heard about the tremendous expense
the Bell companies were now incurring. Although the costs were already
mounting with months of hearings and negotiations still to come, AT&T's
top executives understood "this was just an additional cost of doing business," as Dan Davis, one of Liebers's personnel managers, explains today. [2]

While AT&T was setting up its document collection process, the EEOC's
AT&T Task Force had been organizing its office. Setting aside typical EEOC
policies, Bill Brown had assigned the task force members a separate space
on the fourth floor of the agency's headquarters at 1800 G Street in Washington. Although not large, this private area helped build them into a team
and kept them out of the day-to-day distractions in the General Counsel's
Office upstairs. Brown also found them a Xerox machine and, far more important, announced that Copus would report directly to the chairman's office for this project. In that simple statement, he placed the imprimatur of
the entire agency on the task force's work. Brown risked offending other
EEOC lawyers, especially Copus's peers, by elevating the team's stature, but
that one change dramatically increased the agency's chance of success in its
assault on Ma Bell. "We lifted as much of the bureaucracy away from them
as possible," Al Golub, the EEOC's deputy executive director in that era, remembers, so that the task force members could just focus on the work. [3]
Plus, under this structure, Brown would be more involved with this case

than any other, getting updates from his assistant Bill Oldaker, who met with Copus daily, and regularly visiting the task force office himself. Both the FCC and, especially, AT&T would understand just how seriously the EEOC was taking this project.

Beginning in late May 1971, however, the task force members spent little time in their new hideaway at the EEOC. They had been transplanted to a far less comfortable space at AT&T's local company office in Washington, D.C., the Chesapeake and Potomac (C&P) Telephone Company building at 2000 L Street. Providing every resource the EEOC workers needed with little of the comfort they might have liked, the company had also dedicated private space to Copus and his team. In this case, it was an empty floor, which had most recently been used as a storage area. The company installed steel bookshelves, a few desks, lights, and, in a concession to the D.C. summer heat, an air-conditioning unit.

Because AT&T insisted that all documents had to stay on Bell System property, the task force members spent most of their days at their "C&P office" over the next three months. Each morning, they got up early, arrived at the EEOC office by seven, did a couple of hours of work, and then headed for the C&P building by nine. The four professional task force members would methodically go through the new boxes of documents regularly arriving from Liebers's New York team, reading each one, paper-clipping the ones that looked most damning to AT&T, and setting them aside for the C&P Xeroxing operation. There was a palpable giddiness in the room when a particularly egregious document came along, most often pointing toward discrimination against women: a pink job application for telephone operators from one company, obviously targeting females only, or a set of classified ads from another, listing customer service representatives' jobs under "Help Wanted Female" and phone installer positions under "Help Wanted Male." Enthusiastic outbursts of *Look at this!* and *Can you believe what they did here?* could be heard at regular intervals over the course of each day throughout those months. To an outsider, the task looked as tedious as reading telephone bills all day long, but to these four young men, it was building to a crescendo of excitement. For the first time, they could see, in black and white, how to prove AT&T's guilt.

Even though Susan Ross had relinquished the opportunity to be an official task force member, she kept Copus and his activities in her sights and, in the summer of 1971, provided some help. In her life outside the EEOC, she taught a women's studies course at George Washington University's law school; one of her students, Katherine Mazzaferri, who had recently co-founded the school's Women's Rights Committee, was looking for a summer job, so Ross recommended her to Copus and his team. Since Ross wasn't on the task force herself, she was happy to provide another feminist in her stead.

Mazzaferri, tall and thin with long hair, was between her second and third years at George Washington University Law School. Despite growing up with a smart mother who believed that women should have jobs and support themselves, she didn't get radicalized about feminism until law school. In her criminal law classes, the professors forced the few female students to "recite the rape cases just to intimidate and embarrass . . . and make [us] as uncomfortable as they could."[4] Later, through the university's Women's Rights Committee, she discovered that the school had higher admission standards for women than for men. As she says now, "It was not a welcoming environment."[5] She committed herself to changing that culture, at the law school and beyond.

When Mazzaferri arrived at the EEOC in June 1971, Copus, glad for the help, set her off on a number of tasks: gathering information from potential witnesses, reviewing documents at the C&P office, taking her turn at the Xerox machine. Even Copus was somewhat aware of the poor image his "white male" team produced, so he was happy to have a woman involved who had at least a little legal knowledge. But she was far from sold on him. She later remarked to Bill Wallace, whom she started to date that summer, that there was an "irony [in Copus's] working hard on these women's issues all day long and then going to Georgetown on the weekend and womanizing in bars."[6] But she believed the work was important, so she tolerated his inconsistencies.

Copus at least treated his task force colleagues consistently, even Mazzaferri and Fagan, the team's secretary, who, by job title, were far lower in status than their male counterparts. Copus ran the task force as nonhierarchically as possible, sharing both grunt work and decision making among all members. Although no one enjoyed making the backup copies of AT&T documents needed, it had to be done, so everyone did it. Xeroxing hours were assigned, two at a time, for Marjie Fagan all the way up to Copus himself. In a joke mirroring the remedies they hoped to place on AT&T soon, every task force member had a weekly "Xeroxing quota." Of course, this egalitarian atmosphere would get strained at times—Fagan's opinion, particularly on a policy question, would never count quite as much as Copus's. But Copus did his best to make the decisions jointly, even when the issue was accepting a settlement rather than copying a stack of paper. As Randy Speck says now, "It was . . . an idealized view of what the work environment ought to be."[7]

Copus was even making strides on Susan Ross's biggest concern, his blindness to sexism, which he had to overcome to fight AT&T successfully. Finally, with Ross's help, he was beginning to understand what the feminists were talking about. Ross had been irritated when she first heard Copus, an EEOC lawyer theoretically fighting for women's rights, denigrating the importance of lawsuits filed by "stewardesses" because he saw them as married middle-class women who didn't need the money. As a result, as Copus recalls, she took him on as a project during the winter of 1970/1971. Knowing he liked to be the star of the show, she created one for him: every day for one week, she and he would have lunch together, but in reversed roles. She would play the man—that is, she would choose the restaurant, pick him up at his office, help him with his coat, open the doors, pull out his chair, order from the menu, pay the bill. And he would play the woman, happily acquiescing to all these niceties that were still the measure of a "gentleman" in that era.

The experiment began as planned. Ross called Copus to tell him they would be eating at a popular Washington lunch spot called Kay's Restaurant and went through the full gamut of what would now generally be considered sexist treatment—door opening, coat taking, bill paying. She was ready to continue with a restaurant selection for the next day, but Copus was a quick study. That first day he realized "all the things I did as a southern gentleman to honor and treat women with the dignity I thought they were due made me omnipotent and them subservient."[8] As he says today, after that one lunch, "a bright light went on, which put me on the right track" toward a feminist understanding.[9]

With that growing comprehension, Copus was in a much better position to analyze the documents AT&T was delivering. And it was the documents that truly educated him about the case. With just a little sensitivity to feminism, he and his male task force colleagues could easily see the magnitude of AT&T's problem. There were so many incriminating pieces of paper beyond pink operator's applications and gender-specific want ads: reports listing women's versus men's jobs and related salary scales, which were higher for the men; descriptions of separate male and female personnel offices; and recruiting brochures using gender-specific pronouns—"she" describing a telephone operator and "he" a pole climber. Although the task force didn't note them separately, some documents even pointed to discrimination against men: a statistical report showing that, out of more than 100,000 telephone operators throughout the entire Bell System, just over a dozen were male, all in one San Francisco office and hired as an experiment; and a note explaining how to refuse a man the opportunity to become

an operator. In any case, with all this evidence and their burgeoning feminist awareness, Copus and his team felt certain that AT&T was breaking
the law.

In retrospect, it seems surprising that AT&T willingly handed over all this
incriminating information. It had established an elaborate and costly process
to bring the documents in from the Bell System divisions to a central office
before passing them on to the EEOC, and one of Liebers's temporary employees reviewed each one before submitting it to the EEOC. It's hard to
imagine they didn't see their own guilt.

In the end, the company delivered the documents to the EEOC because
it had to. AT&T was required by law to act on Denniston's orders including
producing all documents the EEOC demanded for discovery, and, as Don
Liebers says today, "John Kingsbury and the legal team were a very, very
ethical bunch of people." [10] They would follow the letter of the law.

But if the company truly understood its culpability, a greater resistance in
other ways would seem logical. Perhaps the company's lawyers could have
argued about the documents' contents rather than their volume, which had
appeared Ashley and Levy's key concern during the prehearings conferences, or Liebers and his team might have presented the documents in a
more confusing manner, perhaps taking Bill Brown's original idea to "just
back up a truck and literally unload thousands of documents" onto the
EEOC's storage room floor at C&P.[11] With a mess of unorganized papers up
to their ankles, completely uncollated, the task force members would have
had far more trouble building a powerful case against the company.

However, such suggestions are moot. Most Bell employees looking at the
exact same pieces of paper would have found it difficult to recognize what
was becoming so clear to the EEOC task force members. The company had
operated like this for so long, with separate men's and women's jobs, that
the policies sustaining them seemed reasonable, or at least inappropriate to
question. As the EEOC had described in its prehearings brief, discrimination
can become institutionalized, and this had happened at AT&T. Men were installers and women operators in AT&T's corporate definition. In 1971, there
were few pockets of awareness within the Bell System that this was inappropriate, never mind illegal.

With the focus of the task force's review of AT&T's documents starting to
move from race to gender, the EEOC knew it needed more than just the facts
those pages provided to prove its position against the company. For one
thing, it needed human drama. Copus's idea to intervene in the rate case, as
strategically brilliant as it was, left the agency without a plaintiff—the poor

aggrieved former employee, in this case preferably a black woman from the South who had been denied a promotion because of her gender and race. In jury trials, the appearance of such a person on the stand often could sway a decision and produce huge damage awards. With no jury and the implacable Denniston at the helm, the appearance of this type of witness probably would count less, but it certainly couldn't hurt. So the task force set off to find one, or more.

Limited to already settled cases, as required by the discovery rules Copus and Levy had negotiated, the task force still found the perfect candidate with little difficulty, an African American woman named Lorena Weeks. Randy Speck flew to Georgia that summer and interviewed Weeks, a former telephone operator for Southern Bell, in her kitchen. Weeks hardly fit that era's image of a feminist, which was probably her best characteristic. Forty-two years old, the mother of three children, diminutive, soft spoken, and from the South, she didn't appear the type to burn her bra, and she hadn't. She was just an average American working mother who had wanted an opportunity for a different job when her operator's position was eliminated. When that alternative was denied her in 1966 because the only other local job available, as a switchman, was reserved for men—as its name implied—she filed suit. The case climbed all the way to the Supreme Court over the next five years while Weeks suffered through a suspension from Southern Bell and then reemployment as a clerk, another low-paid, females-only job in which she sat five feet from a supervisor who despised her for taking action against the company. In the meantime, denied the overtime typical of a switchman's job, she was forced to put her kids through college on 12 percent interest loans. Finally, late in 1970, she won her case. She started as a switchman in Southern Bell on March 3, 1971. Speck's success in guaranteeing her testimony gave the EEOC just the unambiguous symbol of female oppression it needed.

Speck found a few other sympathetic witnesses, too, including Helen Roig, another telephone operator (this time from South Central Bell in New Orleans) who had won at least one discrimination case against the telephone company. He also traveled to New York to recruit additional aggrieved phone company employees to testify. He met with several low-level women on New York Telephone's Albany payroll who couldn't get switchman jobs and with members of a Hispanic group in the Bronx who had faced racial discrimination. Through all these individual faces, the EEOC hoped that AT&T's poor employment policies would come to light.

In addition to compelling stories, the agency needed expert witnesses who could further prove its position. These well-educated individuals would take the stand, under oath, and provide their opinions that women weren't genetically predisposed to avoid high-paying jobs, as AT&T had contended, or present their well-documented studies proving that women, or men, can be pushed into wanting certain kinds of jobs based on the advertising they see. Bill Brown knew exactly the person to pull this expertise together. Phyllis Wallace, a former EEOC researcher, had the contacts necessary to track down the needed experts; plus, she happened to be female and black, just the type of person Brown wanted working on the case.

Phyllis Wallace couldn't have had a more unlikely background. With her dark skin, flat nose, and omnipresent "funny little black hat," [12] she looked more like a choir member in a rural southern church than a woman with an undergraduate degree from New York University and a Ph.D. from Yale, which she earned in the 1940s. She eventually went on to jobs with the CIA (as an economist, not a spy), the EEOC, and the New York–based Metropolitan Applied Research Center (MARC) before landing a professor's appointment at MIT's Sloan School of Business in the mid-1970s. An unmistakable outsider in most of these experiences, she remained remarkably open minded, building a reputation as a caring person who nurtured young talent. She was also a committed civil rights activist and feminist. Jim Crain, an executive with NET in the 1970s and 1980s, remembers her dogged determination in educating him about why women had to be hired at middle management levels and moved quickly up through the ranks. As he says now, she had "a very quiet, persuasive, penetrating style." [13] In addition to these personal characteristics, she had a solid reputation as a labor economist, having been one of the first researchers at the EEOC to use corporate EEO-1 reports to analyze and prove employment discrimination.

Wallace had left the EEOC in 1969, just after Brown arrived, frustrated that an individual with little research experience had been promoted over her head to run the agency's research division. In her typical low-key but determined style, she fought the possibly discriminatory treatment by just moving on to a better job as the vice president of research at MARC, the country's first think tank targeting African Americans' issues. Brown realized the error his predecessor had made early in his own tenure and traveled to New York to entice Wallace to return to Washington, D.C., and work for him. But she declined the offer. Now, a couple of years later, Brown contracted with her to pull together the expert witnesses needed for the AT&T case.

By early July 1971, Wallace had identified more than a half dozen experts, some at the very top of their field. Most came to Washington to meet with EEOC and FCC staff members on July 12, 1971, to review the EEOC's objectives in the hearings and begin strategizing their testimony. One of Wallace's finds, Orley Ashenfelter, was a leading economics professor at Princeton who specialized in the economics of discrimination, and another, Judith Long Laws, taught sociology and psychology at Cornell and had initiated research to refute the often quoted assumption that women were naturally inclined toward certain types of, usually low-paying, work.

Wallace also brought in Bernard Anderson, the African American Wharton School professor who had written the book on blacks' employment in utilities industries included in the original EEOC petition. She even got Lester Thurow, a nationally known economist, to attend that first meeting. Thurow, a frequently published professor at MIT, worked in the same field as Ashenfelter. Copus would have liked to use Thurow because he was "the smartest guy we talked to by a mile."[14] Plus, with today's perspective on Thurow's fame, Copus says, "Every once in a while I kick myself when I see his name [because it] would have been nice to count him among people I worked with." There was just one problem. He was *too* smart. The EEOC team "couldn't understand one thing he said." His name came off the witness list.

Copus also enlisted others to find expert witnesses for the EEOC. One of Katherine Mazzaferri's best contributions during her EEOC summer was recruiting Sandra and Daryl Bem, married psychologists at Stanford University, who designed a study about the impact of sex-targeted job ads for the case. The task force also found two doctors—Andres Hellegers and Robert Henry Barter—who could testify that women were capable of working during pregnancy. Adding these experts to Phyllis Wallace's team, the EEOC had found the best, most clearly communicative people in the field to state the agency's case against AT&T.

During these spring and summer months of 1971, AT&T was just as busy as the EEOC. Don Liebers had assigned Copus's priority request, the detailed analysis of AT&T's employment in thirty of the United States' largest Standard Metropolitan Statistical Areas (SMSAs), to one of his most knowledgeable staff members, Dan Davis. In the early 1970s, an SMSA, a geographical tool used by the U.S. Census Bureau prior to 1983 to make demographic comparisons, encompassed a city with at least 50,000 residents. The EEOC was interested in both the very biggest SMSAs—ranging from New York, with a population of nearly 8 million residents, to Indianapolis, with 750,000—and smaller SMSAs that housed large Bell System facilities and were home to significant minority populations, like Mobile, Alabama, and El Paso, Texas.

In each of these urban areas, the EEOC had made a simple request. Count the number of Bell System employees by gender and race under three umbrellas: their department, their job category, and their job title. In that era, Bell companies consisted of five major departments of interest to the EEOC: Plant, where craft employees who wired the circuits, spliced the cables, and installed the phones worked; Traffic, home to telephone operators; Commercial, housing service representatives who took orders for new phones; Marketing, filled with employees who worked closely with business customers needing more expertise than service reps could offer; and Accounting, whose staff counted each company's financial results. Within each department, there were a range of specific job titles—for example, telephone operator, clerk, switchman, PBX installer, service rep, along with a host of management positions—and each title fit into a job category that defined its level of pay and status within the corporation. For example, all job titles considered to be skilled craft, which would include both the switchman and PBX installer positions, would fall into the same job category because they were paid at the same rate. The EEOC had asked for a snapshot of the company's personnel based on these criteria on December 31, 1970, which would illuminate the results of AT&T's employment practices to that date.

When Liebers selected Dan Davis to do this study, he didn't know him well, having brought him into his personnel group only a month earlier, in February 1971. But he was aware of Davis's reputation as one of the Bell System's most knowledgeable and concerned employees when it came to equal employment opportunity. Davis not only shared AT&T top executives' intellectual commitment to fair treatment of their workers but had also allowed it to alter the fundamental way he saw the world. As he says now, his commitment to civil rights became "a personal philosophy that we're all interconnected and that if we are to succeed, everybody has to succeed for long term progress." [15] Coming from a white male born in the 1920s, this unique perspective made Davis, in the eyes of Liebers, a great candidate to work on this project.

Individuals who previously worked with Davis, a thin man with a gentle face, elfin ears, and a slight southern accent, remember him as impossible to dislike. His upbringing in eastern Tennessee, perhaps counterintuitively, had enhanced his understanding of civil rights. He often sensed that blacks from New York or New England kept him "at arm's length," but he felt an affinity with those from the South. That connection contributed to the empathy he felt toward people, from any part of the country, of any ethnic background, who were discriminated against because of the color of their skin.

Davis even had a feminist perspective, something his best-intentioned bosses on AT&T's twenty-sixth floor had never developed themselves. He saw the careers of his bright and well-educated grandmother and sisters top out when they were hired as teachers. Within AT&T, he lamented the stunted career of the secretary to Western Electric's president, who had graduated from college, Phi Beta Kappa, and also reached the pinnacle of her field by becoming an executive secretary. To Davis, the issue was economic. Not only were these women missing an opportunity to achieve their maximum potential, but, as he says today, "you had a lot of bright people who weren't able to contribute their talents to the success of the economy."

Even before his involvement with the EEOC case, Davis had found ways within AT&T to promulgate his beliefs quietly. As a public affairs and community relations manager at Western Electric in 1963, he wrote a white paper about the Negro revolution, designed to educate AT&T's managers about the problems in American black communities at the time Malcolm X's violent approach to fighting racism was gaining support. Three years later, Davis took a temporary assignment with Plans for Progress, the voluntary minority hiring program, recruiting other companies to commit to hiring more minorities. Although never agitating anything or anyone aggressively, Davis had used his influence to effect change for AT&T's African American employees.

Just a month after he started his new job at AT&T headquarters, he was at it again, this time trying to influence the company's reaction to the EEOC assault. On March 15, 1971, he drafted a memo to AT&T's steering committee for the case, which George Ashley and John Kingsbury led, suggesting that the company's energies should be put into "planning and developing solutions to the known problems in the personnel area" as opposed to fighting the EEOC's charges aggressively in front of Denniston and the FCC.[16] Davis's suggestions, aimed at improving nonmanagement promotion plans, eliminating discriminatory hiring practices, and reevaluating preemployment testing among other things, proved prescient, as many of them were incorporated into the final settlement. However, in the spring of 1971, the company's executives were resistant to making those kinds of major concessions. For now, Davis's job was to collect data, a lot of it, about how many Bell System employees of which race and gender were employed where, for the upcoming hearings. In March 1971, he set off to find those facts.

In most court cases, before the conflict erupts in front of a judge and jury, producing long hours of damaging testimony and spilling buckets of money, the involved parties try to settle. The EEOC action against AT&T in the FCC hearings was no exception. On August 11, 1971, two teams of three negotiators each, one from the EEOC, the other from AT&T, sat down to talk in

AT&T's suite at the Hay Adams Hotel, across from the White House. Today no one involved can remember the specifics of why these discussions got started, and there was no obvious impetus that summer. The EEOC task force members had already reviewed many of AT&T's incriminating documents and, as a result, were feeling confident of their case against the company, while AT&T wasn't worried because the EEOC hadn't yet turned its confidence into a written summary of AT&T's culpability. Neither party had a clear reason to push for negotiations.

Perhaps Dan Davis's egalitarian arm was felt here also. Within his first few weeks in his new assignment, he drafted another crucial memo, this one to Bob Lilley, the executive vice president responsible for personnel issues, noting the political challenge the Nixon administration was facing owing to high unemployment in and strained relations with America's minority communities. Drawing the connection to the EEOC intervention, he wrote, "The interests of the Bell System, the Country and our future relations with the EEOC would be best served by making certain concessions to the EEOC Chairman [to resolve the charges against AT&T]." [17] Davis's idea wasn't entirely altruistic: he also noted in his memo, "It is widely recognized that [the Bell System's] . . . future success is dependent to at least some degree on the survival of the cities . . . [and] the long-term success of the major cities is dependent on resolving the problems of fully integrating the minority communities into American society." [18] Seeing the problem as racial only, the company figured that starting a conversation with the EEOC about resolving the charges would be both good corporate citizenship and good business.

It's unclear how much circulation Davis's proposal received, but its philosophy eventually filtered into the series of discussions that began in mid-August 1971. As George Ashley described it at the January 21, 1972, prehearings conference, in his legalistic language, the EEOC and AT&T had decided to hold "exploratory discussions to see whether [the] parties could report back to their principals [about whether] there was sufficient common ground to obviate the necessity of hearings." [19]

The initial design of the negotiations made fast, easy results seem unlikely. David Copus, reluctant to let any piece of the case slip out of his fingers, held one of the three seats on the EEOC's team, which predicted a somewhat contentious atmosphere. With a sign on his office door stating "AT&T: Public Enemy #1," Copus hardly qualified as the open-minded negotiator likely to facilitate progress in controversial discussions. That partisan perspective added to his commitment to the case and lack of negotiations experience predicted he would fight, not compromise. Bill Brown, feeling it important for both the EEOC General Counsel's Office and its Office of Conciliations to be involved and wanting to balance Copus's aggressive outlook, assigned two more mature staffers to the EEOC team. Jack Pemberton, the acting general counsel, gave the team weight at the table, and Charlie Wilson, an African American who headed the Conciliations group, provided it with tremendous credibility. But since Copus knew the facts of the case—in some instances, better than AT&T—and believed so fervently in its legitimacy, he still played the EEOC's lead role.

AT&T had chosen its participants with equal thought. Hal Levy, AT&T's number two FCC lawyer, and John Kingsbury, number two in the company's Personnel Department, took the top roles on their team. In their areas of expertise and their place near the pinnacle of the corporate hierarchy, they balanced each other, but both had long histories in the structured monopolistic world of AT&T, which meant they'd had little experience negotiating with anyone at any time in their careers. Even though Levy's Jewish heritage had made him vulnerable to discrimination in the Bell System's historically WASP culture, he would never bring personal perspectives to the workplace. He would depend on his intellectual knowledge of the law in the negotiations and argue the case on its merits, just as he planned to in the hearings to come. And Kingsbury, who was known as kind, thoughtful, and by the book, was unprepared for the give-and-take necessary to achieve successful results in a complicated series of negotiation sessions.

AT&T did assign one lawyer, Lee Satterfield, who was far more up to the task. An African American who had worked briefly at the EEOC, he had gotten involved with the EEOC case when he first transferred to AT&T's Washington office from Bell's C&P division earlier that year. With chief responsibility for monitoring the federal government's activities on labor and equal employment matters, politics, and therefore negotiations, ran through his veins. For now, however, Levy and Kingsbury were taking the lead.

Although an immediate clash between these two teams seemed likely, the negotiations started uneventfully on August 11, 1971, with a few more meetings held that month. The teams followed a structured process, with agendas provided, notes taken, minutes produced and circulated throughout AT&T's and the EEOC's top echelon. The issues to cover were obvious: ending sex-stereotyped recruiting, offering women the opportunity to get nontraditional jobs, agreeing to back pay for the employees wronged by past policies, and, most important, ensuring that women and minorities filled better-paying jobs in appropriate numbers in the future. One demand the EEOC made, however, was unexpected. The agency wanted guarantees of women getting jobs men had traditionally held *and* men filling jobs currently reserved for women. The agency's task force had eventually focused on the Bell System documents demonstrating that men had been prohibited from the vast majority of operator jobs, and, as Bill Brown says today, "the basic law is you are no more allowed to discriminate against men than against women."[20] The phone company negotiators didn't agree. Although the operator's job had been referred to by company executives as providing "interesting and satisfying work" for tens of thousands of women, they apparently didn't see it as an enticing enough job for men. They were loath to set goals to make that type of transformation happen.

Although the parties argued over that issue and several others, few fireworks erupted in the initial weeks of negotiations. Nonetheless, little progress was made. Perhaps if AT&T had seen the EEOC's case against the company, it would have felt more urgency and produced more results. But without that motivation, the two parties simply muddled along, trying to argue their way to common ground.

Now, nine months after the EEOC had announced its intended assault on AT&T, one key party with regard to the issue remained on the sidelines. The unions that represented the hundreds of thousands of Bell System nonmanagement employees nationwide had declined, to date, to participate in the FCC hearings process. One union, the Communications Workers of America (CWA), representing about half a million Bell employees, was by far the largest; smaller unions, such as the International Brotherhood of Electrical Workers (IBEW), with members in New England and several other states, and the Federation of Telephone Workers of Pennsylvania, represented smaller cross sections of the company's low-level workers. Each of these unions had contracts with the Bell System company or companies where their members worked, which addressed personnel policies and employee treatment, exactly the issues the EEOC was demanding AT&T change. The unions' lack of interest in getting involved appeared wholly illogical.

The unions had been given the chance to participate. On January 25, 1971, less than a week after the FCC's decision to hold hearings on AT&T's employment practices, Bill Brown had had lunch with Joseph Beirne, the president of the CWA, pressuring him to become a party to the case. With all the female and minority union members the CWA represented, Brown remembers telling him, "It seems incumbent on you to come in on our side in this case."[21] But Beirne refused, which infuriated Brown. Beirne took the position that the case was about rates only and therefore not relevant to his union. Neither Brown's anger nor the fact this perspective was patently false, since the hearings for FCC Docket #19143 would be about employment issues only, fazed Beirne. He had his assistant keep up to date about the goings-on of the case through periodic phone conversations with Copus yet otherwise declined to participate officially.

Initially the IBEW, too, avoided any involvement. For the unions, the issue was far more complicated than an outside observer might perceive. If a company's employees were being treated unfairly, one would think the union that represents them should protect them. Certainly this was the EEOC's view. As Copus says today, the EEOC saw the unions "as an evil blot on civil rights, as obstructionists," because they would not fight for the blacks and/or women they represented.[22] In fact, they often aggressively defended their existing seniority rules that harmed women's chances for advancement.

But from the unions' viewpoint, they represented many more employees than just the minorities and women who were facing unfair treatment. They also represented the white men who had been getting the advantage for all these years. If they agreed with the EEOC and fought AT&T to change its policies, there would be losers, white men who wouldn't get the promotions and raises they would have received without these new "enlightened" policies. The unions were stuck. Although avoiding the issue might not have been the best way to deal with it, the strategy could claim a modicum of logic after all.

During the summer of 1971, however, one union, the CWA, did make an appearance in the case, albeit without its leaders' knowledge. In July, on a nationwide strike against the company, the CWA had produced yellow T-shirts boldly emblazoned with the Bell System logo—a large bell—on one side and "Ma Bell is a Cheap Mother," in large letters, on the other. With innocent intentions of relieving a little tension in the middle of fourteen-hour workdays, one of the EEOC's AT&T Task Force members wrangled a few shirts from the union, handed them out to his colleagues, and scheduled an outing on the Washington Mall. On the appointed day, the five of them, including Mazzaferri, packed a picnic lunch, grabbed a football, invited the official EEOC photographer along, and headed outdoors for an hour or two. As Randy Speck says today, "We were frolicking on the Ellipse at our picnic and [the photographer] was snapping lots of pictures."[23]

An irate Bill Brown, after confiscating the roll of film, demanded they destroy the shirts and challenged them on their behavior. *How could you when you're supposed to be professionals?* he asked. In retrospect today, with years of experience behind them, the task force members agree he was right. As

Copus says now, "[We] should have gotten into trouble, shouldn't have done it, it's not the objectivity that a government employee needs to typify, the opposite in fact."[24] But Brown's interception saved them from themselves. The Bell System never found out about the prank, and the team blew off some steam. The five EEOC participants have only one regret today. They listened too well to their boss's order—none of them can find their shirt.

6

The Case

By the early fall of 1971, David Copus and his task force colleagues had a lot more serious matters on their agenda than touch football. They were no longer working on an initial quixotic petition against the country's largest company, which Copus had worried would be stopped before it gained legal traction; nor were they preparing a generic paper defining employment discrimination to educate the hearings examiner. They now had to prepare a legal document that could stand up in a binding proceeding before a federal agency. They were about to enter the big leagues.

Although just as legally valid, the FCC hearings process differs slightly from a courtroom trial primarily because it depends more on written material. To begin, each side, starting with the plaintiff, or accuser, must develop a written statement of its position, including an overall summary and individual accounts of each scheduled witness's expected testimony. Before the hearings' start, the defendant's lawyer is given time to review the plaintiff's position paper and prepare a counterargument, which he or she will carry out in front of the examiner in the FCC hearings room. Then, when the actual hearings begin, as in a jury trial, each witness is called to the stand for questioning. However, in a time-saving measure, the plaintiff's lawyer never questions his or her own witnesses about their testimony. Since all parties already have each witness's testimony in writing, the defendant's lawyer handles almost all the inquiries, primarily via cross-examination. Once the defendant's lawyer has completed the assault on the plaintiff's case, the roles are reversed. The defendant must produce an equivalent written summary of its position and witness testimony, the plaintiff has time to review and develop a challenge for it, and then the parties go back into the hearings room with the plaintiff's lawyer now pursuing the defendant's witnesses through cross-examination.

In this case, the EEOC, as plaintiff, would go first, and by early September 1971, the task force members had what they needed to put their case statement together. At a prehearings conference held on September 8, Copus agreed that he had received "99 and $^{44}/_{100}$ %" of the documents requested, including Dan Davis's statistical study;[1] Phyllis Wallace had confirmed the availability of her experts; and Randy Speck had the aggrieved employees lined up to testify. As a result, Denniston could finally set dates for the hearings to start. The EEOC would have to produce its written case by December 1, 1971, and the hearings would begin on January 31, 1972. Now the EEOC team had to turn the information it had gathered into an unassailable written case against AT&T.

This was no small challenge, considering that the EEOC later estimated it received close to 100,000 documents from AT&T as part of the discovery process. All these pages had arrived from Liebers's document collection team in New York in the format in which they were originally requested, but now that the task force members had seen the documents and understood their strongest arguments against AT&T, they had to reorganize them to make their case most clearly.

Fortunately a Federal Judicial Center publication called the *Manual for Complex Litigation* (1969) addressed this challenge. The manual suggested that when documents become too massive to be included effectively in a trial, each should be summarized into the points making it relevant to the case at hand. Knowing they "had a gazillion pages of documents . . . [and couldn't] introduce all of them as an exhibit," Copus and his team dove right into this process, each member responsible for translating one stack of documents into bite-sized information scribbled onto individual index cards.[2] For example, one team member boiled a 1971 New York Telephone recruiting brochure called "The Modern Telephone Operator" down to the fact that only women were depicted as telephone operators. When one document produced more than one relevant fact, additional note cards were inscribed. Once the pile became overwhelming, Speck, assigned to put them in a manageable order, numbered the cards, reaching 4,932 by the time he had finished. Using a common term in EEOC investigations, he named the index card stack "Findings of Fact" and contributed it to the efforts of his task force colleagues.

While Speck categorized the cards, Bill Wallace was organizing the statistical data from Bell's SMSA study. Over that summer, the EEOC had contracted with Applied Urbanetics, one of the first companies able to take raw computer data and produce reports based on criteria their clients supplied. Wallace worked with Matthew Degnen, the EEOC's main contact at the company, to identify alternate ways of laying out and reporting the data and double-checking the accuracy of the system's output, a major concern in the early days of computer technology. Copus and Gartner, now working on a strategy for their first-ever trial, lent a hand to both Speck and Wallace when asked.

Weeks later, the task force members had amassed another vast amount of information, now on index cards and in computer files. But it was still just discrete data, not a legal argument, and their due date, December 1, 1971, was fast approaching. Part of their problem was the noisiness of their supposedly private EEOC office. The phones kept ringing; colleagues kept stopping by. Feeling overwhelmed, the four key players decided they needed "to get away, to think, write and be by ourselves."[3] Speck suggested a week at Graves Mountain Lodge in the foothills of the Shenandoah Mountains, and Copus got Brown, with little resistance, to cover the cost. Today Brown says it "wasn't an unusual expense to approve if I felt they needed to get away to produce a document to put my name on."[4] Plus, the weekly rate of this rustic, homey resort hardly stretched the EEOC's budget.

The four task force members fell into a comfortable, if intense, routine at the lodge for that week in the late fall of 1971. Each morning they got up early, headed from the log cabin they were sharing to the main farmhouse for a family-style breakfast that Old Man Graves himself, dressed in his worn overalls, served. Then they spent their mornings, afternoons, and evenings turning their facts, statistics, and ideas into a written account of AT&T's culpability in its employees' mistreatment. They allowed themselves occasional breaks, for lunch and dinner at the farmhouse or to play Frisbee or touch football, this time without a photographer in sight.

The work was mind numbing. In those five days, in addition to writing drafts, reviewing them individually, hashing them out with one another, and then producing them all over again, the task force members had to cross-reference each section of the narrative carefully to its source, whether it was a specific Bell System document, one of Speck's Findings of Fact, or a chart or table that Wallace's computer analysis had produced. That citation process was especially time consuming. With Speck working, at times, "a day and a half just on one footnote," they were busy the whole week and even when they got back to their D.C. office.[5]

Finally, on December 1, 1971, the four task force members proudly unveiled their written case against AT&T. They took its title, *A Unique Competence,* from an AT&T vice president's quote in 1968: "We think our experience as an employer, hiring some 200,000 persons each year, provides us with a unique competence to play a leading role in the improvement of equal opportunity."[6] Employing the same literary trick they used in the original FCC petition—turning the company's own words back on itself—the EEOC's AT&T Task Force members had imbued the entire document with an unambiguous disdain, matching their personal attitude toward AT&T.

A literary approach was certainly appropriate because with *A Unique Competence* the EEOC team had produced a book. Or actually several books. The basic written narrative itself, describing the EEOC's findings against the company, was unimpressive, at eleven chapters and about 300 pages. But the related exhibits and backup data caught one's attention. Just the list of Bell System documents that the EEOC drew upon to build its case totaled more than 400 pages; Speck's Findings of Fact, organized by subject and BOC involved, filled another 1,719. The team also included four other exhibits: a package of charts and tables; testimony from each of the seventeen expert witnesses the EEOC planned to call; a list of twenty-four documents "of more than routine interest," which, at only two pages, qualified as the most readable section of the paper, until you dug into the couple of hundred pages of attached documents; and a presentation of the statistical data gathered in the Bell System's SMSA study that Dan Davis had pulled together. None of these, however, compared with the 20,000 pages of backup—all those documents, directly relevant to the EEOC's argument, that had traveled from Bell operating divisions to AT&T's New York City headquarters to the EEOC Task Force's office in the C&P storage room to C&P's Xerox machine to this final statement of the case.

The document, in fact, was so large that Denniston called a special prehearings conference on December 1, 1971, the document's publication date, just to hand it out; the FCC had no intention of incurring the mailing costs. Under Denniston's suggestion, only the narrative and six attached exhibits "represent[ing the EEOC's] summation and the conclusions [drawn] from the underlying 20K pages" were filed in the case record, although the parties placed copies of the entire document, including the thousands of background pages filling several boxes, in an EEOC office and two FCC locations for public viewing.[7] Two and a half months later, on February 15, 1972, the *Congressional Record* published the document's narrative, taking up a full twenty-five pages and ensuring easy access for anyone interested.

So what did the EEOC say in all those pages? First, thanks to Susan Ross's influence and the power of the documentation that discussed the Bell System's female employees and their jobs, the task force officially changed its primary focus, placing the sex discrimination issue front and center. After an introductory chapter, which painted a picture of the best and worst jobs found in each of the five BOC departments, the task force devoted the next five chapters, or nearly 150 pages, to the gender issue. The race issue also rated five chapters—four addressing discrimination against blacks and the last, titled "The Invisible Minority," focusing on concerns about hiring Hispanics, called alternately the Spanish-surnamed or Spanish-speaking American issue in that era. However, the racial discrimination section followed the gender discussion and comprised twenty-five pages less in the report.

The narrative itself moved from disdain into full-blown venom. Throughout, Copus and his team had published comments one might think appropriate only for a task force strategy session in which a little private vitriol was being enjoyed at AT&T's expense. The Bell companies were "uniquely *in*competent," in a play on the complaint's title; their efforts to improve the status of women workers "have been incredibly timid and reactionary"; and Bell's failure to provide true equal opportunity for blacks "must be considered a national tragedy."[8] Far from feeling bad about using such acrimonious language, the task force members were proud of it. Randy Speck did admit that the task force debated using his line "The Bell monolith is, without a doubt, the largest oppressor of women workers in the United States" in the paper's summary of their sex discrimination argument; they realized it might seem too inflammatory.[9] But, in the end, to his satisfaction, they used it. Today he remembers, "I was . . . pleased that phrase always got quoted in the headlines."[10]

Whether the task force members' words were appropriate or not, their summary of AT&T's employment discrimination was comprehensive and clear. For each category—women, blacks, and Spanish-speaking Americans—they laid out what jobs these individuals filled, historically and at this time, and what specific company practices had led them to those positions. In the case of women, the paper delineated the efforts AT&T executives had used to avoid meeting the requirements of equal employment law.

Women in the Bell System were found, essentially, where men were not. In that era, eight out of ten female nonmanagement employees at AT&T worked in one of four jobs: telephone operator, service representative, clerk, or stenographer. The numbers were starkest for operators: at the end of 1970, only 224 of 165,000, or 0.1 percent, were male. Service representatives' statistics were just slightly, slightly better—99 percent were female. These jobs, along with the clerical and stenographer positions, qualified as the lowest paid in the company, averaging between $5,000 and $7,000 annually. In contrast, men primarily occupied the better-paid nonmanagement craft positions. At the end of 1970, 99 percent of the company's 190,000 craft workers were male, earning average salaries of $7,500 to $10,000 a year, nearly 50 percent higher on average than the typical female nonmanagement employee's wage. Beyond the salary differential, simply put, the women were stuck in bad jobs. The operator's position was particularly unpleasant. Doing dull repetitive work, limited in what they could wear to and discuss at work, and required to raise their hand to go to the bathroom, the women toiled just one small step above a sweatshop.

Women in management did little better. Although they filled 41 percent of all management positions at the end of 1970, the vast majority occupied the first, lowest-paid, level of professional jobs. Only 6.3 percent of women managers had made it to the next step up. Moreover, in the Traffic Department, populated almost exclusively by female telephone operators, the managers from second level and above were nearly three-quarters male. Even in a department they overwhelmed in numbers, women had little chance to advance.

Unbeknownst to the former executives of Michigan Bell, they had developed a policy that, in one simple decision, clarified the reality of sex discrimination in the Bell System. In every BOC other than Michigan Bell, the position of "frameman" was filled, as its name implied, by men. This position was a craft job, commanding wages of $7,500 to $8,500 a year. However, in Michigan Bell, based on a decision made at least twenty years earlier, the frameman position had a different title—switchroom helper—and was filled by women. Not only was it populated exclusively by women, but it was treated just like the other "women's" jobs in this BOC. Applicants had to be between 5 feet 3 inches and 5 feet 10 inches tall, they had to pass a clerical test to qualify for the position, their only chance to move within the company was laterally to another clerical job, and, most important, their pay fell at the clerical level of approximately $6,000 per year, at least $1,500 less than a male employee in another Bell company doing the exact same work would be earning. Based on that one simple example, the Bell System would be hard pressed to claim it didn't explicitly segregate its jobs by gender.

How had this dire situation for women come to pass? According to *A Unique Competence,* it came from the "sexist system" AT&T had designed and followed. Recruitment played a key role. Using employee referral, women and men recommended friends for jobs they knew were open, typically those in their own office, which was likely to reinforce the sex-segregated structure. Recruiting materials used at high schools showed women in operators' jobs and men as installers. Classified ads recruited service reps in the "Help Wanted Female" and craft workers in the "Help Wanted Male" columns that newspapers offered at that time. If you were considering a job with the Bell System in that era, the type of job that welcomed your gender was easy to discern.

During the hiring process, another set of policies came into play. The company maintained separate hiring offices for women and men where officials directed applicants to a certain type of job based on their gender; recruiters offered clerical tests ("the female test battery") to female applicants and craft tests ("the male test battery") to men; and interviewers asked female applicants a series of questions shocking by today's standards: Do you plan to get married? Do you have child care arranged? Are you pregnant? How does your husband feel about you working? Worst of all, female applicants might be subjected to a "home visit" whereby a Bell manager could see in person the woman's house and family and determine whether, in his opinion, she was fit for the job.

Once hired into their "women only" position, female Bell employees had little hope for promotion into a higher-level nonmanagement job for a host of reasons. Promotion procedures were never written down; there were only certain types of jobs—other female jobs—into which women could be promoted; the seniority needed to qualify for promotion, which union rules dictated, counted only within one department, so cross-department promotions—for example, from Traffic to Plant, a female to a male job—were almost impossible; new hires into craft jobs were preferred over transfers from other internal—read: female-dominated—departments; to be promoted, an employee had to pass the craft test, which women were never offered; promotion to some craft jobs required experience in a lower-level craft job, which women never held; and female employees had few role models of women at higher levels whose footsteps they could follow. In short, AT&T had stacked the deck against any woman trying to escape the company's lowest echelon.

The Bell System's maternity leave policy also left the company's female employees at a disadvantage. Eight of the twenty-three BOCs required pregnant women to leave their jobs by their seventh month, no matter how well they were feeling; Bell employees out on maternity leave received none of the benefits they would get if they had been off because of an illness; and twenty companies gave a pregnant woman no guarantee of being reinstated in an equivalent job when her maternity leave was up. These policies guaranteed that women who became mothers while on AT&T's payroll would have less income, fewer benefits, and, potentially, no ongoing job.

The task force's narrative also illuminated the policies that guaranteed that nonmanagement women could almost never rise into management positions. Bell companies required first-level managers to have experience in the work they would now supervise, ensuring that women could oversee only operators, service reps, and clerks but not craft workers. In addition, AT&T's programs of management assessment, for internal candidates, and management development, for new college hires, limited women's participation. Only in the late 1960s did women already on Bell's payroll begin to get a chance at promotion to management, and for college hires, the Bell companies who pursued women at all developed separate programs for them with a lesser objective of promotion than the men's programs targeted. At higher management levels, the structural problems were just as clear and echoed several challenges nonmanagement women faced: women rarely got above first-line supervisors' positions because they didn't have the correct—read: Plant—experience required for higher management jobs, they had no female role models to emulate, and they had to suffer at the hands of male bosses' stereotyped understanding of their capabilities and role in management.

Although, to date, the Bell System had publicly maintained its excellent treatment of its female employees, the task force reported that the company had essentially ignored its legal responsibilities to Title VII in regard to gender. In 1965, when Title VII went into effect, no Bell Company had an affirmative action plan. Actually, the companies were focused in the opposite direction, trying to use the BFOQ exception to allow their craft jobs to stay free from women and operator jobs free from men. These BFOQ claims against women in craft jobs were supported, the company believed, by state protective laws, which earlier in the century had been passed, in theory, to aid women workers. Limiting the hours they worked or the amount of weight they could be required to lift, the laws were useful for AT&T in restricting women's employment in the Plant Department. Even though the legal basis of the BFOQ exception had essentially evaporated by 1970 and many of the state protective laws had been successfully challenged, the Bell pattern of sex-segregated hiring continued. As the task force's narrative said, "All [Bell System jobs] were just about as segregated in 1971 as they were in 1965." [11]

The racial discrimination case *A Unique Competence* made against AT&T had notable similarities to the one for gender. Blacks, particularly black females, were concentrated in the lowest-paid, most demeaning Bell System jobs, many as telephone operators. Blacks were also unlikely to be found in management jobs. A white AT&T employee was 4.7 times more likely to be promoted to management than a black. And just as in the case of gender discrimination, these inequities stemmed from the Bell System's personnel policies. In recruitment, Bell Companies expressed a preference for craft candidates to hold a high school diploma even though they had no objective proof that achievement predicted better job performance. Because of the relatively lower rate of blacks graduating from high school, the only thing it definitely predicted was that fewer blacks would qualify for those positions. Moreover, the employment tests given for craft jobs limited blacks' opportunities because they were passed by 2.5 to 3 times more whites than blacks, although, again, a direct correlation between passing scores on those exams and good job performance had never been shown. The low rate of blacks in management stemmed from poor policies, too. At the end of 1970, more than 40 percent of all black Bell System employees worked in the Traffic Department. The company had done relatively well at hiring black women—although not if they were unwed mothers from the South—but had directed most of them into the lowest-level job in the company. And once they were there, they were stuck. With two strikes against them—being both black and female—they had almost no chance of ever rising into management.

Finally, AT&T's proud claim that it was a leader in hiring minorities had to be questioned. *A Unique Competence* showed that, despite the vocal statements and true beliefs of Hi Romnes and the other top Bell System executives, the company was doing worse than the industry average at just putting blacks onto the payroll in twenty-six of the thirty SMSAs studied. The same was true for Spanish-surnamed Americans: in twelve of the SMSAs where the Hispanic population was the largest, Bell's employment of them wasn't even close to the industry average. The statistics that the EEOC's AT&T Task Force had dug up belied AT&T's national image as a fair and caring employer for all employees.

It was difficult not to be moved by the EEOC's case against AT&T. With the knowledge that *A Unique Competence* was based on and cross-referenced to both the Bell System's own documents and a statistical study of its workforce done by an internal employee, the story the EEOC narrated appeared tough to refute. No matter how you looked at it, AT&T's "good corporate citizen" armor was showing some tarnish.

When an American icon is attacked, there is never a shortage of interested parties willing to exploit its misfortune. After the publication of *A Unique*

Competence, AT&T fell under the critical assault of media outlets, activist groups, and concerned citizens within days. The media came first. The *New York Times* page 1 story on December 2, 1971, opened with Speck's quote: "The EEOC charged today that AT&T and its operating companies . . . were 'without a doubt the largest oppressor of women workers in the United States.'"[12] Walter Cronkite reported the company's alleged employee mistreatment on the *CBS Evening News with Walter Cronkite* during the next two weeks, and the *Los Angeles Times* ran a cartoon on December 6 depicting an EEOC official, with a copy of *A Unique Competence* on his desk, finding it difficult to reach a telephone operator. The word was getting around.

At the same time, concerned Bell System employees wrote letters, although, in one piece of good news for the company, they weren't all on the government's side. One, from Houston Hughes of Texas, exclaimed that the EEOC's charges were false because all *his* employees were women and more than half were black. Activist groups were measurably less supportive, however, with several new ones, including the Harlem Consumer Education Council and the New American Movement, joining an already long list of civil and women's rights advocates wanting to testify against AT&T. Even the CWA seemed to wake up a bit. On December 14, 1971, Beirne, its president, wrote to Bob Lilley, AT&T's executive vice president at that time, expressing concern that the union and the company should "pursue vigorously a policy of eliminating any discrimination on the basis of sex, race or national origin" and asking for immediate discussions on the issue.[13]

For one activist group, *A Unique Competence* prompted more than just letters of complaint or petitions to testify. NOW, which had been founded in 1967 to fight for American women's rights, took it as a catalyst to act. NOW had always had AT&T in its crosshairs as the country's largest private employer of women, so when the EEOC's pursuit of the company began, the organization added its influence. Its leaders joined other civil rights groups in the early prehearings conferences to support the agency's petition, and its local branches staged protests at Bell System offices nationwide on March 29, 1971, the scheduled start date for the hearings, and delivered a "Happy New Year 1972" lump of coal in Christmas stockings to many of the same Bell locations. But even though these efforts drew headlines in some communities, they weren't enough to satisfy NOW's leaders.

NOW's president in 1971, Wilma Scott Heide, struggled herself to get media attention. A heavy-set woman, typically attired in a flowery dress or female leisure suit, her hair a mess of curls, Heide was known as both nurturing and pragmatic. She typically tried to educate her opponents rather than annihilate them, but since that guaranteed neither a good picture nor a good fight, she and her organization didn't interest the press very much. As a result, she was constantly looking for new angles from which to effect change. The EEOC's case against AT&T, which now had a sex discrimination focus and appeared to have a chance to make a real difference, offered an excellent candidate. Sticking with her nonconfrontational approach, Heide and her NOW colleagues planned to ensure that the agency knew what components were essential to its case against AT&T to successfully aid America's working women. The December 1971 publication of *A Unique Competence* gave them an opening to pursue that goal.

Heide and her colleagues realized their effort would be challenging. They were well versed in the EEOC's poor record fighting for women's rights and were also aware that the only feminist directly involved with the case was Katherine Mazzaferri, a part-time EEOC employee and law student. The EEOC obviously needed NOW's help, but exactly what type of help wasn't clear to NOW's leaders. In any case, first they needed to understand the approach the EEOC had taken so far. Heide asked NOW's FCC coordinator, Whitney Adams, to get a copy of *A Unique Competence,* which would give NOW leaders the information they needed to help them decide their next step.

Adams, an attractive young blonde woman who exuded intensity, had volunteered for NOW after receiving advice from a local branch when she faced sex discrimination while pursuing a doctorate. To date, her primary responsibility as NOW's FCC coordinator had been to monitor the commission's broadcast side, trying to improve the depiction of women on television. However, since the EEOC had filed its complaint against AT&T in front of the FCC, she would cover this case for NOW, also. Early in her career and not a lawyer, she lacked the experience to analyze the EEOC's report when she got a copy, but Heide and Ann Scott, NOW's legislative director, read it in detail. Although they could see that the task force had emphasized sex discrimination, the EEOC's lousy track record on women's issues sparked caution in the two women. They wanted to be sure, in the actual pursuit and resolution of the case, that women's issues were properly addressed. As a result, they asked Adams to talk to the EEOC lawyers involved to find out if they could be trusted to represent women's interests, which she set off to do.

After *A Unique Competence* was published, AT&T's situation was simple. The company's name was in the mud, and its executives had to fight to reclaim it. The EEOC, on the other hand, might have liked to wallow in its accomplishment of producing this document, which Jim Juntilla, an FCC lawyer involved, called "the most significant thing" the task force members would do in their lives, even though all except Copus were under thirty.[14] But these four young men still had the actual case to prosecute. They had set a high standard through their written narrative and now had to live up to its potential in the hearings room.

In January 1972, the two parties agreed to restart the informal negotiations that had begun in August and been abandoned by November. At that point, the original prediction had come true, with the negotiations deteriorating into loud debates between Copus and AT&T's most vocal participants, Hal Levy and John Kingsbury, over paying back pay and setting goals for male telephone operators. During the fall of 1971, these disagreements had become so significant that, three or four times, Bill Brown met privately with AT&T's Bob Lilley at the company's suite in the Washington Sheraton, a neutral location where no one who didn't need to know would be aware they were meeting. Lilley, a craggily handsome man whose looks and personality brought to mind Robert Young in *Father Knows Best,* had by then become the lead Bell System executive responsible for resolving the EEOC conflict. In his discussions with Brown, their focus was "to try to get some understanding" and determine how each could help move the process forward.[15] At least once, Brown and Lilley brought their respective negotiating teams to a meeting, as Brown remembers, admonishing them: *You all have to learn to work together, you've got to get your gut out of this case, you have to try to find some middle ground if we're going to settle [it].*

Since these initial efforts had failed, the two executives met at the end of 1971 to jumpstart the talks again, resulting in a restart date of January 19, 1972. The same negotiators would participate on each side, but this time around, they would try to "reduce what needs to be handled in the formal hearings" by focusing on specific issues, such as AT&T's use of sex-biased advertising, rather than attempting to settle the entire case.[16]

The EEOC's other focus, the upcoming FCC hearings, had produced another change. Copus had come to understand that he and Gartner needed help beyond what their task force colleagues could offer. The trial was no longer a distant prospect, and they had little idea how to pull it off. Bill Brown couldn't have agreed more. Based on his knowledge of their case and experience as a trial attorney, he added an experienced litigator to the team before the hearings' first day. Susan Ross, observing the case's progress from her feminist corner of the EEOC, heard of Brown's plan and recommended Judy Potter, the best female candidate she knew. With a feminist lawyer involved, Ross could be absolutely certain the gender angle wouldn't be shuffled aside.

Ross had met Potter when they, along with several other female activists, founded the NOW Legal Defense Fund earlier that year. Potter, a lawyer with nearly four years of courtroom experience as an associate at the prestigious Washington law firm Reeves, Harrison, Samms and Rivercomb, would fill both Ross's own agenda and the agency's needs, a combination not easy to find in late 1971. Aware that Potter might consider a career change, Ross and an EEOC colleague pitched the position to her. After a little thought, Potter agreed to take the job.

Potter, a pretty, slender woman who wore her dark hair off her face and maintained a much more conservative wardrobe than her future colleagues, looked like the competent lawyer she was. She had graduated from Cornell in 1960, an era of sororities and cashmere sweaters and decidedly not of civil rights. It wasn't until she arrived at the University of Michigan Law School in 1965, after a five-year sojourn to Italy, where she worked as a Venetian tour guide, that she became interested in activism of any sort. And her sort was a bit lower key than that of some classmates. While the first meetings of Students for a Democratic Society (SDS), which occurred on the Michigan campus in 1960, proved a breeding ground for radicals like the Weather Underground and the Chicago Seven, Potter and her more conservative classmates gave legal assistance to their disadvantaged peers, preferring to use the system to effect change.

Potter worked for a year in Michigan after law school graduation before moving to Washington, D.C., where she sent out many résumés with no response. Unlike Copus and his colleagues, who were just a few years younger, she wanted to work for a private law firm, and law firms weren't hiring women in 1967. Then she had her own brilliant idea. She began attaching one of her headshots from a part-time modeling job in Italy to the résumés she mailed out, and suddenly the offers came pouring in. Once Reeves, Harrison had hired her, the partners would often introduce her at parties with a canned statement, *This is Judy Potter. We hired her for her brains,* followed by a chuckle. "But then they found out I was actually a pretty good lawyer," she remembers today, "so I got a lot of responsibility." [17] She quickly built the expertise that was so crucial to the EEOC's case.

From the day she graduated from college, Potter had been committed to controlling her own career. That attitude combined with her law school activism and her own experiences of sexism produced a dedicated feminist soon after she settled in Washington. A proven litigator and a champion of women's rights, Potter was the best candidate to ensure that the EEOC's sex discrimination case against AT&T was fought and fought well. She came to work at the EEOC on January 24, 1972, just one week before the hearings would start and the fight would begin.

In the wake of *A Unique Competence*'s publication, AT&T was taking several approaches to address the EEOC charges against the company. At least on the surface, the first had little to do with the EEOC's complaint. The company was actually working hard to change the personnel policies *A Unique Competence* had highlighted with contempt. Although the EEOC had given the company no credit for it, this effort had been going on for years. As early as July 22, 1965, just three weeks after Title VII went into effect, a NET traffic manager informed his subordinates they could no longer use sex-biased ads. Activity increased significantly once the new decade arrived. In January 1970, Pacific Telephone and Telegraph (PT&T) dropped its restrictions against hiring men as telephone operators; in May, South Central Bell eliminated its long-standing, if unwritten, policy against hiring mothers and fathers of illegitimate children, having decided "that there are some applicants who would be viewed by our contemporary culture as being socially quite acceptable [to be hired] despite the fact that he or she is the parent of an illegitimate child";[18] and in April 1971, AT&T's Corporate Labor Relations staff recommended a more generous maternity leave policy, and its engineering vice president ordered managers to recruit women and minorities aggressively for engineering jobs.

By the second half of 1971, the memos rolled out more quickly. At least five companywide personnel policy changes were issued between July 9 and November 24 under the signature of Kingsbury, Mercer, Romnes, or another top corporate executive on issues of sex-biased advertising, hiring women into the Bell System management training program, hiring minorities, and promoting telephone operators. And the publication of *A Unique Competence* escalated their efforts even further, producing corporate memos to revamp recruiting procedures, promote more women in the Commercial Department, end pregnancy testing of job candidates, and try harder to get women into management training programs, all before the end of January 1972.

At the same time, the Plant Department was going beyond written memos to ensure that women and minorities got opportunities for craft jobs and above. First- and second-level managers in that era remember the pressure to hire blacks first, primarily through the Plans for Progress and JOBS programs, and then, by 1972, women. Although companywide goals or quotas had not been agreed to, each district of fifty to one hundred employees was being encouraged to set its own internal targets for getting women into technical nonmanagement jobs. Later that year, at least one Bell division's Plant Department began hiring NOW leaders to make periodic presentations to its technicians and clerks about "Women's Liberation." The law, the EEOC's threats, and the results of Dan Davis's SMSA study had all combined to motivate AT&T to push for change.

An observer might wonder if these aggressive overhauls in the Bell System's personnel policies were in the company's best interest, as they could appear an admission of guilt. But AT&T had little choice now that the EEOC had awoken it to the company's culpability. The law required Bell System managers to hire and promote more women and minorities, so John deButts was going to make sure they complied, even if his order was six years late. Just as important, the company's culture demanded that all managers treat their employees well. With Bob Lilley, the Plans for Progress advocate, running the company's response to the EEOC charges, these changes would be made. As Copus later said, "Once we got [AT&T's] attention, . . . they moved mountains to change the world's largest company."[19]

AT&T also had to get ready for the hearings. And like the EEOC, it needed to augment its legal team. In this case, the hearings lawyers chose to add an outside counsel with more equal employment knowledge than Ashley and Levy, which even Ashley agreed was a smart decision. The EEOC also tried to influence this move. By the late fall of 1971, Copus and Gartner had observed their opponents in the prehearings conferences and had read their responses to the EEOC's prehearings brief, and Copus had sat across the negotiations table from Levy in their sessions that fall. As Copus says now, "We felt we wouldn't make much headway if we didn't have someone who understood more about employment law" working on AT&T's side of the case.[20]

In a way, that perspective seems counterintuitive. Wouldn't the EEOC want its opponent's lawyer to be as inexperienced, unknowledgeable, and ineffective as possible? In the hearings room, perhaps, but not if the agency hoped to reach a settlement, which, despite its lack of progress in negotiations to date, continued to be an important option. As Copus explains today, "My experience is that often the lack of skill and knowledge on the part of your adversary makes it exceedingly difficult to settle a case because the other lawyer can't adequately evaluate the situation."[21] As a result, in one EEOC meeting with Lilley, Copus remembers, carefully, trying not to sound condescending, suggesting to Lilley that it would be in AT&T's best interest to hire the best equal employment legal expert the company could find.

Whether Lilley took Copus's advice directly or had already made the decision to bring an outside lawyer onto AT&T's team is unknown, but the company did act. In late 1971, it hired Thompson Powers and the resources of his firm, Steptoe and Johnson, to support Ashley and Levy on the case.

In that simple decision, AT&T had significantly improved its chances against the EEOC. Powers, a ruggedly handsome man with an athlete's build, was known to be one of the country's top authorities on equal employment law. He had graduated from Harvard Law School in 1959 and been hired five years later by Franklin D. Roosevelt Jr., the EEOC's first chairperson, as the EEOC's first executive director, and although his tenure at the agency was brief, he developed as much expertise on equal employment law as a lawyer could. Then when he moved to Steptoe and Johnson, he committed himself to developing a team of equal employment specialists. His involvement in the AT&T case fit exactly with that effort.

Not only was Powers knowledgeable in a field no one else at AT&T knew, but he also had one of the best reputations of any lawyer in Washington, D.C. Everyone seemed to respect him, a sentiment that continued through his work on the AT&T case. Government employees remember him as taking a "cultured approach to the practice of law" and having "finely tuned ethical antennae," while his employers at AT&T have called him "a fine gentleman" and an "excellent representative of the legal profession."[22] He may have taken himself a bit seriously, once delineating his dress code to an associate: while a dark suit, white shirt, and plain tie were required during the week, a sports jacket was acceptable on weekends. Still, his knowledge and integrity provided a huge asset to the AT&T team.

AT&T made one other key personnel change that winter essential to its future success on the case. Even with the excellent credentials Bill Mercer brought to the company's efforts as personnel vice president, he hadn't achieved the goal Bob Lilley needed fulfilled. The company had been embarrassed by the EEOC's written case, and the negotiations to resolve it had made no progress for a second time and were dead by the end of January 1972. Although these discussions had prioritized resolving the EEOC's complaint against AT&T's sex-biased advertising, they ended with Copus and his colleagues demanding $175 million in back pay for the female and minority Bell employees who had suffered discrimination. Today no one remembers why this collapse occurred, but the outcome was clear. Settlement could happen only with a new strategy and, from Lilley's viewpoint, a new vice president in place.

The individual chosen to replace Mercer, Dave Easlick, was as loose and laid-back as Tom Powers was cautious and dignified. Tall and robust with a tendency to tell stories punctuated by bursts of laughter, Easlick belied the Bell System executive image. In fact, many longtime AT&T employees have wondered how he managed to reach the top of the company's hierarchy. He was unpredictable, disinterested in rules, innovative, and prone to telling jokes that often came off as more rude than funny. One of his former employees remembers Easlick calling him Gitlo in honor of a subservient black character featured in a popular movie, *Gone Are the Days*. Easlick saw the movie, a satire aimed at exposing concerns about race relations, as an educational tool for a personnel vice president and so probably didn't mean any harm by the comment. The employee, being neither black nor particularly sensitive, laughed it off but wondered how such an offbeat guy could have gotten to AT&T's twenty-sixth floor.

However, Bob Lilley had a specific reason for bringing Easlick there—his negotiating skills. When Easlick had been the assistant vice president of personnel at Michigan Bell, he had successfully bargained two pattern-setting contracts with the local union. As he says today with a laugh, "They knew I was a sneaky sort of guy."[23] When he offered Easlick the job, Lilley made it clear that Easlick had one key goal: to resolve the EEOC case without spending a lot more money and jeopardizing the company's bottom line.

Easlick was a better candidate for the job than observers might have surmised. In addition to his skill at negotiating, he had years of personnel experience at both Indiana and Michigan Bell and had written a white paper on the Bell System's vulnerability to race discrimination charges on a special assignment at AT&T headquarters in 1963, two years before the EEOC went into business. Moreover, as an individual with a creative streak, willing to think "outside the box," he was perhaps just what the company needed to extract itself from the complicated situation in which it had landed.

By the time Easlick moved to New York City in December 1971, AT&T had one other resolution effort already under way. When Dan Davis had seen the dismal results of his SMSA study, he hadn't just moved on to another assignment. Aware that the Department of Labor had just expanded Order #4, its requirement for corporate affirmative action plans, to include women, and wanting to fix the problem everyone knew existed, he had proposed what he saw as an obvious next step to his boss, Don Liebers. Since the statistics showed that the company had a problem in hiring and promoting women and minorities into the Bell System's better jobs, why not devise a program to correct the problem? Davis had no interest in joining AT&T's hearings team, which was preparing for a fight. He wanted to resolve the conflict calmly, factually, and by doing the right thing. Liebers agreed to give Davis the chance, so Davis embarked on updating the company's affirmative action program and drafting other policies to ensure women and minorities could and would advance.

In the meantime, Ashley and Levy, along with their new teammate, Tom Powers, joined the EEOC lawyers in the last prehearings conference on January 21, 1972. For more than two weeks, AT&T's lawyers had been pushing the FCC to grant the company a continuance and postpone the hearings' start for another four months, claiming they needed more time to review the EEOC's voluminous record, prepare objections to documents, develop cross-examination questions, and receive still missing data from the EEOC. But Denniston wasn't having any of it: "I think if we keep putting off the evil day of getting started, that this might remove the pressure of the fire that might otherwise cause the parties to proceed with more haste." [24] He had set January 31, 1972, as the day the hearings would finally start, and start they would.

The Testimony

Winter/Spring 1972

Monday, January 31, 1972, was a cool, cloudy day in Washington, D.C., yet the crowd that jammed inside Room 252 of the FCC's headquarters building had driven the temperature way up. Just a little bigger than an average living room, with low ceilings, gray and white paint, and fake mahogany furniture, the room looked more like an industrial-issue conference room found in a Bell System plant building than a regal room where justice would be adjudicated between the federal government and an American corporate icon. The low-key atmosphere hardly fit the important case that was about to be tried.

Three groups of lawyers occupied a series of tables set in a U shape at the room's front to face the FCC hearings examiner's desk, which was raised a foot or two above floor level. With the witness stand to his left, the examiner, Frederick Denniston, looked out on the lawyers he would monitor over the next year. To his right, Judy Potter, now one week on the job, took the EEOC's lead chair with David Copus and Larry Gartner at her side, with AT&T on the left. AT&T's FCC experts, George Ashley and Hal Levy, and their new colleague, Tom Powers, were joined by a couple of Powers's Steptoe and Johnson colleagues. At least in numbers, AT&T appeared to have the upper hand. The two FCC lawyers, Jim Juntilla and Ruth Baker, who were representing the public as they did regularly in FCC hearings, sat in the middle section of the U while Dave Cashdan, appearing for the interested civil rights groups, filled the last chair.

Behind them sat a throng of people occupying the three or four dozen spectators' chairs. All the parties had sent big teams that day, with EEOC,

AT&T, and FCC staffers wanting to show their support as the hearings kicked off. Those seats wouldn't stay filled for long, however. As the sessions migrated from the opening day of a potentially historic hearing to the mundane daily testimony of expert witnesses, the audience dwindled to the witness coming up next on the stand and those key to the case on each side—Wallace and Speck for the EEOC, Liebers for AT&T. Bill Brown came occasionally to demonstrate how seriously he was supporting his three young lawyers, although not often enough for them to feel his breath down their neck.

That first day was huge for David Copus. His more-than-a-year-long crusade was finally getting its moment in court; in addition, he was litigating a case for the very first time. After Denniston had laid out the day's schedule and before any witnesses were called to the stand, Copus got up to speak on a scheduling issue. Observers in the room remember that he sounded fine, but as he stepped forward to say "Mr. Denniston," his hands shook. Even David Copus, known for his bravado, could get butterflies.

The EEOC lawyers had chosen their fellow task force members, Randy Speck and Bill Wallace, to present the basics of their case on the witness stand. Since Speck knew Part One, the Findings of Fact, best, he went first. Copus himself would have loved to sponsor this testimony and might have if Potter hadn't appeared in time to explain a basic legal fact: a lawyer representing a party to the case can't get on the stand himself. Speck would start off.

When Denniston called Speck to the stand at a few minutes after ten that Monday morning, Speck shared Copus's butterflies. Copus and Gartner had done little to get Speck ready because they had "no idea about preparing witnesses," and Potter had arrived too late to be of much help.[1] Plus, as first up, Speck would face the intimidating Tom Powers. Since "none of us really knew what to expect," Speck had every right to be anxious.[2] For his part, Powers, exuding calm, quiet self-confidence, was focused on destroying any confidence Speck himself might have had.

Powers had planned the basic two-pronged approach of any attorney questioning the opposition. First he would discredit Speck's background, then his testimony, thereby attacking the EEOC's entire case. He started with Speck's education. Noting his undergraduate and graduate schooling, he asked, "Did you take any courses in equal employment law?"[3]

"No, I did not."

"Have you had any training in the profession of law?"

"No, I have not, no formal training."

"Have you had any training or education specifically in the field of evidence?"

"No formal training, no, sir."

This building chorus of noes sounded bad for the EEOC and, although Powers probably didn't know it, was cutting deeper into Speck's confidence. After nearly a year working eighty-hour weeks side by side with two lawyers, Copus and Gartner, and often feeling he was working a lot harder than Gartner, Speck resented not being a lawyer himself. Powers's emphasis of that fact certainly wasn't helping calm his nerves.

Powers's next series of questions, about Speck's experience in pulling together the Findings of Fact, seemed easier. After Speck acknowledged he had worked on previous investigations at the EEOC, Powers asked, "In connection with those investigations, have you made summaries of documents?"

Finally Speck could answer affirmatively. "Yes, I have."

"Have those summaries ever been submitted in a court of law?"

Another yes.

"Has their admissibility specifically been ruled on?"

Speck's run of positive responses was over. "Not to my knowledge."

But help came from another source. "Could we turn this around a bit?" Denniston asked. "Has any been rejected by a court of law?"

"Not to my knowledge." A drop of credibility back in the EEOC's column.

Then Powers moved on to Speck's other weaknesses, which, in Powers's questioning, sounded significant. He didn't have personal knowledge of every document used to build the Findings of Fact because other task force members helped prepare them, all the Findings hadn't been appropriately cross-referenced, Speck and his colleagues were looking only for documents "unfavorable" to AT&T and were not taking an objective view. Despite Powers's polite denigration, Speck held up well, answering as many questions as possible with "not to my knowledge" and welcoming Denniston's occasional interventions to clarify his responses. When Powers got to equal employment opportunity law, however, the tide turned. Speck, now out of his league, simply nodded along as Powers recited the executive orders and amendments that had been enacted since 1961 prohibiting employment discrimination. After almost an hour and a half on the stand, a break was welcome.

When the hearing reconvened ten minutes later, the stakes had risen. Powers was moving on to the second half of his strategy, attacking the contents of the summaries at the base of the EEOC's case, which would appear the more substantive challenge for Speck. But, in fact, Speck faced only

limited questioning. Soon after Powers began to individually pick apart a series of the Findings, the legal proceeding deteriorated into a three-way debate between the AT&T and EEOC teams and Denniston, which ended only
when Powers finally got to his point. "I think that this discussion indicates
there are significant questions as to whether these purported summaries in
fact are objective, non-argumentative and whether they are fair characteri-
zations of the total material in the documents," he stated. The EEOC might
consider them Findings of Fact, but AT&T wouldn't go along without a serious fight.

This wasn't a trivial counterattack for the EEOC. Following the Houston
hearings' innovation, the agency's primary emphasis was numbers—how
few women and minorities had high-paying jobs in the phone company—
but Speck's Findings of Fact were crucial to support that strategy. They could
illuminate the discriminatory Bell System policies that had created those
abysmal statistics in a way that expert and anecdotal witnesses could not.
This hearings room discussion would cut to the core of the direction the
case would take.

No resolution came that first day, but, fortunately for the EEOC, AT&T's
protestations made little headway with the hearings examiner. At one point,
Denniston reminded the AT&T lawyers of the source of the EEOC's raw materials, noting, "I assume you understand [the documents] have all been
supplied by Bell and the various companies except where the index indicates otherwise," and he wondered aloud how this unwieldy case could
go forward without using some form of summaries. After all the squabbling,
Speck was off the stand by early afternoon, the EEOC's case went forward
as it stood, and the AT&T lawyers were resigned to writing specific objections to try to squash the documents and summaries they didn't like. The
EEOC had won the first round.

Two more witnesses took the stand that afternoon. Matthew Degnen, the
computer analysis expert from Applied Urbanetics, spent an hour defending
his company's work processing the thirty-city AT&T SMSA study requested
by the EEOC during discovery; then the EEOC's second lead, Bill Wallace,
was on. As the EEOC guy who had designed the models to analyze the
SMSA statistical data, Wallace was directly in AT&T's line of sight for attack.
His testimony included the charts and exhibits that had been part of *A Unique
Competence,* and, much to his dismay, he would spend parts of three days
on the stand defending his work. However, unlike his EEOC colleagues,
he didn't feel particularly nervous about speaking in court. Judy Potter had
found time to help him practice the previous week, and, more important,
with a self-image of being "cool," he willed himself to believe he was relaxed.

From the start, Hal Levy's questioning gave him little cause to change his mind. Levy, taking the same "discredit the witness, discredit the testimony" approach, started by going after Wallace's background, particularly trying to attribute time unaccounted for on Wallace's résumé. "You indicate that you received your BA degree in philosophy in 1963 and that you joined the EEOC four years later," Levy said. "What did you do in the intervening four or five years between 1963 and the time you joined the EEOC?"

Perhaps, as Wallace surmises today, because of his appearance, Levy thought Wallace had been "running around the Caribbean or hitchhiking across North Africa," but if so, it was a faulty conjecture.[4] "I guess my principal activity was attending grad school for four years," Wallace answered.[5]

It wasn't the answer Levy had expected. "What?"

Wallace was happy to say it again. "Attending graduate school in those four years." It had taken Levy only a few minutes to break a litigator's cardinal rule: never ask a question to which you don't know the answer. Instead of discrediting Wallace's credentials, Levy had enhanced them.

Wallace wasn't on the stand much longer that day, but on Tuesday he spent from 9 A.M. to 4 P.M. there, being quizzed about the data he had presented. Levy believed that Wallace's comparisons were frequently invalid—for example, one based on geography. "Taking, for example, New Jersey Bell," Levy asked, "you assumed the service area . . . was the entire state of New Jersey?"[6]

"Yes," Wallace replied.

"And for Illinois Bell, you assumed the service area was the entire state of Illinois?"

"Yes."

"And for Bell of Pennsylvania, you assumed the service area was the entire state of Pennsylvania?"

"Yes."

"Mr. Wallace, what is the basis for the assumption you have made that Bell's service areas are co-extensive with the states?" Wallace may have been well educated, but Levy was doing his best to prove he wasn't that smart.

"I guess it comes from maps and other information which suggested those were the . . . boundaries of the Bell service area."

"Are you aware that there are over two thousand independent telephone companies serving substantial geographic areas in the US and in each state?"

"I am not sure of the exact number," Wallace responded. Levy had made his point.

Levy made at least one other as the day went on, noting that comparing Bell System craft jobs to jobs as "make-up man, hand painter, wig dresser, shoe repairman, cheese maker, corset fitter," the professions considered craft in generic data summaries, was inappropriate. As a result, Denniston agreed that Levy had "raised interesting questions" about the data and "how much weight can be given to the comparisons," handing AT&T a bit of credit. But Denniston refused Levy's requests to exclude any of the EEOC charts and tables. Despite first-day jitters, the EEOC lawyers were holding their own.

Levy helped the EEOC in another way that day by giving voice to the sexist and racist attitudes the Bell System had been accused of promulgating. At one point, he asked Wallace, "What is the basis for the assumption that minority employees are qualified for and interested in all jobs in the company?"

"I don't know that I said they were interested in all jobs in the company," Wallace responded. "The assumption was . . . this would be the case and that is what one would expect if in fact they were employed in all job titles."

"Is it a fair restatement then that this is a hypothetical based on the assumption that all black employees were in fact qualified for and interested in all jobs in the company?"

"Not that all blacks were qualified for all jobs but that blacks would be qualified on the same basis as whites." Wallace wasn't interested in conjecture, just the legal perspective he was required to follow as an EEOC employee.

Legal or not, Levy disagreed. "Mr. Examiner, I do not believe that any basis has been laid in this record for that assumption and I would move to strike [that chart]." The Bell System's racist view of its minority employees was on the record.

Levy went after the company's women, too, later asking, "What is the basis for the assumption that a fixed proportion of women . . . would be qualified for and interested in highly technical inside craft jobs, hazardous or arduous outside craft jobs, or jobs requiring overtime and weekend work on a regular basis?" This again seemed out of the realm of possibility to him.

But Wallace knew it was both possible and true. "Certainly a number of women are employed in those occupations in various places inside and outside the Bell System. There is no reason to assume that no other women would be interested in those jobs," he responded.

Later Levy accelerated his attack on minorities, asking Wallace to speculate on who would be more likely to hire black immigrants with little schooling or English-speaking ability—a restaurant or piece-goods factory, or a local Bell division? Wallace, managing to maintain the objectivity a witness requires, stated that he could draw no conclusion from the scenario, but, with Levy's questions getting under his skin by now, he let out a little of his own perspective. "It is obviously a very strange and unusual hypothetical, it seems to me," he concluded. Levy's attitude was actually not that strange and unusual considering the era, yet it would still undermine AT&T's expressed vow that it was committed to meeting its social responsibility as the country's largest private employer.

Wallace had just one more morning on the stand, on Wednesday, February 2, which proved to be a relative breeze. Ruth Baker, an FCC lawyer, and Copus each led him through a friendly line of questions, primarily allowing him to strengthen his direct testimony. When he left the stand at noon, the EEOC's case, although suffering a few cuts and bruises, was still standing tall. The ragtag EEOC team, with its excellent coach, Judy Potter, had done well.

The parade of EEOC expert witnesses began the next afternoon, beginning with Sandra and Daryl Bem, the married psychologists who would become the EEOC's stars by providing both powerful evidence of AT&T's gender discrimination and a bit of comic relief. When Katherine Mazzaferri had spoken to them the previous summer, she had asked them to design a study on sex-biased job ads specific to AT&T. They visited the senior government relations class of a mixed-income high school in a San Francisco suburb armed with three stacks of "Help Wanted" ads they had written, each pile classified as sex-biased, sex-neutral, or sex-reversed. Twelve jobs were offered in each group, four phone company jobs that matched that stack's gender classification and eight nontelephone, which were nonbiased and simply included as filler to make the study more realistic.

The Bems found the sex-biased ads the easiest to write, as AT&T had already done the work for them. They simply copied verbatim the AT&T ads the EEOC had provided, including a classic ad for a service representative that began: "If We Were an Airline, She'd Be Our Stewardess! She is the telephone company." They then used these gender-directed ads' formats as a basis for creating the sex-neutral and sex-reversed ads. By removing all sex-biased wording and adding another gender, they transformed a telephone installer ad that typically targeted men: "We're looking for outdoor people! Are you a man or woman who likes fresh air and exercise?"

The sex-reversed ads, designed to recruit men as operators and service representatives and women as craft workers, were the most fun to create. To entice men into the service rep job, a stewardess image simply wouldn't do, so the ad the Bems created appealed instead to the male thirst for power: "If We Were a Government, He'd be Our Ambassador!" And in their ads for installers, they were now looking only for "outdoor women" who might like fresh air and exercise. The reversed words sounded simply awkward, emphasizing the apparent sexism behind the policy.

The Bems' study, completed in October 1971, reinforced that sense. After showing each stack of ads to one of three groups of forty different students, the Bems found what they had expected to find. The sex-biased ads, in one direction or the other, encouraged individuals of that gender to apply for those jobs. Only 5 percent of the women in the group who read the ads aimed at men were interested in applying as telephone craft workers, while 45 percent who read the craft ads focused on women expressed interest. Likewise, after seeing an ad recruiting women specifically, only 30 percent of those men wanted to pursue a telephone operator or service rep job. That percentage more than doubled, to 65 percent, for the group reading ads for those jobs targeted specifically at men. Based on this study, AT&T's policy of running sex-biased ads that directed women to low-paying operator and service rep jobs and men to higher-paying craft jobs appeared blatantly discriminatory.

The EEOC task force, thrilled with the study's results, confirmed the Bems' participation in the hearings, which was scheduled for the end of the first week of testimony, February 4, 1972. The EEOC never invested the money to have Speck or Wallace travel to Stanford and meet with the Bems ahead of time or provided the two psychologists much advice about testifying. Copus and Gartner had simply suggested they avoid "yes" and "no" answers and be as expansive as possible, knowing Denniston needed education more than anything.

On the morning of their testimony, Denniston met with the Bems, as he typically did with new witnesses, to explain the procedures specific to an FCC hearing. During the meeting, the doctors made their standard request: *Can we testify together?* As professionals working in the gender discrimination field, they argued that by taking the stand at the same time they would be seen as equals, whereas if each testified separately, Daryl, who was both male and older, might be viewed as the senior partner. This was an unusual request from the perspective of almost any lawyer, and it was even more surprising when Levy agreed to the arrangement. Levy apparently believed that he and his colleagues would have a better chance of tripping up the two doctors with both on the stand at the same time. Tom Powers, a far more experienced litigator, wasn't able to offer his input, as he was absent from the hearings room that day according to the hearings transcripts, so the decision stood. But unfortunately for AT&T, Levy's belief would prove 100 percent wrong. He had simply made a mistake, as almost anyone knowledgeable in a courtroom would say. Bill Brown put it most bluntly: "I thought that was the dumbest thing I ever saw a trial lawyer do."[7]

Hal Levy was far from a dumb lawyer. With an Ivy League education and previous experience in a Manhattan law firm, he drew unanimous accolades from his Bell System colleagues. George Ashley remembers him as "brilliant," Bill Mercer calls him "an astute capable lawyer," and Don Liebers says Levy was "one of the smartest people I ever met in my life."[8] Even David Copus, Levy's rival, reflects today on how much he learned from his Bell System opponent. After each meeting or telephone conversation the two of them held, Levy would send Copus a detailed letter, summarizing his view of their discussion. As Copus says today, the letters "made for a great record, communicated what AT&T's position was, didn't leave anything to chance. [They were done in a] very professional studied way."[9] As a beginning lawyer, Copus adopted the approach immediately and has used it effectively throughout his career.

Despite Levy's legal strengths, however, the decision to allow two witnesses to testify simultaneously quickly proved faulty. Even Levy realized he wasn't sure how this approach would play out when he introduced the two doctors to the hearings room. "This is a new experience for me and I guess it is for everyone here," he said. "I guess we will have to feel our way to see how the procedure eventuates for dealing with two witnesses on the stand at the same time."[10] His open-mindedness wouldn't last.

First, Levy wanted to get the doctors' perspectives on general gender differences on the record. "Doctors Bem, are you familiar with studies demonstrating differences between men and women in . . . ability to discern spatial relationships . . . ?" he asked.

Sandra Bem answered first. "Yes, there are a variety of tests which demonstrate the average sex difference [although] . . . there is . . . very little evidence which addresses . . . where these differences come from."

But Daryl Bem had an additional, perhaps better, answer, which he had had time to formulate while Sandra was speaking. "I would further add in every one of these differences you can usually find correlated . . . socialization differences," he said, leaving Levy waiting to ask his next question.

This pattern continued for the Bems' entire time on the stand, with first Daryl enhancing Sandra's testimony, then Sandra correcting Daryl's. On that Friday, the two doctors seemed like participants in a 1960s TV game show like *The Price Is Right* or *Let's Make a Deal*. After Daryl gave an initial answer, he didn't need to turn to the audience and hope someone would shout out support for his comments or a suggestion of a better response. He could just look down thoughtfully as Sandra jumped in with her perspective, typically

an enhancement or reshaping of what had already been heard. Since Denniston appeared honestly interested in learning about the Bems' study, he
imposed no time limit on their answers, which gave them the luxury to ex-
pound on them at length. The doctors were careful to be polite in their fol-
low-up comments, opening them with "To put it slightly differently" or "Let
me just add" before launching into a several-minutes-longer statement. As
Daryl Bem says now, "The second answer was always better."[11] On that one
day in the hearings, they, and the EEOC by default, were the game show's
big winners.

This turn of events must have frustrated Levy because he had prepared
carefully for the doctors' appearance. For example, he had researched Menlo
Park, California, the study's location, ahead of time and discovered it was an
affluent community where most high school graduates went on to college.
As a result, he surmised that study participants weren't likely candidates for
Bell System nonmanagement jobs in any case, a fact, if true, that would fundamentally compromise the study results. However, even though Copus and
Gartner hadn't done the same research and Potter hadn't had time since her
arrival, the Bems were ready for the question. Trying to point out their error, Levy asked them, "Which of these [area] schools would you call more
typical of working class . . . Ravenswood, Sequoia, or Menlo-Atherton [the
Menlo Park school's name]?"[12]

Sandra responded first. " I guess I would agree with [your] implication. . . .
I forget the names but the two with the lower percentage going on to college would seem more typical of a working class community."

But Daryl was there to expand on her comments. "But not necessarily
more typical of applying for these telephone jobs," he added.

Sandra wanted to make sure they were 100 percent correct. "Again, I
would stress within Menlo . . . we attempted to select students who were
not going on to four year colleges." Even on one of Levy's strongest issues,
the double brain trust was racking up points.

In the areas in which Levy had little knowledge, the Bems were even
more successful. Not a statistical expert himself, Levy had brushed up on statistical analysis before that day's hearing in the hope of tripping up the Bems
in a realm key to their testimony. He questioned them on their statistics education and expressed doubts about the statistical significance of such a
small study. But the Bems knew more than Levy realized, with Daryl, at one
point, noting that Levy's interpretation was "precisely the kind of practice
someone reporting research would be severely criticized for picking out. Essentially that is what is called torturing the data in order to find a pattern."
The importance of politeness was starting to recede.

Levy, not surprisingly, was skeptical of Daryl's response, but when he turned to his statistical expert at the AT&T lawyers' table, he got only a grimace and a comment whispered in his ear, which obviously supported the Bems' viewpoint. Levy dropped both the line of questioning and another two to three pages from the stack of papers he held and moved on.

By early afternoon, the folly of the shared witness stand had become clear even to Levy. Hoping to reduce any further damage, he suggested to the Bems, "Where I am putting to you a question that can be answered by a 'Yes' or 'No,' let us see if it can't be limited to that so we can move ahead with the cross-examination." But Denniston even overruled that Levy request. Levy had created his own hot seat, and he would have to withstand the sizzle.

At the beginning of the day, Levy had suggested to the Bems that they would be on the stand into the following week, but by midafternoon he was nearly finished. Between his arguments falling short and the Bems' ability to cover wide territory in each multipart response, he had gotten through his questions in a fraction of the time expected. When Denniston adjourned the hearings for the weekend at 3:30P.M., the members of the EEOC team couldn't wait to hustle the two psychologists out of the hearings room and express their exuberance over their performance. But Sandra and Daryl Bem actually felt a bit sad for Levy. He had treated them professionally, calling them "Doctors Bem" throughout the questioning with nary a hint of sexism toward Sandra. Plus, he had appeared better prepared than his EEOC opponents. They could see he was a committed lawyer taking on a case they were sure he was going to lose, a position with which they sympathized.

Over the next five weeks, the EEOC brought out the rest of the expert witnesses Phyllis Wallace had recruited. Although they couldn't compete with the Bems for courtroom drama, each would illuminate a key part of the agency's case. In a corollary to the Bems' joint appearance on the witness stand, Potter and her team were now thinking in pairs, presenting two witnesses for each issue addressed.

Bookending all the testimony were the EEOC's two substantive speakers, Judith Long Laws and Bernard Anderson, who had been brought in to address, respectively, gender and minority discrimination. Laws, an assistant professor at Cornell, took the stand on Monday, February 7, 1972. A feminist who had been called on as a discrimination expert in earlier cases, she had reviewed the EEOC's description of employment conditions for Bell System female workers after Katherine Mazzaferri called her the previous summer. Her conclusions matched *A Unique Competence's* narrative: the Bell

System was a sex-segregated company that most women entered through the lowest-level telephone operator job with little hope of promotion. This sex-segregation in jobs had led to sex-segregation in wages whereby women were almost always paid less than men. As a result, sexism had become institutionalized throughout the company. Her testimony went beyond the EEOC report's scope, too, and talked about solutions to the problem: restructuring and recruiting men for the operator's job, recruiting women into management and technical jobs to serve as role models, and re-educating all managers in the company about appropriate treatment of female employees.

The AT&T team had assigned its most knowledgeable lawyer, Tom Powers, to cross-examine Laws, and he was in for a fight. For the better part of three days, they went at each other, Powers unfailingly polite but committed to exposing the fallacy he saw in her remarks, Laws unconcerned with politeness and equally committed to sticking by her findings. Early on, Powers suggested that her work suffered in quality and objectivity because she qualified more as an advocate for her gender than the serious academic she claimed to be. Whether he knew it or not, he had hit on a sore spot that feminist professors both before and after Laws have often faced. As a result, she was prepared to respond. "To the extent that I have a reputation in the field is in spite of being a feminist," she said. "That is considered to be a disqualifying characteristic." [13]

Whether his suggestion had gotten under her skin or she just felt frustrated at having to argue points she saw as obvious, she began to exhibit irritation in her answers. "By the way, I have much to object to being presented with things out of context," she noted at one point and later commented, "I don't have to do that because that is not the argument that I am making."

Powers retained his cool composure, answering her last complaint, "I am not engaged at the moment in a direct argument with you. I am just trying to clarify what you have presented to this proceeding." But the rancorous debate returned when she was brought back to the stand for two more days two weeks later. As Powers continued to pick at Laws's testimony, item by item, she bristled more and more until she had had it. To a particularly lengthy and confusing query, she exclaimed, "That is the most complex double-barreled question I have ever been exposed to. . . . The classic example of a double-barreled question is: when did you stop beating your wife?" [14] Powers's condescension toward her had finally caused her anger to explode freely.

Denniston himself had had enough with both of them. "You are giving dissertations on all his questions as a whole and it is not very helpful," he told Laws, and then he immediately remonstrated Powers to clarify his question. By midday on Thursday, February 24, when Laws was finally let off the stand, Powers had achieved a few concessions from her—her results were only specifically relevant to the cities where her analysis had been done, women might leave their jobs for other reasons than lousy pay and no promotional opportunities—but, overall, she had held her ground.

Bringing up the other end of the EEOC case presentation, Bernard Anderson took the stand across from George Ashley on Monday, March 6, 1972. Anderson, the African American assistant professor of industry at the Wharton School, was familiar to the EEOC team, as he had written the book *The Negro in the Public Utility Industries,* which Copus, Ross, and Gartner had included in their original petition. The book came in handy again, now forming Anderson's written testimony about discrimination against minorities, particularly blacks, for this case. Compared with Laws's time on the stand in late February, Ashley's cross-examination of Anderson resembled the taciturn NBC news anchor Chet Huntley interviewing a member of Congress about rising inflation rates. Anderson got his major point on record— that AT&T had done little to bring blacks affirmatively onto its payroll—but he did make a few concessions to the company, agreeing that it had hired many black females and participated in past job-training programs designed specifically to help blacks get hired.

On the same day, during testimony about an issue not directly relevant to the EEOC case against AT&T, the company's image took another black eye. Juntilla asked Anderson about his research: "Doctor, on page 185 [of your testimony] you make the statement: 'The dominant telephone company refused to participate in the study.' I don't suppose there is much mystery about who [that] is"—Juntilla was certain that everyone in the hearings room knew Anderson was referring to AT&T. "Could you give the circumstances that brought up that statement?" [15]

Over Ashley's objection, Anderson explained. "In 1967, correspondence was initiated between myself, Professor Herbert Northrup and representatives of AT&T asking their cooperation in participating in this study [of minority employment]. . . . AT&T, through Mr. Kingsbury, refused to cooperate, . . . we continued to press him for a more affirmative reply." At a subsequent meeting, Kingsbury gave Anderson three legitimate, if flimsy, reasons for the company's refusal: Bell of Pennsylvania had already participated, and all Bell companies' data would look similar; company policy didn't permit researchers unless they were invited by an AT&T manager; and the statistical information requested was in the EEOC's possession, not AT&T's.

When Anderson pushed Kingsbury, asking what action he'd take if they went directly to the BOCs, Kingsbury made the company's position clearer, saying he would "do everything in his power to dissuade any other BOC to participate in [Anderson's] study." And he did. When Anderson visited the personnel director of Southwestern Bell in St. Louis, whose office bore a remarkable similarity to that of the personnel director of Bell of Pennsylvania—"same type of furniture, same color carpet . . . same books on the credenza, same position of the desk in relation to the windows"—he refused to participate. Apparently he had received a letter from AT&T headquarters suggesting that the company should decline, a letter that also made its way to the PT&T personnel director, from whom Anderson also got a "no." To Anderson, this belied AT&T's supposed commitment to treating minorities well. As he noted, "Across twenty-seven industries, the only corporation in the US that refused to cooperate in this series of studies conducted by a reputable university research team was the AT&T System."

In between the anchor witnesses of Laws and Anderson, the EEOC's other experts appeared in their sequential twos. Orley Ashenfelter and his protégé, Ronald Oaxaca, both economics professors, each took the stand with Levy questioning. On February 25, 1972, Ashenfelter based his testimony on the laws of economics, noting that if there was no demand for women in high-paying craft jobs, their salaries would fall, an outcome already realized in the Bell System. The following week, Oaxaca testified to the same point from the opposite perspective, describing findings that, at present telephone operators' salaries, enough qualified men could never be found to fill the jobs. Levy had little success refuting their claims or cutting off Ashenfelter's long-winded, circuitous responses.

Two obstetrician/gynecologists testified about the flaws in the Bell System's maternity leave policies. Dr. Andres Hellegers and Dr. Robert Henry Barter, professors of medicine at Georgetown and George Washington universities, respectively, both confirmed that women could work as late in their pregnancies as they wanted. The absurdity of AT&T's position came through when Levy asked Hellegers, "If there were a job that required continued attendance at a station for . . . hour-long intervals and a normally pregnant woman could not sustain the bladder pressure for that long, . . . could [this not interfere] with the efficiency of that operation?"[16]

Hellegers could only produce the obvious reply. "Yes, if you have to go to the john, you have to go to the john—man, woman, pregnant woman or anyone else. I must agree."

A Steptoe and Johnson lawyer, James Hutchinson, filling in for Tom Powers, who was out of town for two weeks, questioned the EEOC's two witnesses, who were both psychologists, on employment testing. Philip Ash, a professor at the University of Illinois, punctuated his testimony with stories about employees attempting to qualify for jobs as furnace operators and airline pilots, making him far more interesting than Bill Enneis, the EEOC research psychologist who had helped Bill Wallace with statistics. But both their conclusions were the same: a passing score on the Bell System Qualification Test 1 (BSQT-1), which a job candidate had to achieve to qualify for most craft positions, was a poor predictor of future success in any craft job.

On the recruiting issue, each of the two EEOC witnesses addressed one of the aggrieved groups. Susan Leake, the assistant director of placement at Simmons College, a women's college in Boston, testified that NET's recruiting program directed women into certain lower-level, nonmanagement jobs. As she said in response to one of Levy's questions, "It makes one wonder if the job[s] for which these women are recruit[ed] and screen[ed] are not those that are specifically geared for women."[17] Felix Lopez, a human resources consultant, appeared a week later to face a two-day showdown with Tom Powers about the impact of AT&T's job selection process on minorities. Lopez contended that the interviews and tests AT&T gave to nonmanagement job applicants were disadvantageous to black and Hispanic candidates. It was like a ten-round boxing match, with Lopez ducking Powers's jabs and Powers rebounding to strike again from another angle. Denniston finally stepped in, admonishing Powers to stop cutting Lopez off. The final winner was unclear, but Lopez had at least gotten his, and therefore the EEOC's, facts out.

Mixed in with this series of, for the most part, impassive experts were the two witnesses the EEOC had found to, it hoped, elicit an emotional response from anyone listening to or reading about the case. Although Helen Roig and Lorena Weeks were both former telephone operators from the South who had won discrimination cases against the Bell System, they presented themselves very differently on the witness stand. Roig, whose career with Southern and South Central Bell in New Orleans had taken her from operator to service rep to clerk to test deskman in twenty-five years, arrived with an eighty-four-page analysis of the discriminatory recruiting and hiring practices of the phone company. Replete with bulleted sections, tables, and attachments, it looked more like the work of a graduate student in Judith Long Laws's sociology class than of a nonmanagement employee of AT&T.

But Tom Powers was determined to discredit both the study and Roig's legitimacy to put it together. "Do you believe that you have the credentials to make a professional statistical survey . . . ?" he asked her.[18]

"No, I only know that I have made such surveys," she replied. "Now, as to whether I would be an expert in it would be a matter of opinion." Powers may have made the EEOC's Randy Speck nervous, but he didn't seem to faze this South Central Bell blue-collar worker.

He tried again. "Are you a job evaluation expert? Have you taken courses in industrial relations?"

Roig didn't see how this could be relevant. "No, I just know how they operate at the telephone company."

As the questioning went on, it became clear that Roig, despite her fast, unpolished delivery and overly detailed explanations, knew how to go after what she believed was right and was happy to speak her mind. When Powers asked her about the specific date of a charge she had filed against the company, she said she couldn't be sure without looking through all her records, "because, as I am sure you are aware, I have numerous charges against the Company." She later admitted she had made hundreds of grievances and had five charges to file when she got back to her office.

Finally an EEOC witness had gotten under the normally phlegmatic Powers's skin. He demanded that Denniston exclude her testimony because "in our judgment, [it] is a concoction of personal anecdotes and conclusions and opinions of law which are intermixed with hearsay testimony of unnamed people from Louisiana to Michigan to Virginia." Much of the hearsay she included did get axed, but she still got in the record the "split tours, miserable working conditions, low employee morale" of the telephone operator's job and her vivid comparison of the craft and operator jobs: "The framemen I have observed . . . go about their work in a very leisurely manner . . . [whereas a telephone operator] is sitting there all day long and she is taking one call right after another; it is a busy, busy job. . . . A frameman is working too but he is not rushing. . . . An operator could perform the [frameman's] job very easily and vice versa. To me, if the frameman is going to be paid this tremendous salary for doing this job . . . , then the operator should be paid a similar salary for the job she is performing."[19]

But her most valuable contribution came at the end of her two days on the stand, when Copus gave her the chance to talk about why she had fought so hard for advancement. "It [goes] back to my background," she said. "I was raised on a farm. I was a sharecropper's daughter. It did not make any difference whether you were a man or a woman. You worked in the field and you were paid the same thing. It just depended on how much cotton you could pick in a day. . . . In my young life, I never did realize I was a second class citizen." Who could argue with that logic?

Roig's counterpart, Lorena Weeks, whom Randy Speck had convinced to testify the previous summer, also took the stand on February 9, 1972. Having flown in from Wadley, Georgia, the night before with her sister as a reassuring escort, she made an unobtrusive entrance into the hearings room. When first questioned by the FCC lawyer Jim Juntilla, whom Levy deferred to temporarily, Weeks was equally unassuming, having to be asked to raise her voice so that others could hear her. Her testimony recounted her efforts to get a craft job as a switchman in the Wadley office of Southern Bell. In 1965, her telephone operator's job in Wadley was eliminated, forcing her to transfer to Swainsboro, Georgia, twenty miles from her home, as a clerk. The following year, a switchman's position opened back in Wadley, and she bid on it. But instead of being offered the job, she found her job performance rating downgraded from excellent to unsatisfactory. "What was the basis for that characterization?" Juntilla asked.

It was simple to Weeks. "To me it seemed a good way . . . [for] the telephone company [to] keep me from getting a job as a switchman."

Juntilla wanted to know how long it had taken for her performance to have deteriorated so significantly. "I believe it was six days," she answered.

After the company told her she couldn't have the job both because it was reserved for men and because she now had an unsatisfactory job rating, she complained to the union. It took the same position but at least came up with a justification for keeping women out: women aren't considered "because the man is the breadwinner in the family and women just don't need this type of job".

Juntilla then moved on to what had occurred after Weeks filed a complaint in 1966, with the EEOC's help, in U.S. district court. As she reported in her written testimony, Southern Bell's management searched for every rule that would prohibit her from legally qualifying for the switchman job, including invoking a Georgia state protective law, which was rescinded two years later, that stated women couldn't lift more than thirty pounds while on the job. The company then immediately produced a relay timing test set used by switchmen that weighed in at thirty-one and three-quarters pounds. The company's efforts prevailed, and Weeks lost her case in district court.

As a result, Weeks decided she had no intention of lifting anything in her clerk's job that weighed more than thirty pounds, including her typewriter. In the hearings room, she explained, "I told [my second-level supervisor] the typewriter on my desk weighed thirty-four pounds and I had to move it and since I had just lost a job and working [closer to home] meant so much to

me, I didn't see why I should have to lift this thirty-four pound typewriter. . . .
I told him I didn't intend to lift the typewriter because it looked to me like
the telephone company was using this both ways and either way I was just
wrong." Wrong perhaps but far from dumb. Still, two days later, after getting no help from the union, she was suspended for the rest of the week.

The next five years went no better. She continued to commute to her
clerk's job and continued to press her case in court, now with a lawyer from
NOW. As she described to the hearings room, "I couldn't even answer the
phone [at work]. If I said 'good morning,' I should not have said it. My desk
was about five feet from my supervisor . . . and just everything I did was
wrong." Even when she finally won her case and started work as a switchman in Wadley on March 3, 1971, the harassment didn't end. "The first thing
I got to the office . . . that morning and I was locked out. I didn't have a key.
I had a little trouble getting in. The two men that were in the office were
not on very friendly terms with me." She had a talent for understatement.

When Juntilla had finished, Levy got up, but not for long. He ran through
the routine series of discrediting-the-witness questions and tried to get some
of Weeks's opinions from the written testimony excluded, but Denniston
didn't agree. "Certainly she is not isolated from the female community . . .
and has some feeling or interpretation of . . . that community and can express it. So I will deny the motion," he said. Weeks was finished in less than
an hour. Her quiet matter-of-fact depiction of her fight for a decent job was
arguably the EEOC's most effective testimony against AT&T.

Late in March, the FCC lawyers called two witnesses of their own. In any
FCC hearing, they had the right to identify their own testimony that would
address the public's interests. In this case, they recruited Barbara Bergmann,
an economics professor at the University of Maryland, and Robert Nathan,
a consultant and frequent FCC witness. Bergmann presented her study that
quantified the progress AT&T should have made in hiring women and blacks
if it had been following antidiscrimination laws over the past decade, and
Nathan testified to the ineffectiveness of the Bell System's existing affirmative action plans. In their role as champions of the average American, Juntilla and Baker had produced witnesses whose testimony simply bolstered
the EEOC's case.

It had been a long seven weeks for all involved parties, and they
wouldn't be getting much of a break. Beginning in three weeks, on April 17,
1972, the entire hearings process would relocate three thousand miles, to
California, to begin a series of hearings involving anyone in the public who
wanted to participate. But even knowing how much work was still ahead,

the members of the EEOC team felt relieved. Having entered the hearings room in early February unprepared and nervous, they were exiting their half of the proceeding with their case fully presented and a good part of it intact. Their Findings of Fact might still be under question by AT&T, but the fundamentals of their argument and their expert and aggrieved employee testimony had held up markedly well in front of the hearings examiner. They had reason to be optimistic as they moved to the next step.

The Field

Spring 1972

Just days after the FCC had announced it would hold hearings on AT&T's employment practices, a collection of individuals and groups started clamoring to testify against the company. Letters poured in from well-established nonprofits like NOW and two West Coast Hispanic groups, MALDEF and CRLA, from upstart activist groups grateful for this type of forum like the Center for United Labor Action (CULA), and from individuals, Bell System employees and customers, who believed they had inside knowledge about AT&T's policies toward its workers. All these potential speakers shared one goal: to document orally why the phone company should itself suffer in exchange for the suffering it had caused its own employees.

Such quixotic aspirations by so many American citizens came courtesy of the successful activists of the previous decade. The civil rights movement had been percolating since the 1940s when black World War II veterans returned to their southern homes and demanded the right to vote. In the 1950s, the movement gained momentum with the 1954 *Brown v. Board of Education of Topeka* ruling, which outlawed racial segregation in public schools, and Rosa Parks's 1955 bus protest. By the early 1960s, it had exploded with tens of thousands of Americans participating in civil rights marches and rallies, many motivated by the televised hosing of black protesters by Birmingham, Alabama's firefighters on Good Friday, 1963. In 1964, when President Johnson signed the Civil Rights Act establishing the EEOC, they could see their efforts had paid off. That success motivated other groups: antiwar activists protested against the conflict in Vietnam until Nixon sanctioned peace talks in Paris and announced the phaseout of the draft in 1972 and signed a final peace agreement the following year. Feminists and environmentalists followed, driving the revision of discrimination laws to include women and the establishment of the Environmental Protection Agency. These achievements empowered individual Americans, making their interest in participating in a legitimate attack on the country's largest company natural.

The FCC did employ lawyers—Jim Juntilla and Ruth Baker on this case— to represent the public in every hearing, which, in theory, gave voice to citizens' opinions. But the commission's mandate to serve all Americans meant it would also listen to individuals' viewpoints directly. In more traditional FCC hearings involving rate increase requests, those voices would often be from Washington, D.C.–based advocates for the poor protesting higher phone bills, but to the FCC the subject didn't matter. All perspectives had to be heard.

However, these EEOC hearings were unusual, and not just because of their focus on employment policies instead of telephone rates. Many of the citizens who wanted to testify didn't live or work in or near Washington, D.C., and lacked the resources to get there, so they were pushing for hearings in other cities. MALDEF and CRLA had petitioned for sessions in California to address the phone company's discrimination against Hispanics, while the CULA wanted them held in New York City to address both racial and gender charges. The FCC, before incurring the significant expense and logistical nightmare of relocating an entire judicial proceeding from one coast to the other, needed to be sure it made sense.

The West Coast groups made their request in February 1971, while the CULA didn't ask until a year later, but both met with a similar, predictable response. The FCC wasn't keen on holding hearings outside Washington, AT&T vehemently objected, but the EEOC was strongly in favor. In the end, the FCC commissioners approved the sessions on each coast and added one more set of public hearings in Washington, D.C. The commission hadn't succumbed to the partisan bickering but simply sided with its own lawyers' argument that it was important to hear the individuals, speaking in their own words, who were actually affected by Bell System policies, as this was the FCC's first hearing of this sort.

The FCC's decision generated extra work for the case's three parties. In mid-March 1972, while the hearings broke between the final EEOC witness and the FCC's two experts, David Copus and Randy Speck flew to California to meet with lawyers from the Hispanic activist groups and PT&T to plan those sessions. The next month, Judy Potter took Speck on his eye-opening trip to New York, interviewing the New York Telephone employees—Hispanics in the Bronx and women in Albany—who would testify in Manhattan about AT&T's failures as an employer. Copus worked with Cashdan, Levy, and the involved civil rights groups to produce appropriate public notices at EEOC expense to recruit witnesses willing to talk about AT&T on the stand. The FCC tracked down conference room space in the Los Angeles Corps of Engineers building and the San Francisco U.S. Post Office, locations deemed sufficiently neutral to the local Hispanics who had had their share of run-ins with the California court system, and an abandoned government building in a not-well-traveled section of the West Village was chosen to host the New York sessions. And, after many protests from AT&T, Denniston finally agreed, with restraints, to filming in Los Angeles by an NBC documentary program and in New York by both a graduate student representing the Women's Film Study Alliance and the local PBS station.

During the third week in April, three weeks after Robert Nathan, the FCC's last witness, had testified, the field hearings were finally ready to start. By the time the core group of hearings participants—Copus, Potter, and Gartner; Ashley and Levy; Juntilla and Baker; and Denniston—along with their local colleagues, entered the conference room in the Los Angeles Corps of Engineers building on Monday, April 17, 1972, the glare of the public eye had cranked up the hearings' atmosphere. There were a hundred or so people in the audience, and an NBC television crew was fussing over lights, microphones, and cameras. Seven Hispanic men sat in the first row of the audience, waiting for their chance to testify against AT&T's discriminatory treatment of them and their Spanish-speaking colleagues. A loud buzz could be heard throughout the room.

Although, as George Ashley describes now, it "wasn't . . . a friendly atmosphere" for AT&T, the testimony that day benefited the company.[1] Without challenge, PT&T's lawyer, William Diedrich, made a platitude-filled statement about the company's commitment to hiring "Spanish-surnamed employees," and the Hispanic groups, theoretically the EEOC's ally, came out in support of the company's efforts based on a deal they had cut just before the FCC hearings crowd had arrived on the West Coast. Having not been forewarned of this strategy, Potter and her colleagues were stunned. In the years since, Copus has come to realize this was a strategically clever move for the Hispanic activists, using the incentive of public government hearings to gain concessions from their corporate adversary. However, it makes both him and Potter angry to this day. From Copus's point of view, "it made it look like we had egg on our face";[2] Potter put it more directly: "We . . . got the feeling we had been sold out."[3]

Fortunately for the EEOC, its image improved over the next few days. During the rest of the sessions in Los Angeles, PT&T and expert witnesses testified about the company's discrimination against Spanish-speaking Americans, supporting the EEOC's chapter on Hispanics in *A Unique Competence*. Then, on Thursday, April 20, the hearings moved to San Francisco, into a smaller space with fewer spectators and no cameras, regaining a modicum of order and changing emphasis. Although the new focus—the difficulties Spanish-speakers faced when they needed assistance on the phone—was outside the EEOC's specific purview, it fell within the charge Denniston had received from the FCC commissioners when he took the hearings examiner assignment. Moreover, its entertaining and embarrassing illumination of the company's service for its Spanish-speaking customers emphasized the gap between the Bell System's spoken commitments and its actions.

Albert Moreno, a lawyer for CRLA, proposed the Hispanic advocates' idea to Denniston early that afternoon. "We have a telephone in [a nearby room] which is hooked up to a speaker," he said, "and we would like to go there . . . [and] . . . place a call in Spanish to Sonoma County, and we would like our client to say that he has an emergency and . . . [needs] a phone number of a doctor or hospital, and we would like to see what the results of that request are when he asks an operator for assistance."[4]

Judy Potter spoke for the EEOC. "We would support that request."

Denniston asked the necessary rhetorical question. "Does anyone wish to object?"

"I object, Mr. Examiner," Diedrich, PT&T's lawyer, responded. "I object on a number of grounds." Not that he had a whole list of them available off the top of his head. "Primarily, I am seriously concerned with violating the Federal Communications Act, for one thing, by placing a . . . by, in effect, having a telephone call into an open room without the other end of the called party knowing about it without a beep tone." This was his best effort on short notice.

But Copus had a quick response. "Mr. Examiner, perhaps the caller could first announce in Spanish that the call is being monitored."

Diedrich needed another reason. "The second part . . . is I do not want my client to be party to, in effect, a false emergency call over its public utility facilities. I think it would be a breech of . . . ." Not bad under pressure.

But Moreno had that one covered himself. "If that is an objection," he interjected over Diedrich's trailing voice, "I really have to speak to my office in Healdsberg, California, . . . [so the caller can ask for] . . . the number of my office . . . and that would remove that problem."

It made sense to Denniston. "I believe that the specific provisions of the [commission's order when approving West Coast hearings] directed that I attempt to observe the difficulties of the language barrier," he said, "and therefore, I will do it."

As soon as the members of the EEOC team heard Denniston's affirmative answer, they began picking up their papers to move down the hall. But Denniston, first, gave AT&T an out. "If the company has any qualms about [this demonstration], they may absent themselves," he said, though he still had an opinion. "I would suggest they be present however."

The Bell System's lawyers weren't interested in Denniston's advice. "The company, Pacific Telephone, declines to participate in this matter at all," Diedrich responded.

Denniston gave Ashley a last chance, but he had no interest either. Most likely, the Bell System lawyers' abdication stemmed more from distaste for the idea than concern about the call's likelihood of success, but it did little to build confidence in PT&T's service.

Denniston recessed the hearings for about ten minutes, and the EEOC, FCC, and Hispanic lawyers migrated to Room 264, where a Spanish-speaking client of Moreno's organization, Guido del Prado, turned on the speaker-phone and called information in Sonoma County. When the operator answered, he requested the phone number for CRLA in Healdsberg, California, in Spanish. She replied in English, "What is that?"

He asked the same question again, again in Spanish. This time, understanding she was in trouble, she said, "Hold the line and I will call [my] supervisor."

After a long thirty seconds, another English-speaking woman came on the phone, and del Prado asked a third time. Now, a few words of Spanish came in response, as if the speaker had studied the language for a year in high school, but she still didn't understand what he was saying and told him so. The EEOC team members did their best to stifle their giggles.

Del Prado, not ready to let Pacific Telephone off the hook, began to spell out his request in Spanish. By the time he had gotten through "rural" and "legal," painstakingly recounted in Spanish letters, his counterpart seemed to accept defeat, admitting she didn't speak Spanish well enough to understand what he needed.

But del Prado was like Simon and Garfunkel's boxer who wanted to stay and fight as long as he could before the bout was called, no matter the bedraggled state of his opponent. He asked if there might be a third person in the office who spoke Spanish more fluently.

His tenacity had now inspired the individual with whom he shared the ring. She tried again, apparently now taking this on as an intellectual challenge. The hearings room crowd waited quietly, expectantly, for several moments until, in hesitant Spanish, after five minutes and ten seconds, she produced the number he had requested. In the end, del Prado was on the line for a total of six minutes and forty seconds before he got the information he needed.

When Moreno described the demonstration a few minutes later in the hearings room to Ashley and Diedrich, no one disagreed with his explanation of the events; nor did anyone draw a conclusion out loud. They didn't need to. Everyone knew that waiting nearly seven minutes to get a listed phone number meant the company's service was simply inadequate. PT&T might have been honestly committed to hiring more Spanish-speaking employees, but it wasn't living up to its stated commitment of adequately serving the Spanish-speaking public.

While the Los Angeles hearings were remembered by some as "festive" and "carnival-like,"[5] they couldn't compare with the atmosphere created when the sessions moved to New York City three weeks later. Anyone arriving at 641 Washington Street in Manhattan on the morning of May 8, 1972, could see trouble brewing. A questionable neighborhood in the first place, it felt even less comfortable with a handful of young people, black and white, marching in front of the old government building's entrance, holding large sheets painted with colorful slogans such as "AT&T's Racism Equals Profit," "Dial '0' for Oppression" and "Stop Bell's Superprofits." Other protesters were distributing pamphlets titled "Let's Give Quigley the Business," in reference to a New York Telephone chief operator, Doris Quigley, who was many of these demonstrators' boss.

After pushing through this outdoor melee and entering the hearings room, an observer arrived at the apparent set for a low-budget film about a group of 1960s radicals like the Chicago Seven. Four klieg lights beat down on the lawyers, judge, and witness stand at the front of the room while camerawomen from WNET-TV and the Women's Film Study Alliance moved around at will, claiming a spot on the floor or in front of a witness in order to get just the right angle for their shot. The room felt stuffy, as if a window hadn't been opened since the day the last tenant left, and chain smokers in the back rows made the air feel even thicker. By 10 A.M., when the hearing was scheduled to start, the outside protesters had come inside and joined a hundred or more of their colleagues, who seemed like extras for the film: They had the right level of passion but little skill in being part of an organized effort. On and off that day, the marching went on. Whenever the hearings' rhetoric moved them, an activist or two would grab one of the slogan-covered sheets, now taped to the walls, and march it in circles around the back of the room. At lunchtime, the smell of Nathan's hot dogs wafted through the air as mothers fed their kids. Throughout the day, the lack of microphones and the mixture of ambient and purposeful noise from the spectators made it almost impossible to hear.

The chaotic environment that May Monday wasn't the only thing markedly different from most other mornings of these hearings. In the front of the room, the lawyers' table had suddenly expanded. The three-piece-suited AT&T lawyers were still there—Ashley, Levy, and a couple of colleagues from New York Telephone—and Potter and her teammates, Copus and Gartner, had claimed their space at the other side of the U, while the FCC lawyers, Juntilla and Baker, sat in their usual seats in between. However, a new team of three had appeared next to the FCC contingent, representatives of the CULA, which had become a fourth legal party to the case. But they were unique among their new colleagues—they weren't lawyers. They were female nonmanagement employees of New York Telephone who had convinced the FCC to grant their organization status as a party to the case.

Represented solely by a company union more aligned to management wishes than workers' rights, these young women had formed a branch of the CULA within New York Telephone to fight for better treatment. They described their organization in a February 10, 1972, letter to the FCC as a "nonprofit . . . based in NYC . . . [made] up of working . . . and unemployed people, Black, Puerto Rican, Chicano, and white. We work together for better working conditions, especially for Black, Puerto Rican and women workers."[6] With offices throughout the East and Midwest, the CULA supported workers from established unions including the International Ladies Garment Workers and the Transport Workers. The organization's letter to the FCC had accompanied the petition asking for New York City hearings and offered witnesses, their members, who could testify against New York Telephone.

The FCC had granted that request easily, but just testifying wasn't enough. The following month, on March 31, the CULA leaders asked if their organization could become a direct party to the case with status comparable to that of the three existing key players. Just five days later, the commission agreed, explaining that the CULA "will be of assistance to the Commission in the determination of the issues herein,"[7] which explained little. Why wouldn't an organization like NOW, which had a national profile, be of more assistance than the CULA, a group even the women of NOW didn't know? But with little funding to support a lawyer's daily participation and little inclination to get involved without legal support, NOW never asked to become a direct party—nor did any other activist group—while the CULA did. The CULA had entered the game.

Before long, several people in the hearings room who supported the phone company would decide they didn't like the CULA women's presence. Mary Pinotti, Kathy Dennis, and Gavrielle Gemma, often dressed in berets and spouting anticapitalist rhetoric, were radicals in an era when being radical meant something. They had no interest in politely presenting their views in a judicial proceeding. They had easily gained a seat at the table and had no intention of occupying it quietly.

Before the CULA women could get up much steam that Monday morning, Walt Maneker, a New York Telephone lawyer who had joined the AT&T team, managed to get his opening statement on the record. First he reported on the company's recent progress: 22 percent of New York Telephone's employees were minorities, he noted, versus only 8 percent eight years earlier, and 23 percent of its 53,000 female employees earned more than $10,000 per year, compared with 5 percent of women employed nationally. But he also admitted, "We do not regard the job as done by any means," and listed the company's hiring objectives to improve these figures.[8]

It sounded good, nearly as good as the report Diedrich, the PT&T lawyer, had made three weeks earlier at the California hearings. But these East Coast hearings would be a lot rougher on New York Telephone. For one thing, the New York company had no agreement from community civil rights groups or their own nonmanagement employees that the affirmative action plans they described would meet workers' expectations, a feat PT&T had managed to achieve before the West Coast hearings' start. Plus, New York Telephone faced a double whammy from the CULA. The behavior of the CULA women, who were both legally unschooled and personally uninhibited, produced a free-for-all environment so unfamiliar to the corporate contingent that it qualified as "bizarre," as Don Liebers remembers today.[9] Moreover, the stories these union women and other employee witnesses would tell over the next five days, of egregious treatment perpetrated by company managers on nonmanagement staff, would embarrass the AT&T team. Whether the CULA women's methods were appropriate or not, their descriptions were undeniably damaging. After this week, AT&T's claim of fulfilling its "social purpose" toward its employees would be further damaged.

The three women from the CULA started their exposé that morning with individual speeches about their personal mistreatment at the hands of the phone company. Mary Pinotti, a white woman not older than thirty who was the CULA's national co-chairwoman, went first with an indictment of "New York Telephone and its parent company, the American Telephone and Telegraph Company, . . . for [their] conscious and systematic policies of racism and discrimination against women workers."[10] Her account of the CULA's key role in bringing a case against AT&T, the unlikelihood the company's announced affirmative action plan would make any difference, and the dismal nature of the telephone operator's position inspired three rounds of audience applause.

A few minutes later, Gavrielle Gemma, a second young white woman, who, with her oversized glasses and hair woven tightly into a bun, seemed more fit for a library reference desk than a radical workers' union, took the stand. Though she had never had a conversation with the EEOC lawyers, her testimony brought *A Unique Competence* to life. She expanded on Pinotti's description of the demeaning operator's job. "When you want to go to the bathroom [when on an operator's shift], you have to ring for the supervisor and say, 'Can I have a minute, please?' Then five minutes later, you have to ring back again. Twenty minutes later, you have to ring back, and if you are very lucky, . . . they will let you go. We are grown women. All we should have to do is put our light key on hold and get up and go when we need to, . . . no questions asked, no one following you into the bathroom, . . . like every other human being has a right to."

Later she noted the operators' undesirable work schedule. "From November until March . . . I would have to work every weekend, split weekends," she described. "Very rarely did I ever get two days off in a row. What's that do to a family? What does that do when you have . . . to arrange your babysitting hours?"

She explained how women were kept out of craft jobs: "I applied for a transfer into the plant department about six months ago. There was nothing done. The only time that women in this city were ever given a chance to get into the plant department was during that strike when New York Tel wanted to bust that strike . . . and they hired women, all white, to work on the frame. That's their idea of opportunity, hire them as strike breakers."

Then she added what the EEOC's narrative could never capture, an insight into the dignity lost when people are treated this way. "We're not slaves, and it's about time that you all learned that, because slaves when they're whipped and brutalized and degraded, they don't work—you can't make them . . . give sweet smiles and pleasant voices. You treat us in a degrading and . . . racist [and] humiliating way and you want us to make all this money for you. We're not going to do it. We want these demands answered right now." If Lorena Weeks had been an outspoken activist instead of a quiet grandmother, one could have expected these exact words to have come from her.

But although Gemma's testimony was both powerful and relevant, Denniston was dismayed that applause had erupted eleven times while she spoke, and not only from audience members. "Miss Pinotti," Denniston said to Gemma's CULA colleague, "I notice that you and Miss Dennis are both joining in this applause. You are sitting at the Counsel table. You are . . . acting in a representative capacity. I would ask that you comport yourself as do the others."

Gemma was on the stand for just a few more minutes, since both the EEOC and AT&T declined their turns to question her, although Potter couldn't resist making one brief comment for her agency: "We'd just like to thank you very much."

Kathy Dennis, a black woman with a tight Afro, huge hoop earrings, and a stare that said no one was getting in her way, then stood for the third CULA testimony, this time about the service rep job. She first touched on another of *A Unique Competence*'s claims, that nonmanagement female Bell System employees couldn't get promoted into management. "There is only one woman [district manager]," she said, "out of four commercial districts in my building. The rest are men who have never been through the stages . . . [of] working there and working their way up. My supervisor has been in the company for eight years. Why isn't she a manager? Is it because she's not qualified when she tells our manager what to do?"

The working environment in the Commercial Department sounded no better than Traffic, where the operators worked. "The supervisor runs around the office . . . screaming to the top of her lungs, 'Watch that CWI' [customer waiting interval]. . . . If you are off the phone too long, your supervisor is screaming down your back."

After observing the CULA women in action for several hours, the Bell System lawyers finally lost their composure. All day, they had tolerated their antics: making pronouncements when they were supposed to be questioning witnesses, introducing issues far afield of these proceedings, and encouraging applause from supporters in the audience. But when Gemma called the company racist because Maneker, representing New York Telephone, had objected to the testimony of Dennis, the sole black woman on the CULA team, the lawyers seemed to reach their limit. Maneker attacked Denniston:

"It is perfectly apparent that you are not . . . in control of this hearing," and then read a detailed description of the look and sound of the hearings room into the record.

Under normal circumstances, a statement like this could be legal suicide, but these circumstances were far from normal. Instead of exploding, Denniston acquiesced. "As to . . . your criticism of the decorum here," he said, "I must confess I have to join with you in that." He had no defense, just another polite plea for help: "And again I solicit the tolerance and good will of those who are here in order that we may get along with this hearing and actually accomplish its purpose. . . . We are very slowly getting witnesses heard." At this point, the practical considerations seemed most important.

With relief for everyone, the CULA receded into the background for most of the afternoon, and the hearings proceeded more smoothly. Not knowing of the CULA's plans ahead of time, the EEOC had found its own witness, Gay Semel, to testify about the telephone operator's job. Semel, a thin twenty-nine-year-old with long dark hair, didn't fit the typical profile of a New York Telephone operator, since she was both white and college-educated. When she had applied for her job two years earlier, the personnel official had tried to hire her into the less humiliating service rep position because, as she notes, "they were trying to put me in a white woman's job."[11] But, unlike almost anyone else in her shoes, she had her heart set on becoming an operator for one reason. She wanted to join the operators' political movement. With a working-class, activist background, when she read about the black New York Telephone operators who launched a wildcat strike on Mother's Day, 1970, the highest call volume day all year, she became determined to join their forces.

Once she was hired, her role became clear. In between suffering the indignities of the operator's job, she began working with the group organizing operators to join CWA, the union that represented most of the company's craft employees. As part of her efforts, she interviewed hundreds of operators, becoming the expert on the reality of the position. As a result, when the EEOC went looking for a New York Telephone operator to testify, Semel came up first on the list.

When Semel arrived to testify that Monday afternoon, she was as nervous as Randy Speck had been on the first day of the hearings. Although she wasn't intimidated by the lawyers who would question her, she was worried about her own abilities. She and her fellow operators had been treated so badly by their management that, as she notes today, "I was concerned that by explaining it, people on the outside of the experience would think less of us for putting up with it. Sort of, if this is going on, it must be because it's needed in some way." [12] Without realizing it, Semel was taking on the job of translator for her fellow Bell System employees—not just for her own peers but also for the women who had testified earlier. While the understated Lorena Weeks and the combative women of CULA had all made points, Semel saw her responsibility as clearly and professionally communicating their same message: Bell System managers' treatment of their low-level, female, often minority employees was both disrespectful and unacceptable in a place of work.

Over the course of that afternoon and the next morning, Semel's testimony achieved that goal. She explained that the dress code for telephone operators was "totally arbitrary," with jeans allowed in some offices on some days and dresses required at others; that "the switchboards are always dirty"; and that operators joke "that Martha Washington trained on my [switch]-board because it is so old." [13] Echoing Gemma's earlier testimony and the on-the-job experiences of both Peggy Falterman and Gwen Thomas, Semel gave a host of ways operators are harassed: supervisors standing "behind you . . . yelling pick up [the next call]," or telling you to "sit up straight," or ordering you to look straight ahead at all times, or listening in on your calls. Through her straightforward words, she clarified the daily contempt these women faced in their jobs.

When Semel left the stand, the CULA women made a final statement, which underscored their frustration. Mad that Denniston had denied their request for subpoenas of AT&T managers, Gemma stated, "[What] you're saying, Mr. Denniston, . . . is that AT&T is above the law, . . . that you are conceding to their wishes that a chief operator who makes over $15,000 a year, who can anytime she wants to keep me on the board for eight hours a day, is not going to be subpoenaed here, that you're siding with AT&T against the operators." She drew a breath. "I have a right to confront my supervisor."

Denniston was tired. "Your remarks are on the record. You're not correctly stating my position, however," was his only defense. Finally, at 4:10 P.M., the day was over.

On the second day of New York City hearings, with a good night's sleep behind him, Denniston had arrived prepared, which he needed to be. As if she had never left the hearings room the night before, never mind slept, Gavrielle Gemma launched into a new lecture almost immediately, but Denniston had his own speech ready when she had finished. "If we have any more outbursts like that," he told her, "by you talking at the top of your lungs and refusing to cooperate in the decorum of this proceeding, no matter how deep your feelings are on the subject, I will find it necessary to terminate the hearing."[14] How would they get through three and a half more days with one another?

But Denniston's threat appeared to work. From that point, the bickering calmed to a dull roar, the applause diminished, and most of the witnesses simply told their stories. Gay Semel went back on the stand to recount her experiences with the recruiting policies *A Unique Competence* had outlined. During her interview, she had been asked if she was married, if she would be getting back with her husband, if her menstrual cycle was regular. (The last comment threw Maneker into another brief fit. "Is there no limit?" he asked Denniston.) Later she explained that a "trick" for a telephone operator is the schedule of hours she works on a certain day, but she made sure to point out, "For men, it's called tours and I was just shocked when I first saw it . . . the only other time I heard that was in prostitution."

With that description and the film that would be shown that afternoon, *Miss Index,* New York Telephone was beginning to appear a bit prurient in addition to discriminatory. An operators' training film, *Miss Index* emphasized the importance of being both accurate and fast in responding to customer calls by working toward a set measurement or "index." 'Miss Index,' the film's naked leading character, maintained her modesty with a printed card covering her torso, its numbers noting either her measurements or those the operator was targeting, based on the viewer's perspective. Larry Gartner, who described the film for the record, also pointed out that the operator depicted was female and the customers male. When Gemma took the stand to explain how the film was used—because none of the Bell System lawyers were up to the task—she mentioned its role in training and then added that it made her feel "like a six-year old." Repeatedly, the point had been made. New York Telephone was no place for a woman to work if she wanted to maintain any self-respect.

The final three days of the New York hearings followed that afternoon's calmer pattern. Witnesses presented story after story, some sounding farfetched, like the claim that some telephone operators' home phones were tapped, and some sounding too packaged, like the monologue from Nelson Benedico, a former New Jersey Bell employee, about the company's hubristic managers, who were completely insincere and put on a "perfect performance every day at the Bell Theater."[15] But others sounded discriminatory at best and terrifying at worst. David Newman, a frameman with New York Telephone, talked about how his supervisor told him that "in the future all the FF frames will be staffed by female frame personnel, that frame forces will be segregated, sexually."[16] Luella Smith, a clerk at New York Telephone, described how she "had to sit and listen to them refer to me as a Nigger, and when I went to my supervisor and complained . . . , she said that she was in no position to answer. And now if that isn't racial discrimination, I don't know what is."[17] Robert Kirkman, a former outside plant craft worker in Manhattan, testified that his foreman said of Kirkman's black partner, "That stupid nigger, I'm going to get his ass."[18] Their unadorned words spoke volumes about the attitudes of New York Telephone's management employees.

One of the issues the CULA women had brought up early in the week would hound the New York Telephone legal and management teams for months. Several employees who had been scheduled to testify in the hearings in Manhattan were disciplined that same week for job performance, and more than one was threatened with the possibility of being fired. Maneker and Ashley made many speeches throughout the week denying there was a connection between the two activities. At the same time, the CULA representatives and other New York Telephone witnesses, operating in an era long before whistle-blower protection laws were on the books, repeatedly emphasized not only the facts as they understood them but the fear they believed was keeping others from coming forward. Over the course of the next several months, Denniston, with no authority to manage a private company's treatment of a specific employee, issued orders requiring New York Telephone to give him two weeks' notice of any witness it planned to fire. The phone company executives hated this oversight, but they had only themselves to blame for either the appearance or actuality of the mistreatment.

On Friday, the last day of public hearings in New York, no one was surprised when Gavrielle Gemma made one last speech about how racist and sexist New York Telephone was. "Very well," Denniston replied briefly, but when clapping erupted a final time, he couldn't help but add, "I notice, as usual, Ms. Pinotti leads the applause for herself."[19] A long week was finally over.

When the parties reconvened in Washington two and a half weeks later on the morning of May 31, 1972, they had been assigned a new, smaller room at the FCC. But otherwise, they were back to their old surroundings—same building, same cast of characters, away from the public, away from the women of the CULA. But, alas, they hadn't entirely escaped them. The intrepid Gavrielle Gemma had arrived at the FCC that day too, if a few minutes late. The combination of the smaller room and her latest speech—this time about not getting adequate notice of this session—produced a sense of claustrophobia that pervaded the space. With only scheduling issues to be discussed, the participants gratefully escaped after only forty minutes.

Five days later, on Monday, June 5, the last set of public hearings commenced in Washington, D.C.. with no one from the CULA in attendance. Whether because of their absence or the testimony that followed, the atmosphere felt dull. The parties had to meet on only three days that week because Juntilla had tracked down few individuals even interested in testifying. Although the descriptions by local C&P witnesses of the mistreatment they faced were just as legitimate as the stories heard in California and New York, most of them sounded familiar. Although this repetition helped prove AT&T's discriminatory policies blanketed the country, it provided little courtroom drama.

But on that Friday, there was new potential for activity. A top representative from NOW, Ann Scott, would testify at last. NOW had been remarkably quiescent throughout the hearings, considering Wilma Scott Heide's vow to get involved once she had reviewed *A Unique Competence*. But the organization's leaders had been focusing their efforts outside the hearings room. In February, Heide had designated an internal NOW task force, named Sally Hacker its chair, and assigned her two goals: to coordinate NOW pressure on Bell offices around the country and help convince the corporate executives on AT&T's twenty-sixth floor to improve their female employees' jobs, salaries, and opportunities. In addition, Hacker was coordinating NOW's involvement in the FCC hearings. She had tried to get witnesses on the schedule at the Los Angeles and New York hearings, although only written testimony in New York made the record, and now she was finally facilitating Scott's presence at these Washington sessions. She had also requested a formal meeting with one of AT&T's top executives, John deButts or Bob Lilley, declining Easlick's offer to meet with her himself because "whole corporations must begin to respond to feminist goals."[20]

At the same time, Whitney Adams, NOW's FCC coordinator, had been pursuing her assignment to monitor the EEOC's work in the FCC hearings. Soon after Heide gave her the EEOC case, she went to the agency's office in search of Katherine Mazzaferri, the one feminist working on it based on NOW's research. By then, Mazzaferri, in her last year of law school and working only part-time at the agency, was tough to find. The receptionist instead sent Adams to the task force's office on the EEOC's fourth floor to find David Copus.

Adams took the direct approach when she marched into Copus's office unannounced, stating, *I'm here to make sure you don't screw up the AT&T*

case for women. With just that proclamation, he probably wouldn't have forgotten her. He was irritated by her intrusion because he "didn't think NOW could make a contribution, thought this is another fly in my ointment"; plus, she had interrupted his workday.[21] There was something else, too. She was "cute, smart, energetic, vivacious."[22] He was attracted to her immediately.

In the months since, she had visited him regularly, often enough for their relationship to turn from one of potential adversaries to romantic partners. By the end of 1972, they would move in together and in 1982 would get married. But despite their personal closeness, she wasn't completely convinced he "got it" when it came to the discrimination Bell System women faced. Her strongest concern was something Copus had been thinking about, too. The death of the EEOC/AT&T negotiations in January 1972 had stemmed primarily from the company's outrage at the EEOC's demand for excessive back pay; however, the parties hadn't resolved another, almost equally contentious issue, either: the government's demand for goals and timetables for men in traditionally female Bell System jobs.

As an equal employment lawyer, Copus understood that all jobs had to be open to both genders to ensure nondiscrimination, and the company had agreed de facto to the same point, since men filled dozens of telephone operator positions at PT&T as a result of a recent hiring experiment. However, NOW was pushing the EEOC to go beyond ensuring that telephone operator and service rep jobs welcomed men. The organization wanted specific goals for men in these jobs as a requirement of any final agreement. The company, on the other hand, was adamantly refusing, believing men wouldn't be interested in such jobs and, therefore, the goals would be impossible to meet. After months of discussions between the two parties, the issue had been left unresolved, although it remained in Copus's mind. He realized a negotiated settlement could, in the end, resolve the case, and therefore he needed to understand the issue's real importance. Since Adams wasn't yet steeped in the feminist arguments that could address Copus's concern, she brought in reinforcements.

Wilma Scott Heide flew to Washington from Connecticut, and Ann Scott arrived from upstate New York. They met Adams and Copus and a few other interested parties at the Yenching Palace, a well-known Chinese restaurant in the upscale Cleveland Park neighborhood of Washington, D.C. They had picked the right place: negotiators had met there to craft the deal ending the Cuban missile crisis in 1962, and nine years later Chinese diplomats had made the restaurant their second home while working out the opening of Communist China with President Nixon. Although hardly on that scale, the NOW meeting had its own drama. There were no arguments or lengthy discussions. Wilma Scott Heide, NOW's "resident philosopher and . . . visionary," made just one key statement:[23] *As long as there are jobs that the Bell System believes are so crummy that only women want them,* Copus remembers her saying, *women won't be free.*

By that point, David Copus had come a long way in his feminist awakening. For months, he had been subjected to Adams's incessant observations of female oppression depicted on TV, in magazine ads, in news stories, and just about everywhere else. He attended a conference that year at which a feminist psychologist described how sex differences were taught from the first week of a child's life, when mothers cuddle female babies more than their male counterparts; Copus finally had an empirical explanation for sexism's start. He had even joined NOW, along with Randy Speck, which had further opened his eyes to women's oppression. With all this foundation at last in place, Heide's single sentence was all he needed to hear to finally "get it." By forcing the company to work toward hiring set numbers of men as operators, the job would have to improve enough to attract those men, which would benefit the female operators already at work and ensure no Bell System job would ever be seen as women's only again. As a result, Copus agreed to battle the company until it agreed to goals and timetables for men in traditionally female jobs. The NOW leaders emitted a collective sigh of relief.

With a definite time finally set on the FCC's public hearings schedule, NOW still planned to testify. Ann Scott, who looked like a light-haired Jackie Kennedy and spoke like a woman entirely sure she was right, arrived in Washington, D.C., on June 9, 1972, well coached for the reserved atmosphere she was entering. She based her testimony that day on a review of the AT&T affirmative action plan legally required by the federal government. She began strategically, finding something for which she could commend the company: its requirement that all Bell System managers be evaluated on their success at meeting affirmative action goals, a priority from NOW's viewpoint.

Then she launched into her critique. The plan lacked large enough goals or fast enough timetables for women advancing in the company, the pay scales for women were too low, and, going far afield of what most companies considered relevant to an affirmative action plan, any settlement should also cover fringe benefits, limits on personal questions during interviews, and the availability of child care. Finally, she made the key point: Bell's plan had no goals and timetables in the reverse, no targets for men in women's jobs.

After all this time, Scott's testimony felt anticlimactic. Even Tom Powers, who had reappeared at AT&T's table now that the hearings were back in Washington, couldn't get much of a fight going with her. Today, her prediction that women would achieve parity with men in the workforce by 1985 draws interest, illuminating how long real change takes. But most of her other comments simply echoed what the hearings' participants had already heard from many other women, most who had faced the discrimination themselves. By 3 P.M., after just a couple of hours on the stand, Scott had finished. She may not have introduced many new perspectives or sparked the audience's attention on this last day of public hearings, but she had gotten on record the things NOW leaders believed essential for any agreement with AT&T. From NOW's point of view, she had done her job.

At 3:05 P.M. that June Friday, Denniston adjourned the hearings for what he expected would be four months. AT&T had earlier agreed that it would provide its written defense by August 1, 1972, and Potter, Copus, and Gartner had committed to being ready to question the AT&T witnesses two months later. The work ahead for all parties seemed clear.

Beneficiary Profile:
Margaret Hoppe

In 1973, seven years before she would take a job with AT&T, Margaret Hoppe was working as the assistant dean of students at Seton Hall University in South Orange, New Jersey. She had arrived there two years earlier after earning a master's degree in higher education, having chosen the Seton Hall position over several similar offers because of its competitive salary, its location close to her family's home, and, most important, the challenge it promised. When the small Catholic university, which had recently gone co-ed, decided to house female students on campus for the first time in its 115-year history, its board had authorized the construction of a women's residence hall. In her first professional job, Hoppe would be in charge of the hall, giving her a terrific opportunity to put her education and ideas into action quickly and make her own mark.

Hoppe, small, dark-haired, and Caucasian, dressed impeccably with never a hair out of place. Since she worked on a college campus in the hippie era, she had the option to wear much more casual clothes than she would when she later started her job with Ma Bell. But with a conservative approach to both politics and her wardrobe, she left the tie-dyed blouses to the students and wore neatly pressed dresses and skirts to her Seton Hall office every day.

Hoppe's mother had never expected her to go to college, never mind work at one. She had never worked herself, except for a few painful weeks as a cashier at a local supermarket after her kids were grown and gone, but the pressure of swiftly ringing up a stream of groceries unnerved her; *I'm not good at this,* Hoppe remembers her saying. With that discomfort in the working world and a husband who had always supported her, her "girls don't have to go to college" attitude wasn't surprising.[1] Hoppe's father, on the other hand, wanted all his kids to attend "whatever college they want." He himself had had dreams of becoming a lawyer but got through only two years of his bachelor's degree before his father died, forcing him to join the family mining business. He vowed that his four children, both the boys *and* girls, wouldn't face the same disappointment.

Neither parent, however, provided a role model for the executive career Hoppe would eventually find. Her father did get out of the mines, once his family's coal reserves were depleted, and moved into professional union jobs, but Hoppe never visited him at any of his offices, instead accompanying him on investigations into workers' compensation claims for the AFL-CIO and noting his frequent absences when he was on the road, lobbying for members' rights. But she couldn't envision herself in either of these roles because the work seemed so unappealing and the world so male. Sometimes she would imagine herself becoming a veterinarian because she loved animals, but that seemed far-fetched, since she had never known a female vet. In reality, the career role models for a young, college-educated, American woman in the mid-1960s were limited. Based on the working women Hoppe had observed, she figured she could "maybe become a nurse, maybe a teacher."

From the time Hoppe was just old enough to talk, she exhibited the independence and tenacity for the professional career she would excel in decades later. In her baby book, her mother documented her first words: "I do myself." Later, at the private girls' high school she attended, she focused on her schoolwork while her peers were busy with other pursuits. "While everyone was going boy crazy," she remembers today, "I was studying, making great friends and learning how to create strong bonds" with her classmates, an ability that would prove essential in climbing the corporate ladder a dozen years later.[2] Combining these traits with her innate drive for acknowledgment and recognition, which she sensed could come from challenging work, Hoppe had all the raw material for a professional career, even if she was the wrong gender.

With this raw material, Hoppe was naturally inclined to listen more to her father than her mother and head directly to college. She chose a small liberal arts college in Virginia, which was located the farthest south her father would allow and had the prettiest campus. Hoppe loved it there from the day she arrived. She made friends who would last a lifetime, she got to know her professors personally, she worked on the college's newspaper, helped with new student orientation, and ran the Pan-Hellenic Council, which oversaw the school's sororities. She was having so much fun soaking up the school's benefits that she hadn't gotten around to choosing a major by the time it became a necessity at the end of her sophomore year. Under pressure, she decided on sociology: she had just finished a sociology course with a professor she loved, she knew it was a field that welcomed women, and, in any case, she had no other sense of what career she wanted. But her dream of pursuing a social work profession lasted only until she started her internship with a family services agency. After just a few home visits, she remembers thinking, Get me out of here, I don't want to do this. After one particularly futile discussion with a mentally retarded couple who had bought an expensively decorated Christmas tree but couldn't afford to feed their child, she came to understand her future fate if she pursued this career direction. Social work provided its practitioners with no leverage or power, just the opportunity to expend their energies convincing and cajoling their clients. It looked like an exercise in full-time frustration to Hoppe.

Concerned that she now had a major but no career direction, Hoppe turned to her mentor, the college's dean of women, who suggested that Hoppe consider a career like hers. Hoppe could use her upcoming sociology degree as a foundation for a high-level college administrator's position. Hoppe loved the idea. She had no model for a business career, but she could imagine doing the same work as a woman she admired and, at the same time, return to the intellectually stimulating and emotionally supportive environment of a college campus. Plus, the college administration field appeared relatively well integrated by gender, even in 1971, which appealed to Hoppe's sense of ambition.

To qualify for this type of job, Hoppe needed a graduate degree, also, which she pursued over the next two years at a gargantuan midwestern university because it gave her the most financial aid. Unfortunately, it also offered the antithesis of her idyllic undergraduate experience—fifty thousand students, twenty-story dormitories, and an atmosphere more evocative of an efficient manufacturing company than a nurturing university—so she focused solely on getting her degree and getting out of town. But even though her experience there lacked the warmth she had enjoyed during her undergraduate days, it still led her to her goal. By the end of her second year, the offer from Seton Hall had come across her desk, and that fall she started work as a college executive, just like her mentor, with the chance to make the impact she had always dreamed about. She had no idea then that AT&T was in the midst of a metamorphosis that would, in a few short years, offer her a career opportunity even beyond those dreams.

9

The First Agreement

Spring/Fall 1972

During the first few months of 1972, AT&T's team of lawyers had been just as busy outside the hearings room as within. They were lining up their own expert witnesses, whose statements would constitute most of their written defense, scheduled for submission on August 1, and whose presence on the witness stand would be required later that fall. The company had assigned Gene Kofke, a New Jersey Bell personnel executive, to fulfill the role Phyllis Wallace had played for the EEOC and track down psychologists and academics to support AT&T's spin on its employment record.

AT&T's corporate lawyers also had to involve the BOCs directly. Although the EEOC's complaint targeted the Bell System as a whole, its specific charges related to policies in each local Bell company. As a result, "for probably the first time," AT&T lawyer George Ashley recalls today, "we had to get lawyers in each BOC to represent their particular company."[1] Twenty-four individuals from twenty-four diverse businesses would testify. They represented the liberal cultures on either coast, the "good old boy" environment of the South, and many other value systems, and each company had its own unique record of hiring and promoting women and minorities. The possibility that these BOC executives might contradict, or "whipsaw," one another, as one Bell lawyer put it, loomed large.[2] As a result, Ashley and Levy decided to add a few lawyers to their New York staff to coordinate this testimony. To fill one of those slots, Ashley asked Ohio Bell's general counsel to release Clark Redick, one of that company's top labor lawyers, for a thirty-day assignment in Manhattan.

In Redick, a tall, lean man, just thirty-six years old with bushy eyebrows and hair, AT&T had again found an individual who could meets its unexpected and pressing needs. Redick had already been working on the EEOC case as the Ohio Bell lawyer with equal employment responsibility; plus, like Tom Powers, he had civil rights experience as the past general counsel of the Ohio Civil Rights Commission in an era in which that knowledge was rare. Moreover, in a company of loyal employees, Redick displayed an unusually fierce fealty despite having only six years' Bell System tenure. Without question, he would do his best on AT&T's behalf.

Redick happily accepted the month-long position. Not only capable and committed, he was intensely ambitious, always looking for a new challenge and more exposure to top company executives. But completing the assignment in just one month proved impossible. By that spring of 1972, thirty days had turned into as long as the job takes, and Redick had gone from temporary New York resident to Westchester County commuter with a full-time position as an AT&T corporate lawyer. Coordinating the BOC testimony now took about 50 percent of his time, with dozens of other duties filling the rest of his fourteen-hour days, seven days a week.

At the same time, the FCC legal experts, Ashley and Levy, along with Tom Powers and the equal employment opportunity lawyers at his firm, were busy since the first day of the hearings with a dogged attack against the EEOC's document summaries, Randy Speck's Findings of Fact. Ignoring Denniston's suggestion that first day that the two teams meet to negotiate mutually agreeable Findings, on February 4, 1972, the Bell System lawyers submitted their official request to jettison Speck's entire package, suggesting the Findings were "not designed to be fair and accurate summaries of the documents to which they relate."[3] However, aware that Denniston might resist taking such sweeping action, Powers also enlisted more than a half dozen of his young associates to develop specific complaints against each summary, a team that included Jane Lang, Steptoe and Johnson's first full-time female lawyer.

As a woman who had graduated from the University of Pennsylvania Law School two years earlier with only 5 female peers out of 120 total law students, Lang seemed an unlikely candidate to defend AT&T in its discrimination against women. But Lang, who had never considered herself a feminist, had a naive, if common, point of view, seeing AT&T's discriminatory policies against women as a reflection of American society. As she recalls today, "It was a learning experience for me to see the role employers played in reinforcing societal problems."[4]

With her uncritical perspective, a true admiration for Tom Powers, and little choice as a young associate, Lang willingly went to work on the case when she returned from maternity leave in February 1972. Powers threw her and her colleagues right into it, starting them with the first five hundred Findings, which had to be individually reviewed to determine, first, if each was relevant to the charges against the company and, second, what legal objections could be raised against it. As Lang says now, with understatement, "It was rather tedious work."[5]

In just four weeks, Lang and her colleagues produced a ream of documentation, illuminating the errors they believed the EEOC had made in those first five hundred Findings. But it had no effect on Denniston. On February 29, he finalized his initial opinion, ordering that each Finding the Bell System lawyers found wanting would have to be individually challenged. All of a sudden, negotiations sounded much more appealing. By early April, Lang had moved on to developing witness testimony for AT&T, while a couple of her Steptoe and Johnson colleagues were meeting regularly with Randy Speck to hammer out summaries they could agree on and document their differences on the others. The job was no less tedious than Lang's had been, with the Bell System often producing a suggested summary "as long as the document itself."[6] Moreover, it was just as low profile. By October 30, 1972, Speck and his counterparts had developed a several-thousand-page document listing each original EEOC summary still in dispute, AT&T's criticism of it, and the company's alternate version, a tome that Denniston alone would review. But what their work lacked in visibility, it made up for in potential impact. As a fundamental foundation to the EEOC's case, the summaries the examiner found most persuasive could ultimately sway his decision toward one side or the other.

In the spring of 1972, a casual observer could have assumed little else was happening within AT&T to resolve the year-and-a-half-long headache the EEOC had given it. Negotiations with the civil rights agency had broken off in January, and Bob Lilley and Bill Brown had had no further meetings to discuss reigniting those behind-the-scenes discussions. Even action by Dave Easlick, the maverick negotiator Lilley had brought in months earlier to resolve the case, hadn't come to pass.

Not that Easlick was twiddling his thumbs in his twenty-sixth-floor office. Since his arrival he had chosen to stay away from the hearings, letting John Kingsbury and Don Liebers represent the Personnel Department's interests to the Bell System's legal experts. Easlick was expending efforts instead on items he considered of higher priority, such as building the internal political connections he'd need to pull off any settlement. Most important, he was building on the policy changes that had been increasingly flowing out of AT&T headquarters in a push to transform the Bell System's treatment of its female and minority employees.

Although making the company over wasn't the primary mandate Easlick had received when he was hired the previous December, both his own staff and his bosses were pushing him in that direction. Dan Davis had written a short paper that spring that summarized the EEOC's damning statistics from the FCC hearings and advocated corporate action to improve them, and Bob Lilley's commitment to treating all employees fairly was well known throughout the company. At the same time, John deButts, the company's chairman, had weighed in on the subject in a speech to his executives in early May. "One thing should be clear," he said. "It is the policy of the Bell System—North, South, East and West—to assure that every employee has a fair and equal chance to realize full potential and to progress to the limit of that potential along any career path he or she may choose. . . . In short, affirmative action to achieve equal opportunity is a major factor in every Bell System manager's job."[7]

Whether policy or not, Easlick genuinely believed in deButts's statement. The Bell System couldn't waste any more time arguing it had tried to do well by women and minorities, its telephone operator job wasn't that bad, its record on promoting women into second-level management was better than most other companies. Now as part of their daily jobs, every AT&T manager needed to be certain that females, blacks, and Hispanics were treated the same as their white male colleagues.

Easlick was going at this company transformation from several directions. More memos were flowing from his subordinates' offices to BOC executives nationwide, announcing even further changes in recruitment, hiring, and promotion policies. In June, Don Liebers appeared on a popular talk show in New York City, "Mid-Day Live," to debate a NOW representative, guaranteeing, on air, NOW members' access to any New York Telephone office to prove the company's changed treatment of women. A Bell System–wide advertising campaign was launched in the spring of 1972 that featured a woman climbing a telephone pole and a man answering calls at an operator's console. When Copus saw the full-page glossy ads in *Time, Newsweek,* and the *Saturday Review,* which read like exact replicas of the sex-reversed ads designed by the Doctors Bem the previous fall, he gleefully wrote to EEOC witness Orley Ashenfelter, "And they said it couldn't be done."[8] Easlick wasn't purposely trying to please Copus and his EEOC colleagues, but it was a side effect he'd have to accept as he pursued his bosses' goal and his own beliefs. By the time Alana MacFarlane, the woman in the pole-climbing ad, appeared as a guest on *The Tonight Show,* there was no question the EEOC had driven Easlick and his team to make changes no one ever expected.

While Easlick was pushing these changes, Dan Davis, always looking for a new angle from which he could agitate, was stealthily spearheading his own effort to resolve the government's attack on the company. He had enlisted a team of BOC employees for a temporary assignment in New York City, similar to Liebers's document collection team, and initiated three task forces within his corner of the company's corporate employment office, named after the materials they would produce: Affirmative Action Plan, Upgrade and Transfer Plan, and Job Briefs and Qualifications.

By 1972, the year the EEOC finally got its own enforcement authority to take alleged discriminators to court, the concept of "affirmative action" for disadvantaged employees had been around American industry for more than ten years. In 1961, President John F. Kennedy signed the first related executive order, #10925, which required companies that did business with the federal government to "take affirmative action to ensure that applicants are employed, and that employees are treated during employment, without regard to their race, creed, color, or national origin."[9] Concurrently he created the Committee on Equal Employment Opportunity, an ad hoc group of federal government leaders chaired by the vice president, to oversee his new order. Kennedy acted in accordance with the times, addressing black Americans' concerns in an era when civil rights stories were on the front page of American newspapers every day, while ignoring affirmative action for women, an issue not yet a worry to the average American.

Four years later, in 1965, the year the EEOC opened as a result of Title VII of the 1964 Civil Rights Act, President Lyndon Johnson took more aggressive action, issuing a new executive order, #11246. On the surface, Executive Order #11246 appeared a Xerox copy of Kennedy's original dictate, adding no new requirements of government contractors' employment policies, but one important change in its administration would significantly strengthen its impact. Abolishing the president's Committee on Equal Employment Opportunity, Johnson transferred the order's oversight to the Department of Labor. With an established government agency taking over monitoring American businesses' compliance with affirmative action regulations, Johnson had dramatically increased the potential the order had to help minority employees. That potential expanded in 1967 when the order was updated to include women as a targeted group of beneficiaries.

But further change didn't come for five years, when the Labor Department must have realized the order, as it stood, was proving ineffective. In truth, this presidential regulation resembled nothing more than a polite request. Without an effective method of measuring results, there was no way to know how many women and minorities had been promoted in any given company. As a result, in 1970 the Labor Department, now under President Richard Nixon's administration, finally issued its own order, #4, which required government contractors to develop written plans with "goals and timetables to correct 'underutilization' of minorities."[10] No longer could companies simply produce a platitude-filled statement about their commitment to minorities' equal employment opportunity. They would now have to produce numbers—how many would get what jobs when—and be evaluated for their ability to achieve them. These affirmative action plans would be submitted annually for approval to the federal government agency having the primary business relationship with the company in question. Again, women were a second thought. It took another year, and another revision, for gender to be included in this requirement, taking effect in December 1971. The revision also emphasized the need for every company's workforce to match the race and gender demographics of its local community.

As a result of this order, AT&T's twenty-three operating companies along with Bell Labs, Long Lines, and Western Electric had been required to submit an affirmative action plan to the federal government for the past two years. Their plans had been filed with the General Services Administration (GSA), the internal government division responsible for handling administrative details for other government departments, like constructing office buildings, setting up purchasing agreements, and providing telephone service. In one way, the Labor Department's decision to decentralize oversight of corporate affirmative action plans made sense, handing the responsibility to the government agency with the most knowledge of that company's business. On the other hand, this dispersed oversight structure increased the risk of uneven implementation and minimized the opportunity for equal employment opportunity expertise to develop. Knowledge was building among Department of Labor staff within the Office of Contract Compliance (OFCC) who oversaw the "overseers" in each government division, but they sat at the second tier. The people on the front line of monitoring compliance—in AT&T's case, the team in the Civil Rights Office of GSA—had a relatively small number of companies on which to build their equal employment opportunity proficiency.

When Davis organized his Affirmative Action Plan Task Force in early 1972, he should have been setting it off on a simple challenge, just updating the plan the company had submitted the previous year. But with GSA dissatisfied with the generality of AT&T's past plans, the Labor Department now demanding targets for women, and the Bell System's corporate executives requiring this new program to serve as a model for the BOCs' own plans, the job was far more complicated. Davis wasn't just concerned about the complexity, though. He was more focused on the plan's potential impact, which had led him to create the other two related teams. If this new plan was going to become the first building block of an equal employment settlement between the phone company and the federal government, as Davis fervently hoped it would, the company needed more than just a statement of what it planned to do to promote women and minorities. It also needed the tactical programs to make that happen, which Davis's other two task forces were designing. The upgrade and transfer plan would "make it possible for any non-management employee to transfer more readily between departments, geographical areas or companies,"[11] enhancing women's and minorities' abilities to advance, while the job briefs and qualifications would provide standard definitions and requirements for each position to ensure candidates would be considered fairly. By defining and publishing both rules for applying for a nonmanagement job in another department and the skills and qualifications required to hold that position, Davis's teams were paving the way for telephone operators to finally have a real chance at craft jobs.

By late February 1972, Dan Davis and his Affirmative Action Plan Task Force had completed their model plan, gotten departmental approval, and submitted it to GSA two months ahead of schedule, perhaps hoping their early action would demonstrate how seriously they were taking this responsibility. But beating the due date didn't mean they were off the hook. Over the next few months, Davis and his boss, Don Liebers, spoke periodically about their plan with representatives of the GSA's Civil Rights Office, often facing a hostile environment as GSA made more and more demands. At the same time, Bob Lilley was bringing his BOC presidents to the New York corporate office to clarify their responsibility to produce their own plans based on Davis's team's model. The entire company was taking action to meet its equal employment opportunity responsibilities.

Although the task force circulated its affirmative action plan draft within the company, Davis had made sure it didn't leak outside, particularly not to the EEOC, since it was never wise to let your adversary in on your battlefield strategy. As a result, David Copus didn't catch wind of this AT&T effort until late March, and when he did, he wasn't happy. GSA's involvement brought out his competitive juices, since he saw every government agency with equal employment opportunity monitoring responsibility as an "archrival" to the EEOC. More important, he viewed GSA as a miserable failure in its equal employment efforts because, in two years of monitoring AT&T's affirmative action compliance, it "had never found discrimination and it was staring them in the face." [12] However, even Copus couldn't be certain GSA hadn't had an epiphany, perhaps inspired by the revised order's new requirement for goals and timetables for women, unless he actually read its plan. Over three days in late March, he nearly begged Levy to send him a copy but got stonewalled in every direction. On one day, the excuse was the unions hadn't yet seen it; the next, that Bob Lilley wouldn't allow its release; the next, the BOC presidents hadn't reviewed it. AT&T wasn't going to hand it over freely.

Bill Brown was as frustrated as Copus when he heard about AT&T's affirmative action plan, but his irritation stemmed primarily from the potential disaster this portended for his agency's case in front of the FCC. In Brown's eyes, AT&T, while politely participating in the daily hearings, "was trying to undercut our case" in the hearings by getting another government agency to approve its affirmative action plan.[13] On March 30, immediately after hearing about this behind-the-scenes effort, Brown fired off a letter to Ed Mitchell, an African American man who headed the civil rights division of GSA, demanding he "be supplied with copies of AT&T's proposed Affirmative Action Plan and associated documents," and, in the hope of "avoid-[ing] any embarrassing public disagreement," suggesting that "representatives of our two agencies meet informally to discuss the matter prior to any formal action any agency might take on the matter." [14] Brown's strategy proved more effective than Copus's, with a copy of the plan arriving on his desk within two weeks.

The EEOC wasn't the only organization exercised about the Bell System's work on these plans. The unions representing the company's employees could also be heavily affected by the work of all three task forces, a fact that finally aroused the union leadership. The IBEW, which represented seventy thousand Bell System employees around the country, was the first to be alerted. In a February 15, 1972, meeting between its leadership and NET, the Bell division with the most IBEW members, NET executives informed the IBEW representatives they would soon submit an affirmative action plan to meet their legal responsibilities. Since the plan's requirements might directly conflict with the personnel policies in the existing union contract, an uproar from the IBEW could have been predicted. Yet the atmosphere remained calm as the company explained the new requirements in Revised Order #4 and the expected components of an upgrade and transfer plan and agreed to negotiate the plan's language with union representatives. The company stood by its word, having at least six contacts through meetings or letters with the IBEW between late April and the end of the summer, giving the union a chance to add its perspective.

On the surface, the other key union, the CWA, seemed far more interested in this issue than with the FCC hearings. In mid-March, Richard Hackler, Joseph Beirne's assistant at the CWA, began meeting regularly with Rex Reed, AT&T's vice president of labor relations, to discuss how the two plans would affect the union's collective bargaining agreements throughout the Bell System. Their discussions continued for three months, but in the end, Reed proved no more successful in getting real participation from the CWA than Brown had been in getting the union at the hearings table. Hackler just wanted to keep the union's finger in the pie, to know what was happening, but, in reality, the CWA's position remained the same: make whatever agreement you want, but if it produces conflicts with our collective bargaining contracts, get ready for the grievances that will follow.

By early summer 1972, AT&T had held a final meeting with Ed Mitchell of GSA, finding only a few outstanding differences between what GSA was demanding and what the company felt it could agree to. But those differences, including goals for female outside craft workers and male telephone operators, proved deal breakers. In July, Dan Davis received a letter from one of Mitchell's staff members, stating the company's affirmative action plan was in noncompliance. Despite all the hard work of the task force and conversations with GSA staff, the company still hadn't produced an adequately aggressive plan for Ed Mitchell and his team.

Finally it was time for Dave Easlick to step in. What spurred him isn't certain. Perhaps he had just breezed through Dan Davis's twenty-four-page status report detailing the results of his SMSA study and discussing his task forces' recent efforts. Perhaps he had just attended a meeting with Bob Lilley, who had reminded him why he had been hired the previous December. Perhaps, on his own, he had realized he'd been on the job for almost nine months and had yet to make any real progress in resolving this conflict with the government. Probably a combination of all three led to the meeting he scheduled with Dan Davis on the morning of August 4, 1972.

With both Don Liebers and John Kingsbury on vacation, Davis made sure he was completely prepared when he reported for the meeting at 10 A.M. that Friday, since he would be meeting alone with Easlick, his boss's boss's boss, a wide divide in the stiff hierarchy of the phone company. He didn't have to invest much extra time, however, because he had produced the report Easlick had already received and, arguably, had thought more about how to resolve this issue than any other Bell System employee.

When Davis arrived, Easlick got right to the point. *Tell me what's going on with this EEO [equal employment opportunity] issue,* he said.

Davis gave the logical response, from his perspective. *I just sent you a twenty-four-page memo explaining it.*

Easlick had no time for reading or Davis's expectation that he would. *I don't read that stuff,* he said. *Just tell me what's going on.* Actually, this was just the opening Davis wanted, a chance to unburden himself of all his knowledge and perspectives on the case. He was aware, of course, that his comments would be a review for Easlick, but he felt he needed "to convey that I knew the problems and also knew a way to solve them."[15] First he explained the requirements of the new Revised Order #4 and the long distance AT&T would have to travel from its present employment statistics to meet the order's demands. He then rattled off a host of other concerns that suggested AT&T's culpability in the mistreatment of its employees, particularly the women: the proof of sex-segregated jobs in Michigan Bell, where women were doing the frame job for low salaries that, in all other Bell companies, was done by men for more money; the overwhelming predominance of women in the low-level telephone operator job; the inequalities produced by the employment tests used. He also mentioned the conflicts with the unions in meeting the government's expectations and the GSA's notice of noncompliance that Davis had recently received.

Finally, Davis addressed what he found most interesting—the steps to begin resolving the conflict. Based on his experience with Plans for Progress, he emphasized to Easlick that "it was essential to have each company identify its own problems," suggesting each Bell company study its own employment statistics and policies before developing plans to improve them.[16] He also pulled out copies of the model affirmative action and upgrade and transfer plans and the job briefs and qualifications package his task forces had been working on for the past several months.

Easlick liked what he heard. After checking his watch in the late morning, he told Davis, *Come back at two P.M. and bring your lawyer,* signaling he was ready to investigate the next step. Davis was at least as pleased as Easlick. "Never in [my] quarter century of service in the Bell System had [I] experienced such a fast response to a proposal," he remembers today.[17] Back in his office, he called Clark Redick, whose knowledge of the case combined with an open-mindedness from being new to the corporate office made him the right lawyer to involve. Davis gave him a brief rundown of his morning discussion with Easlick and asked him to arrive in Easlick's office at two o'clock.

The afternoon session focused first on the legality of actions the company might take. Easlick put Redick through his legal paces, proving he knew more about what was going on and its potential implications for the company than his casual, uninhibited exterior might suggest. Redick, who believed negotiated settlements were almost always a better solution to a legal problem than litigation, strongly advocated the use of a consent decree to get AT&T out from under its government cloud, an idea Davis had also recently floated with the company's general counsel, Horace Moulton, who supported it enthusiastically. Redick also suggested one or more opinion letters, signed by the top government lawyers from any involved agencies, which would give AT&T the additional cover it would need to ensure that future complaints didn't haunt the company.

An hour later, with the meeting winding down, it was Redick's turn to be surprised with the speed with which Easlick made decisions. Easlick charged Redick and Davis first with resolving the GSA issue, some way, any way. He wanted to get one government agency's approval of AT&T's equal employment opportunity efforts on the record. When Easlick asked, *Are you ready to go to D.C. and meet with the GSA?*, Redick, who had a full plate coordinating the BOC testimony and was accustomed to the typical slow pace of Bell System action, looked on in astonishment. But Davis responded, without hesitation, *Yes,* and the company's new negotiations team had its initial assignment. Before Redick and Davis left, Easlick clarified that their job would not end with GSA. He also assigned them to work with whomever they needed in the government to address the EEOC's concerns and end the hearings in front of the FCC. That's where they all hoped a consent decree and opinion letters could be instrumental.

To accomplish either of these tasks required negotiation skills, one of the few areas Davis couldn't claim as an expertise. As a lawyer, Redick had more experience at bringing parties together, but he typically played the "bad cop" in negotiations, so he needed a balance. Dan Davis knew just the right person to add to their team: Lee Satterfield, the African American lawyer from C&P who had participated in the first set of failed negotiations with the EEOC. Satterfield first came to mind because of his friendship with Ed Mitchell, AT&T's obstacle at GSA. But with excellent negotiating skills, many more federal government contacts including a personal relationship with Bill Brown, and credibility within the BOCs as "one of us," he had all the attributes Easlick's team might need. Easlick quickly added Satterfield, completing his team of midlevel AT&T managers who, he was convinced, would resolve this conflict with the federal government.

But Easlick had skipped one unwritten but crucial Bell System protocol: he never asked anyone, other than the three managers themselves, whether they were available for their new assignments. Once he'd gotten their commitments, he had simply written a blanket memo announcing that they now reported to him and distributed it widely. This posed little problem for Dan Davis, who already worked in Easlick's organization, but reassigning Redick and Satterfield proved a little trickier. When an uproar erupted after Easlick's memo got out, Easlick had to meet with Redick's boss, Charlie Ryan, to get him taken off other projects, and Satterfield's boss forced him to write a memo of his own, stating he had had no advance knowledge of Easlick's decision.

All this consternation over a simple reporting change seems excessive even in the hierarchical world of AT&T, where the desires of the company's top personnel executive would seem nearly paramount. But the widespread discomfort with Easlick's action had little to do with reporting structure and all to do with results or, actually, the lack of them. Kingsbury and his team had been working on this project for more than a year and a half and, from Easlick's viewpoint, were "obviously never going to get the job done."[18] Although Kingsbury probably wouldn't have agreed, the empirical evidence supported Easlick's opinion: the Kingsbury-led negotiations had failed twice, and Denniston, the FCC hearings examiner, had overruled most of the company's objections to the EEOC's testimony against AT&T. Kingsbury's team hadn't achieved Easlick's goal, so Easlick was bringing in new recruits. He was ready to live up to the activist reputation that had brought him to New York in the first place.

Within just a couple of weeks, Davis, Redick, and Satterfield achieved their first goal of updating the affirmative action plan to address GSA's objections. First they met among themselves day and night so that Davis could bring his two teammates up to speed, and then they brainstormed their strategy with Tom Powers and traveled to Washington to work out the details with Ed Mitchell and his staff. By then Mitchell's prime concern was appeasing the white southern congressmen who he believed would never accept an agreement that benefited only women and minorities. The AT&T executives had already fought this battle with Copus in earlier negotiations and weren't entirely comfortable with the solution Davis had devised, the same solution Copus had come to see, with NOW's help, as essential: include goals for men in telephone operators' jobs. It wasn't that the company begrudged men getting these jobs; it just didn't see it as much of a benefit because the operator's job was so unappealing. But now more motivated than ever to get the government off their back, they agreed to a 5 percent target for men in telephone operator jobs within one year.

On September 19, 1972, Bob Lilley met with Arthur Sampson, Ed Mitchell's boss, to sign off on the affirmative action and upgrade and transfer plans and related job briefs and qualifications, with the news hitting the papers on Wednesday, September 20. GSA management couldn't have been prouder, calling it a "landmark agreement" that was "an immensely important milestone in the history of equal employment opportunity for this country." [19]

AT&T itself was simply relieved. It had successfully gained one federal government agency's approval of its affirmative action programs, the first step in Easlick's overall strategy to rebuild the government's trust in the company's equal employment opportunity commitment. The company realized there was much more work to be done, work that would be much more difficult. But at least it felt like it had finally scored some points.

10

The Explosion

Fall 1972

When Bill Brown heard about GSA's approval of the AT&T affirmative action plan, he was neither pleased nor relieved. He was infuriated. He'd been annoyed when he found out that AT&T and GSA were discussing such a plan back in the spring of 1972, but GSA approving it, without one conversation with him, made him "so mad [he] was climbing the walls."[1] Moreover, he learned about GSA's action when everyone else did, since Arthur Sampson, GSA's administrator and Brown's peer in the Nixon administration hierarchy, never gave him the courtesy of an advance call.

Brown was equally angry at his government peers in GSA and his opponents at AT&T. Just six months earlier, he had sent his polite but direct letter to GSA's Ed Mitchell, emphasizing the importance of both the FCC hearings and their two agencies working together to advance Bell System equal employment. This wouldn't be the only time Brown would encounter another government agency working at cross-purposes to him, but because of his apolitical, just-get-it-done nature, this type of maneuvering drove him crazy.

As for AT&T, Brown understood that its executives had no responsibility to be honest and open with him or his agency, but he still felt betrayed. The EEOC lawyers had been working with the company as openly and honestly as possible, from their point of view, for more than a year and a half, in both the hearings and negotiations. Moreover, Brown had developed a personal connection with Bob Lilley, whom he respected. For the company to have behaved in such a premeditated and underhanded way outraged Brown. "They were going behind our backs," he says today, with still audible anger.[2]

Copus was "pissed" too. The organization he saw as an incompetent arch-rival, which had failed miserably at monitoring AT&T's affirmative action compliance, was now setting foot into the middle of his case, "trying to grab a headline." To him, GSA's action was simply "a kind of one upsmanship that was par for the course."[3]

However, when the EEOC filed its twenty-two complaints against the agreement a few days later, its concerns came in much more objective terms: the plan used inappropriate methods to calculate goals and timetables, it featured a transfer procedure that would never get enough minorities and women into better jobs, it didn't define "affected classes," it never discussed back pay, it avoided the testing issue. Concurrently, the EEOC's supporters in the civil rights community, including NOW and the NAACP, chimed in with strongly worded press releases and similar lists of complaints. Even with their anger level at boiling, AT&T's adversaries made a clear, well-argued case against the company's affirmative action plan.

At that time, AT&T took a strong stand that "there is no direct relationship between our discussion with the GSA and the EEOC case that is currently before the FCC," which Easlick stated in a widely publicized question-and-answer session the day after the GSA agreement was signed.[4] And today, confronted with Brown's charge that they were deliberately going behind the EEOC's back, the AT&T executives maintain their virtuous stance. They weren't holding clandestine meetings to strategize how to embarrass the EEOC; they were simply addressing a troubling business issue that surfaced when Dan Davis received GSA's noncompliance letter that summer. But while their actions may not have been malicious, they were clearly political, to which even they admit. For one thing, although they weren't flagrantly playing one government agency against another, they also felt no compunction to make sure that EEOC staff members, with whom AT&T lawyers were meeting nearly every day, knew about the company's negotiations with GSA. As Lee Satterfield explains, "The government was always split . . . they had no coordination that kept each agency in contact with another. Well, we didn't go around saying, you guys need to be in contact with each other."[5] AT&T was happy to take advantage of the government's inefficient equal employment opportunity design that had spread responsibility across dozens of agencies.

In truth, the AT&T executives understood clearly they were running a risk by leaving the EEOC unaware of their GSA talks. But it was strategically calculated, as Clark Redick explains today; the Bell System executives were trying "to break the logjam between AT&T and the government" in order to advance their own objectives.[6] They did try to minimize their exposure, asking

Ed Mitchell of GSA repeatedly in their meetings, *Do you have the authority to negotiate the final solution?*, suggesting a nervousness over the potentially messy fallout if that answer was no. But Mitchell always said *yes,* and Davis and his colleagues did nothing to verify Mitchell's veracity. They took him at his word, probably because they liked his answer.

When the EEOC and civil rights groups exploded in anger immediately after the GSA approval was announced, the AT&T negotiators remained surprisingly calm. As Davis says today, "We had scored our point with the GSA agreement in that our programs were acceptable," the first goal Easlick had set for them.[7] In any case, Davis, Redick, and Satterfield had prepared themselves for an EEOC outcry and had briefed Easlick on that possibility. But they were skeptical about the EEOC lawyers' reasons for their fury. Publicly the government agency could list its complaints and privately express its outrage at the company's duplicity, but the AT&T team saw the agency's anger as more personal. As Davis now says, "We had stolen Copus's show."[8] The company's executives now understood that any agreement would have to meet both Copus's and Brown's requirements and be credited primarily to the EEOC.

While the mute CWA maintained its sideline spot, the other key union, the IBEW, joined the EEOC in its wrath. Just four days before Sampson and Lilley announced that GSA had approved AT&T's affirmative action plan, IBEW representatives had met with Ed Mitchell and his colleagues to discuss the plan's status, leaving with the understanding that they could still submit an alternative proposal and negotiate a compromise. Now that the plan had been blessed without any union input, they agreed wholeheartedly with the EEOC that the company had acted in bad faith.

No matter how angry civil rights and union leaders were with AT&T, they had no legal influence. Without direct intervention within the government, the company's approved affirmative action plan would stand, an outcome Bill Brown and David Copus weren't going to allow. Brown called Sampson or Mitchell—whomever he could find—to "rais[e] hell about it,"[9] while Copus tracked down Bill Kilberg, a young lawyer he knew vaguely who had a big title in the Department of Labor: associate solicitor for labor relations and civil rights. Copus knew that the group Kilberg worked for within the Labor Department, the OFCC, had final sign-off on the AT&T plan. Copus was going to ensure that the plan never got that signature.

Bill Kilberg, only twenty-five in 1972, had a big job to match his big title. As head labor relations lawyer for the OFCC, the Labor Department division responsible for ensuring that companies doing business with the federal government followed their contracts, he and his staff of fifteen handled all legal matters related to equal employment opportunity. In the phone company's case, GSA was the front-line cop, but the OFCC was the enforcer, the last stop.

In some ways, Bill Kilberg seemed a carbon copy of David Copus. He wore long sideburns and kept his curly hair piled on his head, looking as much like a 1960s college student as Copus. Kilberg was also as bright, having attended Cornell, a college even more prestigious than Northwestern, and also graduating from Harvard Law School. Moreover, they both exuded a confidence not earned by either age or experience. But in other ways, the two men were very different: Copus was lighthearted, Kilberg serious; Copus openly supported liberal causes, and Kilberg deliberately leaned to the conservative; Copus was on a mission to change the world, while Kilberg simply wanted to ensure that right triumphed over wrong more often than not.

Kilberg might not have been trying to change the world, but wherever he was headed, he was in a hurry. In 1969, at the age of twenty-two, he was named the youngest-ever White House Fellow, a one-year federal government position, typically within a cabinet-level staff, designed to grow young Americans into future leaders. Colin Powell would become a White House Fellow three years after Kilberg, and any number of senators, congresspersons, and corporate CEOs have claimed the distinction both before and after Kilberg's tenure. Just four years later, at twenty-six, Kilberg again took "youngest ever" honors when he was confirmed by the Senate for the sub-cabinet post of solicitor of labor. He was a very young man whose seriousness of purpose was producing significant career opportunities.

Kilberg's adolescent years didn't necessarily predict this meteoric career ascension. As a teenager, he worked as the social director and MC at a summer resort in the Catskills and became an apprentice electrician, getting admitted to the local union thanks to his father's connections as an electrical engineer. Although the jump from apprentice electrician to government "mover and shaker" appeared to scale several classes and income levels, his union work actually led directly to his law career. He attended Cornell on an IBEW scholarship, and his summer work among his union peers showed him the importance of giving an individual opportunity, the objective he took on when he became a labor lawyer. With that value system, he was well suited to help bail out David Copus and his case against AT&T.

When Kilberg got Copus's frantic call, he responded in his typical deliberate fashion. He got a copy of the plan in question and, methodically and cautiously, reviewed it. But he really didn't need to be so careful. On his first read-through, noting the plan simply laid out goals and timetables for women and minorities in craft jobs and men in clerical and traffic jobs, he could see it was "markedly deficient" in resolving the government's complaints against AT&T.[10] Under other circumstances, it may have stood as a legitimate affirmative action plan, but that minimal standard would be far from adequate, at this point, to resolve the government's conflict with the phone company. In addition, Kilberg, despite his conservative outlook, was a civil rights lawyer who believed "requiring more was a legitimate thing for government to do."[11] Perhaps the plan should redress, financially, the wrong done to employees, he thought. Perhaps it should require changes in the company's hiring policies. Perhaps it should order upgraded salary ranges for certain jobs. Perhaps it should do all three.

But a final decision to reverse GSA's approval fell in the bailiwick of the OFCC director and Kilberg's client, Phil Davis. A thoughtful African American, Davis didn't take the issue lightly when Kilberg filled him in. He hadn't been in his job long, and overturning the work of another agency could alienate colleagues, individuals whom he respected and might need on his side later in his career. Plus, since the OFCC typically just rubber-stamped affirmative action plan approvals, this would be an entirely unexpected reversal. In addition, Davis didn't see AT&T as the worst corporate actor. Steel mills, for example, had "hot," dirtier jobs specifically targeted at blacks while the "cold," cleaner jobs went to whites. At least the phone company consistently hired both blacks and whites for telephone installer and operator jobs.

Davis may have been conflicted, but more than anything he was fair. After several conversations with Kilberg over the next week, Davis made the difficult decision to overturn GSA's approval. On September 28, 1972, he notified AT&T and GSA that the AT&T affirmative action plan did not meet government standards and that the OFCC would now take responsibility for monitoring AT&T's compliance with equal employment opportunity laws instead of GSA.

In the meantime, Kilberg, confident that the OFCC would stay involved in some way, had already taken a next step, brainstorming ways to resolve Copus's conflict with AT&T, an issue he had actually already thought about because of the company's well-known reputation for poor equal employment statistics. He considered the solution under the OFCC's closest control—canceling the company's contract with the government—but that was obviously out of the question. Since AT&T had a monopoly on phone service and essential government business was conducted every minute of every working day over the phone, the government couldn't cut off the relationship. Kilberg needed an alternate answer.

Another option Kilberg had contemplated in discussions with David Rose, a Justice Department colleague, was suing AT&T in federal court for breach of contract, which at least had judicial power behind it. But to implement this approach, Kilberg would be involving Justice, *another* government department, because only it had authority to sue; in addition, a successful outcome would produce a paltry penalty for AT&T. The company would simply be subjected to a more aggressive, court-ordered, affirmative action plan without any of the tenets of a settlement about which Kilberg had mused. Although Rose was willing to attempt it, the potential result just didn't seem powerful enough to Kilberg, so he kept thinking.

One issue stood out in Kilberg's mind: the number of government resources being expended in various battles against the phone company over treatment of its employees. He ran down the list of agencies: the EEOC, which was tied up with the FCC hearings and had hundreds of complaints on file from individual Bell System employees that needed attention; GSA, which had been arguing with the company over its affirmative action plan; the Justice Department, which had discrimination complaints against Bell companies on its lawyers' desks, waiting for action; and the Equal Pay Act, also within the Labor Department, which had formed a task force to target Bell System companies violating the Equal Pay Act of 1963, a statute prohibiting paying female employees less than men for doing the same work. The government was investing enormous resources into this war on AT&T.

But Kilberg's thoughts went far beyond money. True to his nature, he was also hoping to right the wrong done to past and present Bell System employees, but he was thinking even bigger, beyond justice to systemic change. As he says today, "My notion was that we could spend a lifetime suing employers and never achieve the same impact as one very significant settlement." [12] And believing it was a "unique point in history . . . especially with regard to gender discrimination," the AT&T case presented an incredible opportunity. [13] If he could bring all these government agencies around one table with AT&T on the opposite side and hammer out an acceptable agreement, the effect could be enormous. He realized that government-wide negotiations had never been tried before, which made them risky, but he also understood the prominence of the phone company, the nation's largest employer. "If that employer would agree to make dramatic changes, that would wake everybody up." [14] Kilberg wanted to place that wake-up call.

For his part, Copus had no idea Kilberg had set off on this course. When Copus had originally called Kilberg, he was simply reaching out to the OFCC, the final federal government arbiter of equal employment opportunity compliance, hoping its lawyer would "tell GSA to go bark at the moon." [15] He was asking Kilberg to use his organization's authority to over-turn GSA's approval of AT&T's affirmative action plan, not use that authority to take over Copus's case. Copus was unaware of any model for government-wide negotiations, and if he had thought that approach might work, he certainly would have planned to direct it. Dan Davis had been right—David Copus was not going to be happy when he found out that the OFCC was planning to steal his show.

Kilberg couldn't know how AT&T would react to his negotiations idea. With the company also expending endless dollars, he did have some hope that it would be willing to try a new approach to settlement. What he didn't know was that AT&T, in the guise of Easlick's anointed team of three, had already begun a similar process itself. Though run slightly off course by the OFCC's recent reversal of GSA's decision, Davis, Redick, and Satterfield had already moved on to their next, much larger assignment from Easlick: resolving the conflict with the EEOC, a challenge on which Lee Satterfield took the lead.

Satterfield, an African American man of medium build who wore dark-framed glasses and dark suits, was more than just a politically astute lawyer. He also had an unusually strong work ethic and sense of responsibility that had enabled him to support his family of four with a full-time construction job while completing a five-year Howard University program leading to bachelor's and law degrees awarded the same year. He could reach any goal set before him, and if it came from a boss, his motivation was even stronger. When the GSA-approved plan died, he received just such a challenge from Mickey McGuire, an AT&T executive in the Washington office where Satterfield worked. McGuire told him, *Well, go fix it, Lee.* Satterfield didn't have to hear it twice.

As a first effort, Satterfield approached his friend Chairman Brown, suggesting that Dan Davis present the contents of the AT&T affirmative action plan to Brown's EEOC team, hoping to make a few inches' progress toward common ground. Although still angry over the GSA mess, Brown agreed, welcoming any chance to move forward. Soon after, Davis led a lengthy presentation of the plan's details to about twenty EEOC employees including David Copus. Although Davis's talk stimulated many questions from the audience, Copus left before Davis had finished, and Brown, either not ready or not motivated to move forward at that moment, never approached AT&T to suggest a next step in this process. Another strategy would be needed.

Fortunately, Satterfield had thought of one. Charlie Wilson, the head of the EEOC's Conciliations group and a negotiator in the first round of discussions earlier that year, was also a longtime Satterfield friend whom Satterfield respected and trusted implicitly. Although he had played number two to the vocal Copus in the initial discussions, Satterfield knew that Wilson, who was older, more experienced, and less ideological than Copus, would be just the type of person with whom to begin a discussion that could end this drama. With Brown's blessing, that's what the Easlick team did.

At the two parties' first meeting, their casual discussion hardly suggested that a historic settlement between the federal government and the country's largest company could be the eventual result. Over dinner at a high-end restaurant in a Washington hotel, Wilson asked the three AT&T executives, *What prominent blacks have you ever met?*, to open up a discussion about race. Fortunately, Redick had gone to high school in Ohio with Nancy Wilson, the renowned jazz singer, who, although no relation to their government opponent, qualified as a good enough answer to break the ice. The conversation remained light that evening, allowing Wilson to feel out his corporate counterparts and learn about their equal employment experience and abilities in and attitudes about resolving this conflict. Quickly he discovered the quality of Easlick's team: two lawyers, one with state civil rights experience, the other with time at the EEOC, and a personnel executive who had worked for years advancing minorities in the country's largest company. They were a far cry from the average Bell System manager the EEOC was trying to reform.

In the meetings the Easlick team held with Wilson over the next few weeks, their conversations slowly turned more serious, beginning to touch on the key issues a settlement might cover, the same issues Bill Kilberg had already pondered: back pay for victims of discrimination, hiring and promotion plans, equal pay for equivalent jobs. But without a wider sanction from their bosses, it was interesting conversation for the four men, but nothing more.

Fortunately, a phone call from Bill Kilberg came to their aid. Now committed to putting his negotiations idea in action, Kilberg was traveling methodically through his Roladex, calling his contacts at the EEOC, the Equal Pay Act, and AT&T, asking for their participation in the government-wide process that would focus on resolving all outstanding equal employment issues between AT&T and the U.S. government. Truthfully, Kilberg didn't want the discussions to be "government-wide." He didn't call the Department of Justice initially, since it was less directly involved with complaints against the Bell System, and he also left GSA out, freely admitting today that "we kind of took it away from them."[16] With Ed Mitchell's past support of AT&T's

record in hiring and promoting minorities, Kilberg "didn't think GSA understood or had the sensitivity" required to effectively negotiate a fair settlement.[17] But he was certain the three groups he'd identified, plus his own team at the OFCC, could effectively resolve this business/government battle.

With the conversations between the Easlick team and the EEOC's Wilson already under way, AT&T's full support of Kilberg's idea was expected. But top executives didn't immediately agree on who should represent the company in the sessions. Easlick was solidly behind his team of three who had pulled off the GSA-approval in just a week's time, even if it had been shunted aside, and were in the process of building credibility with a key EEOC player. But his AT&T peers, particularly in the Legal Department, didn't share his exalted view of his three chosen ones, not having as forgiving a perspective of the GSA debacle. More important, they worried that the Easlick team wasn't high enough in the corporate hierarchy, having participants from only the fourth (Davis) and fifth (Redick and Satterfield) levels of management, compared with the first negotiations, in which a sixth-level executive, John Kingsbury, led the team.

Charlie Ryan, AT&T's general attorney for labor law and Redick's original boss in New York, visited Redick in his office one day in the early fall of 1972 to present the lawyers' concerns. *Some people upstairs are worried you guys aren't heavy enough,* he said. *They're worried Kilberg and his crowd will balk at negotiating if you're the team sitting across the table.*

Redick had worked in government before, and he knew the truth. *Those guys at Labor would love to have our jobs,* he responded. *They'll be happy to negotiate with us.*

Redick spent a while longer providing Ryan with a stream of reassurances that he and his peers, with their solid experience and great chemistry, could handle the job. Emphasizing that, as negotiators, they would actually be in the lesser role, he added, *this all has to be done under your supervision,* meaning Ryan, Ashley, and the twenty-sixth floor. Redick and his colleagues could do the job, whatever job AT&T's top executives wanted done.

Redick's speech proved effective. Ryan asked one last time, *You're certain you can do it?* With Redick's final *Yes,* he gave his blessing. Easlick had won. His team of three would be at the negotiating table.

When Kilberg brought his suggestion to Carin Clauss, the head of the Equal Pay Act, a sister division to the OFCC within the Department of Labor, she was just as amenable to government-wide negotiations as AT&T had been. In the eight years since the Equal Pay Act had been passed, her organization had been wrapped up in a battle against the phone company over dozens of cases filed by underpaid women, so Clauss was looking for any creative way to hold AT&T responsible for its malfeasance. She was happy to invest time in an effort to resolve all the cases at once.

Of all the groups Kilberg contacted, the EEOC was the least enthusiastic. Copus was the true opponent, feeling his agency was being manipulated by both the phone company and its fellow government agency, the OFCC. On AT&T's part, he saw this as further evidence of its "divide and conquer" strategy, which had started with its blatant effort to secure GSA's approval of its affirmative action plan in order to undermine the EEOC's case. And even though that effort had ostensibly failed, the company was now using a divisive approach again, to gain an audience with a government agency other than the EEOC, in this case the OFCC. Moreover, a blessing from the OFCC, the agency that audited BOC affirmative action plans nationwide, could prove invaluable.

As for the government, Copus, as expected, strongly resented the OFCC taking a lead role in his case. Since he had called Kilberg to gain assistance, not relinquish control, he personally resented the organization's involvement. In addition, he saw the OFCC as just as ineffective as GSA in improving opportunities for the company's women and minorities. As he explains today, "The OFCC had had jurisdiction over the Bell System for many years and they had done nothing with it. They had given rubber stamps to AT&T [on its equal employment efforts] at every opportunity." [18] The OFCC's involvement, appearing like the heroes of the government, also was playing right into AT&T's hands, providing the company another way out of its conflict with the government. Just as important, Copus believed the OFCC "had nothing to contribute to the process." [19] Copus had been at the FCC hearings every day, he knew how well the EEOC was doing against AT&T, he believed Denniston would eventually decide in favor of the government and hold the Bell System accountable—he and his EEOC colleagues had everything under control. Finally, even though he had been purposely excluded from Charlie Wilson's discussions with the Easlick team, Copus knew about them, understanding they were a foundation to a final EEOC/AT&T settlement, if and when it was deemed appropriate and necessary by Bill Brown. Why did the EEOC need another government agency, totally ineffective in promoting equal employment opportunity, to help it out?

Bill Brown had a markedly more generous view of the potential of government-wide discussions with AT&T. Although he prioritized the EEOC getting maximum credit for the case's resolution, he figured that battle could wait until the resolution was at hand. For now, he figured, "you never give up an opportunity if you can settle a case on favorable terms."[20] Plus, even if Denniston decided in the EEOC's favor, he was wary of appeals that could drag the issue on for years. As a result, "as long as I was satisfied that it was [going to be] a good agreement, I would have encouraged any negotiations," Brown says today.[21]

Brown's viewpoint, of course, won out. With Copus steaming, Brown agreed that the EEOC would participate in joint negotiations with AT&T, the OFCC, and the Equal Pay Act. The players would all be in the same room. Now they would have to figure out if they could get from here to there.

On the morning of Wednesday, October 18, 1972, in a large third-floor office in the Labor Department's Washington, D.C., headquarters building, Bill Kilberg called to order the first session of negotiations between the federal government and AT&T about the company's equal employment practices. Since Dick Schubert, the solicitor of labor, traveled constantly, Kilberg had usurped his office, a twenty- by thirty-foot colossus replete with crystal chandeliers and eighteen-foot ceilings. The participants sat around an oversized conference table on one side of the room, which also housed a huge desk at the office's center and a sitting area the size of a small living room on the opposite side. The portentous surroundings seemed appropriate for these first-ever government-wide negotiations over equal employment opportunity.

Representatives of the four involved parties had arrived for the morning's kickoff session. The AT&T team of Redick, Satterfield, and Davis sat opposite Kilberg, while the EEOC threesome, Copus, Wilson, and Pemberton, reprising their roles from the first negotiations, sat to his right, with Carin Clauss and Karl Heckman of the Equal Pay Act filling the seats on his left. Kilberg's job that morning was simple: open the discussion, solicit and document his colleagues' concerns and objectives, and begin planning a strategy to meet them. Some of the attendees weren't very impressed with the discussion—Davis recalls it as merely "show and tell"[22]—but Kilberg achieved his goal. The EEOC men talked about their hot buttons—goals and timetables or, preferably for Copus, quotas, along with back pay for the aggrieved employees—and Clauss emphasized the importance of ensuring that all AT&T jobs paid the same rates for the same work effort, no matter what gender filled them. The company's team, meanwhile, mostly listened, focused on identifying exactly what it would have to relinquish to get the government off its back.

From that first day, both the personalities and roles of each of the groups burst to the surface while their objectives for these sessions burned just underneath. The members of the AT&T team, laboring under the weight of Clark Redick's commitment to Charlie Ryan, were as serious as they could be. Their briefcases were stuffed with copies of the affirmative action and upgrade and transfer plans that Dan Davis's task forces had produced, in the hope they might be included in a settlement, but the team members remained committed primarily to reaching an agreement their bosses could sell to the BOCs, no matter whose vision it was based on.

Carin Clauss played a quieter role in the discussions, just angling for an agreement that would negate the Equal Pay Act cases she had outstanding. But the data she brought, which summarized those stacks of cases revealing the Bell System salary scales that were disadvantageous to women, would provide crucial evidence against the company.

Kilberg himself tried to stay as neutral as possible. Copus was right: Kilberg and the OFCC had nothing substantive to offer these discussions. They were uninvolved in the EEOC's effort in the FCC hearings and had no cases of their own against the company; the office's only direct involvement in AT&T's equal employment efforts had been its near endorsement of an AT&T affirmative action plan the EEOC considered absurd. But while Copus saw Kilberg's involvement as worthless because of his ignorance of the EEOC's case, Kilberg and the Bell System negotiators viewed his outsider status as a boon to the process. Kilberg could act as an honest broker, keeping the government agencies at the table and convincing AT&T, even at the worst moments, that some type of settlement could and would be reached. And a settlement, powerful enough to make newspaper headlines, was Kilberg's only objective.

The EEOC provided the most knowledgeable and least unified front on that Wednesday morning. Although Copus had come with his wealth of incriminating data against the company, he had little else to offer. He was a reluctant participant, at the table because Bill Brown had told him he had to be there. Over the next several weeks, he would sometimes not attend the sessions, putting most of his energies instead into the FCC hearings he led for the EEOC. In this negotiations room, he was no longer the dashing young knight, leading his team of inexperienced crusaders on a charge against the most powerful lords of the land. He had become a disgruntled soldier, who had been remonstrated by his commanding officer to follow orders and grapple through this drawn-out battle until it was resolved. He didn't wear the transformation well. All he wanted to do now was leave his enemy, AT&T, with the worst wounds possible.

Fortunately, Copus had come to that first meeting with two far more will-ing colleagues. Charlie Wilson, the agency's leader this time around, arrived fully prepared to represent the EEOC's interests in negotiating a fair and reasonable agreement, as long as it gave the EEOC primary credit. Jack Pem-berton, the agency's acting general counsel, had a less demanding assign-ment, responsible primarily to appear at each session. With the EEOC's top lawyer at the negotiations almost full-time, Bill Brown was demonstrating to both the Labor Department and AT&T the priority he had placed on these proceedings.

At the beginning, the players made an unusual choice. No notes or min-utes would be taken to document each session's discussion. Unfocused on the historical importance such notes might have today, all four parties agreed that written accounts of their conversations would add little value but might hinder progress by enabling finger-pointing over who made what comment about which issue. All notebooks in the room would remain closed.

Over the next several weeks, the negotiators met regularly, with Redick and Davis, the two New Yorkers on AT&T's team, commuting regularly on the New York to D.C. shuttle. In between the multiday sessions in Washing-ton, the government and company negotiators would hold separate strategy meetings, and over time, they brought in experts to advocate for their posi-tions. Bill Kilberg included Labor Department colleagues when he needed certain expertise, and AT&T invited Tom Powers to some of the sessions, with Ollie Taylor, an AT&T labor relations executive, participating later to help predict the unions' likely reaction to any agreement.

Meanwhile, one of the unions had again resurfaced. While the CWA was maintaining its stance of nonparticipation, even declining direct invitations from both Copus and Kilberg to participate in the new sessions, its union colleague, the IBEW, had decided to take the opposite approach and, finally, get involved in any way possible. In a conversation with an IBEW attorney soon after the GSA explosion, Bill Kilberg, living up to his responsibility as a Labor Department lawyer, offered the union a chance to comment on the plan the negotiations would produce, which the attorney accepted. When the negotiators developed a sample agreement later that fall, Kilberg arranged to meet in Washington with Elihu Leifer, a lawyer representing the IBEW, and members of the union's Boston Local to hear their comments about it.

In addition, on September 29, 1972, the IBEW officially asked to inter-vene, just a little bit late, as a party in the FCC hearings, which the FCC agreed to on October 17. Then, on October 6, IBEW representatives met with David Copus to discuss the affirmative action and upgrade and transfer plans that were being considered. So much sudden activity seems somewhat surprising, but, with momentum in the air, the IBEW wasn't going to miss its chance to get its desires on the record.

11

The Defense

Late Fall 1972

By October 1972, the FCC hearings had been on hold for four months, making the Kilberg-coordinated negotiations seem the only route to resolving the case, but that presumption wouldn't have been accurate. Behind the scenes, lawyers from both AT&T and the EEOC had been busily preparing for the hearings' impending recommencement. As optimistic as Kilberg and his corporate colleagues were about their informal discussions, no one could be sure they'd go any further than the first set, so both AT&T and the EEOC needed to stay exceedingly serious about winning over Fred Denniston.

With AT&T scheduled to take the stand in its own defense on October 30, 1972, John Kingsbury and his personnel office colleagues had delivered their written case to Denniston on August 1. Resembling *A Unique Competence* in miniature, it had an introductory memo summarizing the company's position preceding the written testimony of scheduled witnesses: Kingsbury and sixteen other internal AT&T or outside experts along with a representative of every BOC. Yet AT&T's summary document was just 103 pages long, as opposed to *A Unique Competence's* 300-page narrative, and the company's entire submission, including all testimony, exhibits, statistics, and backup, was merely 10,000 sheets, a shadow of the EEOC's 20,000. By any other measurement, however, it was a voluminous stack of paper to plow through.

In its opening memo, the company took as positive an approach as possible, with chapters titled "The Bell Commitment to Equal Employment Opportunity," "The Results Have Been Good," and "Looking to the Future." Within these sections, the company reiterated, with much more backup, the points it had made in its initial defense against the EEOC attack. Hiring of blacks in the past three years had risen by 44.3 percent and of Hispanics by 92.8 percent, while the total workforce had grown only 14.1 percent. A third of all female Bell System employees were managers, and more than half of them earned more than $10,000 annually in an era when full-time female workers' yearly salaries averaged less than $6,000 in the United States. The opening summary also outlined the company's historical commitment to equal opportunity through, first, its voluntary efforts to hire disadvantaged individuals, starting in 1962, via President Kennedy's Plans for Progress and later through the JOBS program of the National Alliance of Businessmen, which the Bell System joined in 1968. The company had carefully picked out its best data to present.

Unfortunately, the ensuing press coverage wasn't all AT&T might have hoped for. In mid-August, *U.S. News and World Report* devoted much of an article about AT&T's defense to its needs as a bottom-line-driven business. About the company's responsibility to prioritize equal employment opportunity, the writer quoted Kingsbury as saying, "The EEOC has failed to recognize that the primary reason the Bell System exists is to provide communications service to the American public, not merely to provide employment to all comers, regardless of ability." About the company's responsibility to train its workers, Kingsbury said, "What the EEOC fails to recognize is that if we eliminated all our hiring standards, our training costs would soar astronomically and those costs would necessarily be passed to our customers."[1] Although some readers may have read in those lines a sympathy for the company's financial plight, others would have discerned a suggestion that the AT&T executives' upfront platitudes about equal employment opportunity belied their true beliefs.

Another quote in the article came from the testimony of Hugh Folk, an economics professor at the University of Illinois, which illuminated the company's sexist attitudes: "The proportion of women in Bell craft jobs will increase but it will not approach the proportion of women in the labor force unless and until rather deep-seated attitudes held by women toward clerical work—as being proper for women—and physical and outside work—as being improper for women—are substantially modified over time."[2] Folk's comment underscored AT&T's claim that it wasn't to blame; it was, actually, as much a victim as the women working within its walls. Society had produced women who wanted certain types of jobs only—the demeaning, low-paid ones, apparently—and how could the EEOC expect good old Ma Bell to do anything about it?

Eileen Shanahan of the *New York Times,* an aggressive reporter who later became a plaintiff in a groundbreaking sex discrimination lawsuit of her own, also documented the company's impotence. On the Tuesday evening AT&T released its package, she called Don Liebers just as he was heading home, in search of details for her next day's story. After noting the report's quote that the percentage of women at third-level management or above would increase to 7.25 percent by 1976, she asked for the same targets for Hispanics and blacks.

Liebers had to be honest. *I have no idea,* he replied. In its recent efforts to develop an effective system to collect employee data and predict trends, Liebers's team had prioritized statistics for women but hadn't yet gotten to those for minorities.

Shanahan thought she was being railroaded. *Don't lie to me,* she said. *But I don't know.*

The company, even Ma Bell, couldn't be this arrogant. *Nobody would sign an agreement if they didn't know exactly what was required of them.*

Well, I don't, he said for the third time.

Heading nowhere quickly, she got his name and title and added, *This is going to be in the paper tomorrow, that you've been uncooperative.*

Oh God, thought Liebers. This was all the company needed now. As soon as she slammed the phone down, he made a call himself, to Dave Easlick. *Dave,* he said, *get ready, it's going to be in the paper tomorrow, it's going to be a mess.*

The next morning, there it was. After noting the information on women's planned promotions, Shanahan had written, "But Donald E. Liebers, personnel director for employment and equal opportunity, said that he could not supply similar figures, on a system-wide basis, for blacks or the Spanish-speaking."[3] More evidence the company wasn't the equal employment icon it claimed.

Yet, in the meantime, the company was continuing to improve its equal employment record. New recruiting brochures were developed, targeting women and men for nontraditional jobs, another bow to the ideas of the Doctors Bem. Kingsbury sent out a memo to the entire company dictating that height, weight, or the need for child care could no longer be used as hiring qualifications, and the company started including women in management assessment centers, which were used by Bell executives to identify candidates for fast-track management training programs that produced many of AT&T's top executives. Despite the negative press reports and the risk that the changes the company was making might point more to its culpability than its commitment to improve, the AT&T executives were push-

ing forward with their corporate transformation because it was both legal
and right.

While the AT&T team had been immersed in preparing its case, the EEOC
had been as busy and, now, with less hands to help. On July 21, 1972, just
before the AT&T defense was published, Judy Potter resigned. Caught in the
conundrum she was fighting to change, she followed her husband, whose
job was taking him to Portland, Maine, far from the Washington, D.C.,
political bustle. She wasn't happy about giving up the challenging work
and high profile that had come with her role in this case, but with a young
daughter and a commitment to her family, she found a good job as an associate professor at the University of Maine Law School in Portland, packed
her bags, and headed north. In any case, she had left her mark. She may not
have been able to resolve her own feminist crisis, but her knowledge of trial
law had enabled the EEOC to put on an effective case against AT&T on behalf of its oppressed female employees over the previous six months.

The Although Potter's departure was unexpected and unwanted, her timing
was impeccable. She had stayed long enough for the EEOC to present its
case, its most important responsibility, and for her two protégés, David Copus and Larry Gartner, to build competence as trial lawyers. Although the
team was diminished by her absence, it was far from crippled, now having
the basic skills to fight the agency's battle against AT&T.

The EEOC team's next step was clear-cut. With a copy of AT&T's written
case in hand, its members now had to discredit it. Beginning on August 2,
1972, and continuing periodically over the next couple of months, Copus
and his task force colleagues wrote to each of the EEOC's outside witnesses,
requesting their comments on the AT&T experts' submissions, which, un-
able to rein in his disdain for his opponent, Copus sometimes called a "puff
of hot air."[4] Concurrently the agency staffers were doing their own investigations into the credibility of the company's witnesses.

On September 22, the EEOC team put that research into action, filing a
fifty-one-page motion to strike the testimony of the five Bell System witnesses most blatantly trumpeting the "it's someone else's fault" defense.
From the EEOC's viewpoint, these five had sidestepped the statistics presented in *A Unique Competence* and instead discussed only the general problem of societal discrimination, justifying AT&T's behavior on the basis that
"everyone else was doing it too." If these experts had found there weren't
enough female or minority job candidates in the local labor pools of Bell
System facilities to meet equal employment opportunity requirements or

that the phone company had made serious, in-depth efforts to hire women and minorities but had failed, that would have been a legitimate argument. But ignoring the facts the EEOC had presented and simply blaming the problem on the abstract "American society" didn't stand up as a legal position. It was a well-argued statement that would have made Potter proud.

But on the reopening day of the hearings, October 30, 1972, despite support from the FCC Common Carrier Bureau, Denniston denied the EEOC's motion, allowing all of AT&T's testimony to stand. The burden was on the EEOC to prove the validity or inaccuracy of each witness's testimony during questioning, Denniston argued. That's exactly why they'd all returned to his hearings room.

With this decision the phone company had won round one of the renewed hearings, but not much else went well for it that first day. Once again, when all the parties arrived at Room 252 in the FCC headquarters building at 10 A.M. that Monday morning, the women from the CULA had appeared too. As an official party to the case, they had every right to be there, but they weren't welcomed when Denniston opened the session. In his first order, he asked them to remove the anti-AT&T signs they'd again tacked to the walls.

"We just did not want to wait all day to make our point," Gavrielle Gemma responded.[5] It quickly became clear that the women had lost none of their combativeness and had not shed any of their problems during the four-month break. They were worried about getting fired, they hadn't gotten copies of the hearings documents or a list of the upcoming witnesses, they were smoking in the hearings room and sleeping on a hotel room floor, they had brought witnesses to testify who were nowhere on Denniston's schedule. Like members of most disadvantaged groups, the CULA women had little power in or knowledge of societal institutions, just reams of experience with mistreatment at their hands, in this case perpetrated by Ma Bell. And, in these women's eyes, that mistreatment had gotten worse in the recent past, rather than improving as the company had been reporting, which the CULA's Kathy Dennis explained that morning. "In the last several months, AT&T has tried, through newspaper and secret 'backroom' government deals, to change its image. We inside know that the racism, harassment, lack of opportunity . . . have all gotten not better but worse since the hearings in May."[6]

The reappearance of the CULA had to be bad news for AT&T's lawyers, but, unbeknownst to them at the time, the women's group's return would be only one of the company's problems as they put on their defense. In twenty-four days of hearings, the EEOC would score a number of points, by both undermining the facts behind the company's testimony and challenging the credibility of their witnesses. The testimony that would be heard in Room 252 over those next seven weeks would pile up, making it even clearer that AT&T had reparations to make to its female and minority employees.

The EEOC's attack began with David Copus questioning the company's lead witness, John Kingsbury, whose testimony, as Copus put it, was the "centerpiece . . . , it brought [the company's case] all together."[7] AT&T's decision to put Kingsbury in this central role made sense because he was the personnel executive most directly responsible for the case and for implementing any affirmative action program that resolved it. Perhaps just as important, Kingsbury had thought about the potential outcomes of the case in more than a cursory way. While the lawyers on either side were tied up arguing over numbers—how many females would have to fill which jobs once the case was settled—Kingsbury was focused on the individual women who would actually get these nontraditional positions. For example, he was concerned that the company provide adequate training and appropriate equipment for women who took outside plant jobs involving climbing telephone poles, particularly after he heard of several women falling during climbs. Kingsbury understood that the push of women into men's jobs couldn't be successfully achieved simply by setting a goal and hiring the people to meet it. A lot more planning would be needed to ensure that all the company's employees were safe. With this thoughtful perspective and his job responsibilities, Kingsbury could represent the Bell System well.

Copus had taken the time to review the "detailed set of charts and tables, showing what enormous strides the Bell System had made, particularly in the employment of blacks," that accompanied Kingsbury's written testimony in the weeks before the hearings restarted. Even to Copus, on the surface they looked impressive. They showed "how much progress [the Bell System] had made, so who would dare question their commitment to equal opportunity."

Nevertheless, Copus believed there had to be a hole somewhere in the figures he read in AT&T's written defense, and, one day, ruminating in his tiny EEOC office, he found it. While Kingsbury's testimony showed that the company had recently increased its percentages of women and minorities hired into high-paying craft jobs compared with years past, it omitted certain pieces of hard data that had a material influence on the level of improvement. For example, when company executives talked about percentage increase in hiring, they didn't mention the actual numbers hired or the employee turnover that year, two details essential to determining the amount of real progress made.

Both the logic and calculations were so simple that it seemed unimaginable AT&T had based a significant part of its defense on this strategy. But there it was in front of Copus's eyes. "They used that analytical model in page after page, in every different kind of scenario, it was their basic template," he says today. Perhaps the company executives used such a flawed approach because, never having had to analyze hiring and employment statistics before, they hadn't developed the proper expertise. Perhaps their statistical experts had suggested they spin their numbers this way. Or perhaps, as Copus speculates today, "[the AT&T executives] were so convinced they were the answer to motherhood, apple pie and the American flag, . . . that they were the model corporate citizen, it never dawned on them these numbers weren't right."

But in either case, Copus was well prepared to exploit the error. With Randy Speck playing Kingsbury, Copus practiced his cross-examination, which used a series of hypotheticals based on his view of the correct statistical analysis. When Kingsbury took the witness stand at 11 A.M. on October 30, 1972, Copus started slowly, throwing a few straightforward questions at him. Then, relishing his opportunity to shine, he moved to his hypotheticals. He may have been squeezed from control in the government-wide negotiations, but things were different here at the FCC. He had left that battlefield behind, donned his Superman suit at a nearby phone booth, and was now set to spring into action. He wasn't just the smartest person in the room; he was the hero who was going to save AT&T's employees.

Copus's first hypothetical was based on statistics AT&T had submitted about hiring blacks. "Mr. Kingsbury, I want you to assume we have two companies, A and B," he began. "Both companies produce the same products . . . and they have the same jobs. They are in the same neighborhood and . . . are the same size, they employ 1000 craft workers, one of who is black. . . . During 1971, [at] company A, 5 percent of the entry level craft workers who [it] hired were black and [at] company B during 1971, 25 percent of entry level craft workers who [it] hired were black. Based on that information, wouldn't you say company B was making considerably more progress in the hiring of blacks than company A?"[8]

"If that is all you looked at, yes, I would conclude company B is doing a better job," Kingsbury replied. Then he added, "I would [also] want to look at the figures as to the numbers hired." He had taken no time to suggest there could be a problem with a key part of the testimony so vital to AT&T's case.

Copus added to his scenario. "Let's assume the following occurred at company A in 1971—no craft workers quit [and] one hundred craft workers were hired, five of whom were black. What would be the percentage increase in minorities at company A?"

"500 percent."

"Now let's assume the following occurred in 1971 at company B: No craft workers quit, twenty craft workers were hired, five of whom were black. What would be the percentage increase in minorities in company B?"

"500 percent."

"Thus the percentage increase was the same in both companies?"

"Right."

"Despite the fact they were hiring blacks at substantially different rates?"

"Right."

"So would it not be fair if you wanted to judge companies A and B using a percentage increase measure, you would want to know also, as you indicated earlier, how many blacks and whites were involved?"

"Right." Kingsbury's response was nearly inaudible.

But Copus hadn't finished making his point. "In addition to the percentage you need the numbers that were actually hired to evaluate the increased figure of 500 percent?"

"Yes."

Having established his premise, Copus moved from his hypothetical to Kingsbury's written testimony, making him flip through the pages to see if he had provided that data for the Bell System. After Kingsbury tried to explain the figures away once or twice, Copus asked him pointedly, "But you don't give us the number of people hired?"

Kingsbury finally had to answer, "Not specifically, that's right."

Copus still hadn't finished with Hypothetical #1, going through each job category—sales workers, professionals, college hires—demonstrating that while Kingsbury's testimony stated the percentage increase in minority employment over the years, he never mentioned the total numbers of minorities hired. When looked at through Copus's eyes, the testimony became meaningless.

And this was just Copus's first hypothetical. When he asked his key question in the second one focused on Bell System Hispanic employment, "Which company was doing a better job of hiring Spanish-speaking individuals in 1971?," Kingsbury had already moved from conciliatory to frustrated. "I don't know for sure," he responded, "I'm not going to hazard a guess."

On it went, through a half dozen more of Copus's concocted scenarios.

By the end, the hearings room dialogue sounded like a tutorial the esteemed professor Copus was leading for the unprepared freshman Kingsbury in front of a packed classroom. "Let's finish this hypothetical by giving you the rest of the information and see if that turns out to be correct." The center-piece of AT&T's testimony hadn't stood up well under Copus's gleeful deconstruction.

When he had finally finished, Copus's exuberance ratcheted down a few notches. After lunch, his questions came slower and seemed simpler, but Kingsbury still answered tentatively more often than not: he didn't know when in the hiring process—the interview, test, physical exam, or refer-ences—minorities were typically screened out because the company didn't keep those statistics; his office hadn't studied the connection between the criteria used to choose a job candidate and later job performance; no BOC had yet implemented AT&T's suggested guidelines to move minorities into management training programs. Perhaps Kingsbury was overwhelmed by the morning assault or simply unprepared, but by 4:15 P.M., when he was let off the stand, he could have felt nothing but relief.

Kingsbury's second day on the stand started no better than the first. When the parties entered the room that Tuesday morning, the CULA's slogans dis-paraging AT&T now covered the hearings room's blackboards, a turn of events that again drove Denniston to step outside his calm persona and lay down the law. With Kingsbury waiting to testify, Denniston launched into a lecture that sounded well rehearsed. "Miss Gemma, I want to make certain observations and one of them has to do with the conduct of the NYC hear-ing. . . . Many times during that hearing you were disruptive . . . and I had to repeatedly threaten to stop the hearings. . . . I realize you are not attor-neys and perhaps not aware of all the implications of that, but . . . I want personal assurances from you that . . . you will observe certain rules."[9] Den-niston then listed those rules the CULA women had to follow: observing the "decorum of this hearing," discouraging audible audience participation, and refraining from making statements, since they were acting as legal parties to the case who would cross-examine witnesses and not serving as witnesses themselves.

Gavrielle Gemma came right back at him. "We are workers who are un-der the pressure every day," she said. "I'm sure you've never been a tele-phone operator before."

For this moment, Denniston wasn't wavering. "I suggest you confer with your associates and later in the day . . . advise me whether you are willing to accept the conditions I stated."

Again, a directive from Denniston seemed to help. That morning, the

CULA women got their collective act together against Kingsbury, living up to the standard Copus had set the day before. When Luella Smith, a new CULA face, asked Kingsbury how many blacks had achieved each level of management, he couldn't immediately produce the figures, and later, after he had dug them up, his report was embarrassing: there were no African Americans out of 413 total managers at sixth level (equivalent to Kingsbury) or above, 7 of 1,170 at fifth, 10 of 3,313 at fourth, down to just over 6,000 of almost 120,000 at first. At no level, from first to the top of AT&T's ladder, did blacks hold more than 5.2 percent of the jobs, and that was at the very bottom rung of first-level supervisor, just a slight step above nonmanagement.

The CULA racked up more points against AT&T that morning during Gavrielle Gemma's questioning. When Kingsbury talked about the company's aggressive new affirmative action plan, Gemma asked him bluntly, "This plan is offered because AT&T realized that there has been discrimination?" Kingsbury could only answer "No, it is not," but Gemma's point had been made. Later, when Ashley and Denniston suggested that her inquiries into New York Telephone's plans to raise its directory assistance rates were irrelevant, she made the direct link. Higher rates would mean less calls would mean fewer operators needed. While the telephone operator's job may have been dismally unpleasant, it at least guaranteed a weekly paycheck.

The day ended in triumph for neither Kingsbury nor his CULA opponents. Late that afternoon, Kathy Dennis made a contrite statement on behalf of the CULA: "As to what you asked of us earlier," she said to Denniston, "we have discussed it over lunch and we have decided we would abide by the rules of decorum as far as our conduct in these hearings is concerned." The CULA women weren't giving up, so they had agreed begrudgingly to play by Denniston's rules.

Kingsbury hadn't given up either, but his appearance on the witness stand had done nothing to bolster his written testimony. Its official title, *The Bell Companies as Equal Employers: A Record of Achievement, a Commitment to Progress* sounded almost like a parody of what he had presented on the last two days of October 1972. Not that it was entirely his fault. Maybe with a little more preparation, he could have answered a few more questions accurately. But in reality, he had been sacrificed by a hubristic company that underestimated its opponent. He would have been better off back in his office, working even more aggressively on changing the personnel policies of the country's largest employer.

Following Kingsbury's testimony, the rest of the first week of AT&T's case presentation remained essentially under the CULA's control. On Wednesday,

November 1, executives from Traffic and Plant, the key Bell System departments under scrutiny, took the stand to defend their employment, hiring,
and promotion rates. Both Robert Ferguson, AT&T's Traffic Department assistant vice president, and Joseph Hunt, the Plant Department assistant vice
president, held their own against Copus's questions about promotions, hiring, job titles, and training, but then the CULA women took over. Kathy
Dennis went after Ferguson, quizzing him about how a telephone operator
could live on a maximum pay of $141 per week, and Luella Smith, even
more effectively pursuing Hunt, forced him to state out loud the company's
horrendous employment statistics, similar to those documented in *A Unique
Competence:* 96.6 percent of the company's clerical jobs were filled by
women (at the end of 1971) at a top pay of $157.50/week while 98.6 per-
cent of all Bell System craft jobs went to the male gender (in mid-1971) at a
top weekly pay of $235, a whopping 49 percent difference. Hearing these
figures from the company's top plant executive had much more of an impact than just reading them in a report. Smith had more good questions too:
Wasn't the more dangerous splicer's position filled disproportionately by minorities? Weren't craft jobs posted where only men could view them?

On the CULA's last day in the hearings room, one Bell witness, Therese
Pick, the company's employment benefits secretary, presented an enlight-
ening spin on AT&T's employment policies. Pick's clerical title belied her
professional position, coordinator of employee benefits, the first woman
ever to hold it. At first, her testimony simply fed the standard fire of Bell System culpability when she explained that although pregnancy testing during
job interviews had been discontinued earlier that year, policy still dictated
that pregnant women couldn't be hired for jobs requiring five days or more
of training or those that might be hazardous to the mother or child, a des-
ignation undefined by Pick or any of her colleagues in the room. No matter
the written description, a pregnant woman would never get a high-paying
outside plant job because it required weeks of up-front training and offered
the highest level of danger—a perfect example of a "caring" Ma Bell policy
specifically keeping women from making more money.

Pick's testimony got more interesting when she next described recent
changes in employee retirement and death benefits that, for a change of
pace, inflicted their pain on the company's male employees. On October 1,
1971, AT&T had set a standard time frame for an employee to retire with full
benefits—sixty-five years old with fifteen years of service—to replace its
former policy requiring twenty years' employment for both genders but allowing women to retire at fifty-five while requiring men to wait until sixty.
The company had also standardized its pension policies, allowing widow-

ers to collect them, not just widows, and company death benefits, such as life insurance, paying them to any beneficiary of a female employee who died, not just a beneficiary financially dependent on the worker. It was reassuring news of a sort: AT&T classified men as the stronger sex in every past policy, even when that policy's outcomes didn't fall in men's favor. The company may have been breaking the law, but at least it did so in a consistent manner.

The day Therese Pick testified was also the last day the CULA women would be seen at these hearings. No longer able to afford a Washington, D.C., hotel room, they left town that evening, having laid out their dissatisfaction with the telephone company in every way they could. They had had moments of brilliance, such as when Smith, a maligned telephone operator, got Kingsbury, a corporate vice president, to admit on the record to figures illuminating the company's egregiously lopsided employment statistics for women versus men. But it was hard to know if they had achieved their goal. With the case's decision left to just one person, Fred Denniston, an older, polite gentleman whose experience lay primarily in judging dry rate cases argued by male lawyers with thin ties and calm voices, the CULA women's radical approach seemed risky. But they had done what they could with the resources they had. They would find out later whether they had made a difference.

Over the next two weeks, AT&T's case presentation proceeded in a more orderly but no less entertaining manner with ten experts appearing on six days between Wednesday, November 8, and Friday, November 17, 1972. The company had already put up its primary witnesses on the facts—Kingsbury, Ferguson, and Hunt—and later, a series of BOC executives would testify, more effectively the company hoped, about equal employment achievements in their own companies. Sandwiched in between, these experts were scheduled to explain away, in AT&T's favor, any facts that didn't look so great. The ten experts took one of three approaches: blame the victim; blame society; don't blame AT&T because its past equal employment opportunity efforts have been exemplary.

The "blame the victim" strategy targeted both women and minorities. Lewis Perl, an assistant professor of economics at Cornell, testified that women didn't get better jobs because they weren't prepared for them, having studied business courses rather than the college track in high school, while Leona Tyler, a professor emeritus of psychology at the University of Oregon, stated that women simply weren't interested in professional, high-paying careers. Hugh Folk, a professor of economics and industrial and labor relations, reported that the problem was the same for blacks—they just hadn't shown they wanted AT&T's better-paying craft jobs.

Four additional witnesses found fault with both groups simultaneously. Two psychologists, Doug Bray and Donald Grant, who were also AT&T personnel employees, and Robert Guion, a professor of psychology at Bowling Green State University, opined individually that since women and minorities didn't score as well on craft tests as white men did, they weren't as qualified for craft jobs. And Brent Baxter, a vice president at the American Institutes for Research in Pittsburgh, asserted that whatever skills and abilities women and minorities had in that era, they didn't predict strong job performance in the company's higher paying-positions.

Blaming society as a whole proved tougher for the company's lawyers, as they tracked down only two witnesses to support that position. Frank Coss, a New York City advertising executive, laid the responsibility on the media, suggesting that newspapers' policy of advertising jobs in sex-segregated columns meant that women and men applied, respectively, for the type they read about. He had thought of the obvious EEOC rejoinder but wrote it off: AT&T *could* have advertised in both, which might have benefited future employees, but it would have been worse for customers who would eventually have to cover the higher costs. Nathan Glazer, a professor of education and social structure at the Harvard Graduate School of Education, declined to focus on one industry, instead arguing that the American capitalist economy was fundamentally structured to favor one group over another—tough luck for women and minorities, apparently.

The final expert argument against AT&T's culpability had been heard many times before. Jules Cohn, a professor at the City University of New York, took the stand to describe the crucial leadership role AT&T had played in the National Alliance of Businessmen's JOBS program, targeted at disadvantaged Americans who were disproportionately minority. Because the company had done one good thing, it was impossible for it to be responsible for anything else bad.

Copus and Gartner faced a tough challenge in responding to this cabal of AT&T experts because they weren't presenting verifiable facts or statistics, so their comments were difficult to absolutely disprove. Moreover, most of these experts were luminaries in their fields compared with the competent, but not yet distinguished, team Phyllis Wallace had found for the EEOC. As Copus says today, "The industrial psychologists [who testified for us] were clearly outweighed by the Bell System experts so we were swimming upstream." [10]

But with the EEOC team's earlier research, Copus and Gartner managed to launch an effective assault on the company. First, they attacked three of the witnesses—Folk, Cohn, and Baxter—for their past and present work as AT&T consultants, suggesting they could benefit financially if they made statements, under oath, beneficial to the company. Next they began their discreditation process, which proved effective for the EEOC and awkward for the company. After getting AT&T's witness list, Copus had focused his team on researching each one's previous work, hoping to find a quote or publication to undermine her or his testimony during cross-examination. In half the cases, they hit pay dirt, finding spoken or published statements that indirectly or even directly supported the EEOC's case. Doug Bray had worked on a book called *A Policy for Scientific and Professional Manpower,* which discussed how discriminatory employment practices, like those AT&T was accused of, significantly limited the number of blacks, Spanish-speaking Americans, and women in scientific and professional fields. Leona Tyler quoted from her own written testimony in this case that, although she didn't believe there should be absolute parity for men and women in jobs, there should be "equalization of opportunities, responsibilities and rewards."[11] Jules Cohn read a passage from his own book, *The Conscience of the Corporations,* which described how the Bell System was aggressively pursuing unemployed blacks for telephone operator's jobs because it couldn't find anyone else to take them. Nathan Glazer had written that members of disadvantaged groups tended to follow the same jobs of other members who had gone before them, even if they were interested in a different career, using the specific example of Jews who had historically become entrepreneurs whether a corporate job was their first interest or not. These experts on AT&T's side had practically covered the EEOC's bases: the existence of discrimination against blacks, the need for equality of opportunity for women, the dismal nature of the telephone operator's job, the subtle discrimination preventing any one group moving into a new career. Their reputations may have been stellar, but their records, on that day, worked in the EEOC's favor.

One AT&T witness's past writing went beyond awkward and became downright embarrassing for the company. It wasn't a theory in a scholarly tome, just an offhand comment in a professional letter that the EEOC had uncovered in its research. On November 16, 1972, Copus began questioning Robert Guion, one of the psychologists he truly respected, about Guion's limited responses to the EEOC expert witness testimony he had been sent for review. Since Guion "was the single most genius expert on either side," Copus had to attack something other than his testimony.[12] Copus started by asking him, "Isn't it true, Dr. Guion, that one of the main reasons you did not comment on the other witnesses that dealt with sex discrimination is because you believed that sex discrimination was blatant in the Bell System?"[13]

"No," Guion responded. He probably realized the goal Copus had in mind and, as an AT&T witness, was going to do his best to force him to miss it. "There are two reasons why I didn't pay much attention to those witnesses. Do you want them?"

Allowing Guion to proceed briefly, Copus could see he needed a more direct approach. "All right, Dr. Guion. Let me refresh your recollection. Your honor, I am going to show the witness a letter from Robert M. Guion, dated July 18 1972, to Mr. Phil Davis, Acting Director of OFCC—"

Despite an objection from James Hutchinson, the Steptoe and Johnson lawyer, Denniston allowed Copus to continue. "For the record, please, Dr. Guion," he said, "would you read the first two paragraphs?"

Now, Guion had no choice. He read the first paragraph and then got to what Copus cared about. "Haste dictates that I respond only to those portions of the expert witness testimony dealing with testing; I have skimmed through the sections dealing with sex discrimination, but have not looked at them carefully for two reasons: 1) they seem unrelated to employee selection tools . . . , and 2) from other sources, I am quite convinced that, at least until fairly recently, sex discrimination was probably blatant at AT&T."

He stopped awkwardly. He would have to find a way to explain this. "May I comment on the paragraph?" he asked.

Denniston gave him the chance, which he used ineffectively, his strongest argument being that the letter "was hastily dictated with no thought to ever having to answer to it again later." The AT&T lawyers must have desperately wished he had been right.

Not that the Bell System was alone in facing embarrassment. Just three days earlier, on Monday, November 13, Frank Coss, the advertising executive who had tried to justify the company's advertising policy, noted that, in his review of classified ads while preparing his testimony, "as I was going through these many newspapers [to compare other ads with AT&T's ads] there were enough ads with sexual connotations to make me wonder whether the EEOC was really operating."[14] Granted he was combing through papers published in 1967, a year before the agency revised its guidelines to target sex-segregated ads aggressively, but his comment reflected poorly on the EEOC. Perhaps its fight against discrimination hadn't been all it could have been. Perhaps it could share a little blame with AT&T.

But Ma Bell still came out looking the worst when one of its key witnesses, Leona Tyler, walked straight into a meticulously designed EEOC trap. On the same day Coss testified, Larry Gartner began questioning Tyler.

"Earlier this morning you testified that books could be factors in determining sex roles," he said.

"Yes," Tyler responded.

Gartner leaned down and picked up a book from the table in front of him. "I would like to show you a book entitled *Come to Work With Us in a Department Store*. . . . Are you familiar with this book, Dr. Tyler?"

"No, I am not," she answered. But in a quick glance at its pictures of women as clerks and men as managers, she could see that a girl reading it wouldn't be inclined to imagine herself in a top job. "I think I see the point," she added. "I must say I agree with you."

But Gartner didn't want his key point made so easily. "At the beginning of the book," he went on, "there is a foreword. . . . Doesn't it say this is a book a child should read to find out what kind of job [he or she] is interested in?"

Tyler again agreed.

"Let's look at some of the jobs described in this book," Gartner said, explaining what Tyler had already seen. "So little girls and little boys reading this book might be influenced as to certain types of occupational roles, wouldn't they?" he asked.

"Yes." She didn't hesitate.

Now Gartner would open the EEOC's trapdoor. "I would like to show you another book," he said. "What is the title of this book, Dr. Tyler?"

"*Come to Work With Us in the Telephone Company*." This was bound to be shakier territory for Tyler.

"It is written by the same authors, isn't it?" Gartner asked, suggesting they probably took the same approach.

"Yes." Nothing seemed incriminating so far.

". . . Let's look at the pictures in this book. On page 13, a little boy is pictured as a communications consultant, isn't that right?"

"Yes."

"On page 15, a customer service representative is pictured by a little girl, isn't that right?"

The little girl in the picture stared right at Tyler. "That is right." She didn't have much wiggle room.

"On page 23, there is a little boy as a lineman. What about on page 27 that depicts a frameman? That is a little boy, isn't it?"

"That is right."

Even though he'd clearly made his point, Gartner wasn't finished. "On page 33, there is a little girl as a long-distance operator, isn't that right?"

"Yes."

"On page 43, who is pictured as the district manager?"

"A boy." Tyler at least had a slight rejoinder in this case. "Of course, he is black."

With his trap only focused on gender, Gartner didn't respond, not wanting to get off track. Now he just needed to tie the book to AT&T, which would be easy. "I would like you to look at the very first page of this book, the title page," he said to Tyler. "At the bottom, the authors and publishers make an acknowledgement to a particular company for this book. What company is that?"

Tyler had no choice but to answer. She read out loud, "American Telephone and Telegraph Co. and associated companies."

Now in the same incriminating situation Guion would face a few hours later, Tyler tried to explain. "I would like to comment on this a little in relation to what I said," she added, but her comments fell flat, at least from AT&T's viewpoint. "I am very much in favor of changing material like this," she added. "It would be an influence [on children who read it.]" At this point, apparently all she could do was be honest.

Tyler may have felt uncomfortable, but AT&T's lawyers were in worse shape. This little kid's book had drawn a straight line from AT&T to gender-specific jobs, a major blow to the company's case. As Copus remembers, later in the day the Bell System lawyers announced they would speak to the book's publishers and ensure that the next edition's pictures provided a more equal gender mix for each type of job. Kingsbury himself autographed a copy of the book and sent it to Copus after the hearings with a conciliatory note. As Copus would later say, "It took [the AT&T executives] a long time to understand that they were dead wrong, but when they [did], they corrected it."[15] But no matter their integrity level, the facts brought out by Gartner's careful questioning of Tyler had unequivocally damaged AT&T's case.

With AT&T's expert testimony complete on November 17, 1972, Denniston recessed the hearings for the week of Thanksgiving, scheduling them to restart on Monday, November 27, with the first of a string of BOC witnesses. Jenny Longo, on the FCC legal staff, had developed a list of standard questions about each company's personnel record, such as how many women and minorities were employed at each job level and what recruitment and maternity leave policies were followed.

Again AT&T's lawyers had invested significant expectations in these men, particularly considering the bruises the company had already taken, and again they would be disappointed. Although each local manager did his best

to emphasize the positive in his company's record, the underlying facts, repeatedly noted in earlier testimony, limited their success. In addition, at
times, they appeared uninformed at best or untruthful at worst.

And in some cases, they clearly highlighted the depths of the company's
discrimination. Harold Dann, the NET vice president of personnel, began
the procession that first Monday morning, admitting that through NET's
present policy of asking female job candidates about their periods, the company had subverted its January 1972 ban on pregnancy testing. C&P, on
the other hand, had simply decided to ignore the company order and was
still giving pregnancy tests to women attempting to get "active" (read: high-
paying, outside craft) jobs, according to Lloyd Dyer, its personnel vice president. Wes Clarke, Bell of Pennsylvania's personnel vice president, admitted
that his company did home visits of female job applicants, while Elizabeth
Edmundson, the assistant manager of New York Telephone's employment
office, described her company's new job applications, implemented just one
month earlier, which no longer asked questions about a woman's marital
status, menstrual period, number of children, and the likelihood she would
reunite with her husband if she was separated.

Beyond the discrimination exhibited in the Bell companies' recruiting
and hiring processes, at least two Bell executives clarified that their companies maintained sex-segregated jobs. J. B. Gable of Illinois Bell testified
that during a recent strike management women filled in for male craft workers on the frame with no difficulty. Moreover, when the strike was over, the
company opened the job to women, briefly making it appear as if it was taking a step, without EEOC encouragement, to integrate one of its job classifications by gender. But in Gable's next sentence, he mentioned that the company had considered changing the "frameman's" job to be filled only by
women, probably to save costs, presenting more proof that the EEOC was
right—AT&T classified its jobs by gender and paid women less for the same
work. Edward Hodges of Michigan Bell reinforced that perspective when he
was forced to recount on the witness stand the well-known story of his company's all-female switchroom helper's job, which was filled by more highly
paid men in all other BOCs.

Two Bell executives added their discriminatory beliefs to this pile of facts.
George Madsen of Mountain Bell stated he thought women who pursued
craft jobs were emotionally and mentally unstable. John Hopkins of South
Central Bell opined that, from his viewpoint, it was still legitimate to deny
jobs to unwed mothers. Bell System women were both held down in low-
level jobs and looked down upon.

On December 15, 1972, with testimony from just two more BOCs to come, Denniston adjourned the hearings for the Christmas holidays, which couldn't have seemed too soon for AT&T and its supporters. Things hadn't gone according to plan. Over those two dozen days of testimony that fall, the witnesses for the phone company had painted a rather guilty picture of America's corporate icon. Ma Bell needed another approach to resolve its conflict with the U.S. government.

12

The Settlement

Late Fall 1972/Winter 1973

While AT&T appeared headed for disaster in the FCC hearings, its negotiating team locked up in the solicitor of labor's office was faring a bit better. Instead of spending their days unwittingly unveiling the Bell System's worst side, Clark Redick, Lee Satterfield, and Dan Davis were focused on the positive: helping create the best settlement possible to get AT&T out from under its government cloud.

In the first weeks of negotiations, the AT&T, EEOC, OFCC, and Equal Pay Act participants met several times a week for seemingly endless hours. Their discussions had started with each party's hot buttons. The EEOC had two: quotas for women and minorities in craft jobs and, thanks to Copus's NOW education, men in operator jobs, and a multi-million-dollar payment to the company's victims. These demands stemmed not only from Copus's desire to inflict maximum pain on AT&T but also from the EEOC's belief that definite hiring numbers, not just goals and timetables, and a big dollar payout would be most effective in improving the professional and financial status of Bell's female and minority employees.

The Equal Pay Act's Carin Clauss remained focused on the phone company's salary structure. Equal work demanded equal pay, which, based on the stacks of cases she had against AT&T, was a policy she knew the company wasn't following. Any agreement these negotiations reached had to guarantee that.

Not surprisingly, AT&T's two primary concerns directly conflicted with the EEOC's priorities. Before walking into the first negotiations session, the members of Easlick's team knew their bosses would never sign any agreement that included the term or concept "quota," no matter how long and loud Copus demanded it. While the company's top executives had driven Easlick's ongoing efforts to advance women and minorities—John deButts to meet his legal responsibilities, Bob Lilley to live out his own values—neither, under any circumstance, would agree to a plan that set hard numbers they were required to meet. They may have worried about their ability to achieve those amounts, but, at least as important, they were concerned about the precedent it would set for the rest of American business. No one on the twenty-sixth floor wanted AT&T known as the company that started such a distasteful trend.

Just as Copus wanted AT&T to pay as much as was financially possible, the company's negotiators were pushing to pay as little as they could get away with. Partially it was a business issue, since the final government bill, however large, would be an unbudgeted expense for the company. But more significant, the Bell System executives wanted to minimize the adverse reaction they would face, both externally and internally. A large settlement would set as bad a precedent as quotas, which was exactly why Bill Kilberg was relentlessly pushing for it. Moreover, the company's New York City executives had to keep their own divisional presidents happy. As Clark Redick says today, there was "the possibility of outright rebellion" among the BOCs, and the larger the settlement's cost, the more likely the revolt.[1]

There were other, less controversial issues to consider also: What special rules, if any, should be followed in recruiting pregnant women? What type of affirmative action plan should each Bell division implement? Could Bell companies continue using preemployment tests that routinely screened out blacks? Which female college graduates should be asked to join a management training program?

None of these specific issues, whether sizzling hot or mundane, concerned Bill Kilberg very much. With the primary objective of reaching a settlement that produced big headlines, he was just trying to keep everyone talking. Knowing back pay had derailed the first negotiations, he steered the teams to leave it until the end, when all other concerns had been addressed, and worked with his colleagues to clear other issues off the table entirely, including those hiring policies for pregnant women and the upgrade of management pay, by setting them aside for future consent decrees. The parties also agreed that AT&T could continue to give its preemployment tests as long as managers didn't use them as an excuse for not achieving their hiring numbers and could still base their affirmative action and upgrade and transfer plans on the ones Dan Davis's task forces had developed. Although the final AT&T affirmative action plan would be stricter than the one GSA had approved, all parties agreed that the format the AT&T task force had devised would be adequate for promotion and hiring plans throughout the company. With these few decisions, the negotiating teams saved hours of time.

Extra time alone, however, wouldn't help resolve the EEOC/AT&T conflict over quotas. But Dan Davis, in his endless deliberations, thankfully produced a creative, if simple, idea to address it, which used an existing resource: those preemployment tests. Typically when a candidate for a non-management job was selected, he or she had been ranked "best qualified" for that position, having scored highest of all candidates on the relevant preemployment test. By this design, Bell System managers were always in search of the top test scorers—the "A" students—even though the tests as effectively identified "qualified" individuals, those who achieved a set minimum score. Just as in high school, when a C minus got you full course credit, if not entrance to a top college, a "qualified" rating meant you had the basic ability to do the job.

To solve the quota question, Davis suggested that AT&T increase the use of the tests and exploit that "qualified" evaluation. If any Bell division couldn't meet its affirmative action goals, it would have the leeway to choose a candidate, female or minority, who was "qualified" for the position—that is, had passed the appropriate test now given also to internal candidates—even if she or he wasn't "best qualified." Company managers would still get individuals who could do the work while women and minorities would get more opportunities for better jobs.

Although the unions would come to fight Davis's idea, since it diminished seniority's importance when company employees transferred from job to job, the government negotiators welcomed it. Their ultimate boss, President Nixon, had been supportive of affirmative action in his ongoing reelection campaign but had come out forcefully against quotas, and Bill Brown, just then, was mired in controversy over the issue. In his November 11, 1972, column, Jack Anderson of the *Washington Post* had suggested that the EEOC, which was part of the "no-quota" Nixon administration, was actually requiring quotas in discrimination settlements. To get around this criticism, the government negotiators embraced Davis's idea, which would allow them to still push for aggressive targets without giving those targets the evil "quota" moniker. The following year, the technique got a name—the affirmative action override—and proved essential to the Bell System in meeting its consent decree commitments.

By the time November 1972 arrived, the parties had gotten into a stable, if uneven, rhythm. After a couple of weeks of meetings that led to agreement on one issue or another, the negotiators would suspend their daily sessions to get their ideas on paper. AT&T took the lead drafting the agreement, as it had already produced a key section, the affirmative action and upgrade and transfer plans; plus, it had Tom Powers and his stable of Steptoe and Johnson lawyers waiting at its offices, ready to write. Powers and his colleagues would get their assignment in the morning and produce a draft by the end of the day. As Clark Redick says today, "We had real-time drafting ability which was a tremendous asset."[2] Once AT&T approved the draft, it went out for circulation, both to the company's opponents across the negotiating table and internally, to John Kingsbury, George Ashley, and the other AT&T executives laboring concurrently in the FCC hearings. Typically the negotiators' corporate colleagues would offer a few questions on any given draft, followed by a stamp of approval, while the government team contributed specific edits to make the agreement acceptable for eventual government sign-off.

Only one active player working on the case was intentionally impeding progress, and that was David Copus himself. While he was pushing forward aggressively at the hearings, he was simultaneously putting on the brakes, to the extent he could, during the negotiations sessions he attended. When he was there, he assertively repeated his demands for strict quotas and big money, no matter the topic of the day. As a result, a palpable tension hung in the air between him and his more mature EEOC colleagues, particularly Charlie Wilson. Bill Brown had given Wilson a clear charge—settle the case to the EEOC's best advantage—and he wasn't going to let Copus stop him from meeting that responsibility. Kilberg also got frustrated by Copus's attitude, enduring more than one lecture about how the agreement would be a sellout without the quotas and back pay Copus was demanding. But Kilberg used his standard rejoinder: *An agreement with AT&T, in which its executives agree to promote and hire thousands of women and minorities into high-paying jobs, will be powerful even if not a single dollar of back pay is dispensed.*

Despite David Copus's recalcitrance, some progress was being made. Like Charlie Wilson a few weeks earlier, Kilberg was especially impressed with AT&T's team. As a kid from Brooklyn brought up knowing he could never get a Bell System job because the phone company didn't hire Jews, Kilberg was pleasantly surprised with the Easlick team's knowledge of and commitment to equal employment opportunity. As Kilberg says today, "[The company] came to the table with a human resources crew of negotiators who were very progressive and had a lot of credibility."[3] With the sage, calming presence of Tom Powers in many of the sessions and Charlie Wilson performing as the consummate negotiator, making a little progress on some issue at every meeting, hopes for a successful outcome were increasing.

Throughout the fall of 1972, the negotiators stayed in close contact with their various bosses. Wilson called Bill Brown regularly, and Brown's special assistant, Bill Oldaker, passed on Copus's less enthusiastic perspective after their regular get-togethers over a beer. AT&T's challenge was more complicated because the company had more to lose and the negotiators had many more people to answer to. One or another of their team of three called Dave Easlick every night, knowing Easlick would update Bill Lindholm, AT&T's vice chairman, during their more than two-hour daily commute from Brookside, New Jersey, to Manhattan. Almost as often, Dan Davis updated Alvin von Auw, his mentor from Western Electric and now a corporate vice president and John deButts's assistant. As a result, deButts and Bob Lilley, who would have the final say on any settlement, always knew where the negotiations stood.

As time allowed, the members of the Easlick team also met with other AT&T executives with an interest in the proceedings. They introduced Mark Garlinghouse, the company's new general counsel, to Tom Powers in a meeting on one of their rare days in New York that fall and responded to Garlinghouse's esoteric questions about feeder pools for employees and other issues he considered important. Later in December, the threesome presented the draft agreement to Rex Reed, AT&T's vice president of labor relations. As the top AT&T executive responsible to the unions, Reed had one concern: Could he make the agreement fly with the CWA, IBEW, and other bargaining units representing Bell System workers? He challenged the negotiating team aggressively, particularly Clark Redick, yet the team members walked out of both sessions with support from their colleagues. Reed's only caveat was the same one they'd heard all along—we can accept almost any agreement as long as it doesn't involve quotas.

While AT&T and EEOC leaders stayed aware of the negotiations progress, President Nixon's White House was never heard from. Considering that representatives of his administration were discussing two issues Nixon felt strongly about—affirmative action and quotas—with representatives of the country's largest employer, several negotiations participants expected a phone call from the White House outlining Nixon's requirements for any settlement. Len Garment, a White House special consultant and advocate for Brown within the Nixon administration, may have been acting as an intermediary by reassuring the president and his top staff that the EEOC had things under control. But more important, this was the late fall of 1972, less than six months after five men broke into the Democratic National Committee headquarters at the Watergate Hotel, a time when Richard Nixon and his top staff were focused almost entirely on news reports plastered across the *Washington Post*'s front page. Perhaps Nixon wouldn't have been happy a capitalist icon was about to agree to a historic commitment to hiring more women and blacks at the expense, some would say, of white males. But he was far too concerned with other things to say so.

Although Nixon stayed out of the negotiations process, Kilberg brought him in, figuratively that is, to serve his own purposes. Since the Watergate story had remained confined to the metropolitan Washington area that fall, Nixon had easily been elected for another four years, with his second inauguration set for January 20, 1973. This would appear to offer little clout as a deadline for major government activities, since the president wasn't being replaced. However, Kilberg suggested to AT&T that Nixon could use this second mandate to bring fresh faces into his government agencies, individuals who might even want to start the AT&T/U.S. government negotiating process over again. In retrospect, Kilberg's sales pitch sounds far-fetched, particularly considering the upcoming escalation of the Watergate scandal, yet at the time it worked. Easlick became convinced the agreement had to be completed by January, 20, 1973, or the clock could start again. AT&T, understandably, didn't want to take that risk.

As a result, when the negotiators hit the inevitable bumps generated by the discussion of goals and timetables and back pay, the Easlick team's nervous reports to its New York bosses never gained much traction. Mark Garlinghouse, AT&T's new general counsel, did get frustrated when Satterfield outlined the difficulties over the phone one afternoon, and he responded, *We're not doing anymore. Come home, Lee, come home.* But since Satterfield lived in Washington and wasn't ready to quit, he shrugged off the admonition, and Garlinghouse never pushed it. About the same time, Clark Redick flew to New York to share his concern about the negotiations' potential collapse with Dave Easlick. Upon hearing Redick's warning, instead of responding with criticism, Easlick doled out unmitigated praise for his team of three, a typical reaction from a boss they loved working for. Often allowing the three to use his private car, authorizing better hotels, and suggesting nicer restaurants, Easlick was "the kind of boss you dream of . . . who did everything he could to give us a feeling of importance," Davis remembers.[4] Sending that message once again to Redick that day, Easlick said, *I appreciate your coming and telling me this, but I've got confidence in all of you guys.* Easlick's opinion won out. The negotiations continued.

With just two issues left to work through, the negotiators tackled the slightly easier one first: the quota controversy. Although AT&T's refusal to agree to quotas never wavered, the government finally got the company to agree to specific goals for hiring women and minorities into craft and other high-paying jobs, and, yes, men into operator and clerical jobs. Copus's pursuit of male goals in these sessions again met with resistance, but this time it came primarily from his government counterpart, the Department of Labor. As Kilberg says today, "Typically you don't worry about the majority, you worry about the minority. [Our] feeling was that would take care of itself over time," but, reiterating the argument of NOW's Wilma Scott Heide, Copus eventually convinced him of its importance.[5] AT&T itself, which had already consented to the somewhat distasteful concept in its agreement with GSA, also acquiesced. The parties agreed that of all the opportunities available in inside craft jobs each year of the six-year consent decree, 40 percent would go to women applicants. Likewise, 19 percent of outside craft (e.g. pole climbers) opportunities would go to women, with 10 percent of operator and 25 percent of clerical opportunities going to men. The negotiators also agreed to an elaborate algorithm, which took into account job classifications and the surrounding demographics of company locations, to set appropriate goals for minorities.

Finally, back pay and its less controversial twin, promotional pay, were the only items outstanding. The government cared little how these two amounts were divided, just wanting the largest total possible, but AT&T wanted to assign most of the payment it would make to the future, to individuals who had been promoted, and as little as possible to paying reparations for past damage it had caused. The less it paid for that mistreatment, the smaller an admission of guilt, perhaps. Because back pay was a one-time payment and promotional pay annual, however, it was a costly decision.

To compute back pay, the negotiators used a formula devised by Labor Department experts, which required AT&T to make payments of $100–$400 to every female or minority employee who had missed getting a higher-paying job in the recent past. The numbers sound absurdly small today, and even back then, they weren't a big deal to the workers who got them. AT&T didn't even consider the cost significant. The company's total initial payment of $38 million, including $15 million in back pay and $23 million annually for new promotions, inspired Rex Reed to remark that the company spilled that much every morning before lunch, a sentiment with which David Copus surely agreed. However, particularly to Kilberg, the amount did have significance. Any two-digit number preceded by a dollar sign with six zeroes following it would turn a few reporters' heads, which would help him achieve his goal. While the settlement would wipe out the EEOC's backlog of discrimination cases, the most important consideration, that dollar figure would also draw national headlines to the fight against sex and race discrimination. A number that AT&T would sign off on and the press would pay attention to sounded like just the right amount.

Before the agreement could be signed and sealed, Bill Kilberg had to fulfill his obligation to the IBEW and was planning to review a draft with the union in mid-November. But Elihu Leifer, the union's attorney, and his colleagues weren't particularly satisfied with the arrangement, since they had hoped to participate directly in the Kilberg-led negotiations. Knowing progress might be impeded with the union at the table, Kilberg disappointed them. But as compensation, he told them, "[I'll meet with you] as many times, as long as you want, as long as you don't delay the process," Leifer remembers. "You give us your input and we'll take it back and discuss it with the company."[6] At the same time, Kilberg tried to expand the union discussions by inviting the EEOC team members to participate, since they had so much knowledge of the case. But busy with their other sessions, aware of Kilberg's extensive labor experience, and loath to set a precedent of negotiating with the union over every discrimination charge, Copus and Wilson declined the opportunity.

The lawyer leading the IBEW delegation, Elihu Leifer, could have been mistaken for one of the government's team—another Harvard Law School graduate, another preternaturally bright, surprisingly young man. In 1972, Leifer was just thirty-three years old, with five years' experience representing unions and another three working in the Justice Department's Civil Rights Division. He had wanted to represent unions from his first semester in law school, and it would remain his only focus throughout his thirty-five-year career. Both his intellectual curiosity and values pulled him toward the labor movement: in his law school classes, he had found union issues intellectually challenging, and, more important, he believed in unions' mission—"to support the efforts of labor to increase their wages and benefits."[7]

Being a civil rights supporter, too, Leifer recognized, as Copus had, that unions didn't always hold up the gold standard for fairness. However, he sat more squarely on the fence than Copus, understanding their plight when the demands of female and minority union members related to "terms and conditions of employment" directly conflicted with those of their white male colleagues. "Unions are political organizations that have a responsibility to represent their members," Leifer explains today. In that type of disagreement, "if the membership doesn't include many minorities or females then the union will support white males over [them]."[8] Plus, unions must follow the tenets of the 1935 National Labor Relations Act that charged them to represent their members by "confer[ring] in good faith" with the employer over employment issues.[9] If a female union activist represented primarily white men, she had a legal responsibility to advocate for them at the expense of all others, even if she was a committed feminist. In any case, Leifer believed unions served a beneficial purpose to American society, which made it easy to work for them.

Not that Leifer's job representing the IBEW was easy. In 1972, the approximately seventy thousand IBEW members employed in the telephone industry were covered by thirty-two local unions under seventeen collective bargaining agreements in eight BOCs. Each bargaining agreement encompassed workers in a specific field, which meant, for example, telephone operators were covered under a different bargaining agreement than craft workers. With such a wide diversity of Bell System jobs, the union and company negotiated and maintained a multitude of contracts, which made effectively representing all these local unions' interests no simple task.

Faced with this challenge, Leifer, when he came to meet with Kilberg and his associate, Ron Green, on November 13, 1972, brought several IBEW representatives with him. Robert Nickey, the director of the IBEW's telephone industry arm, joined him, as did a few members of NET's bargaining unit, since that unit had been the most vocal about the potential settlement, along with a representative of Illinois Bell's local. Kilberg welcomed them warmly, noting in a friendly tone *Oh, I see the IBEW has brought the big guns* when he saw Leifer, a lawyer Kilberg had encountered in previous labor negotiations. Leifer didn't mind having his ego stroked a bit even if he knew it was a diplomatic move by Kilberg to soften up his opponent.

Leifer and his colleagues went to Washington only three times because, in fact, they had only one issue to discuss with the government: the affirmative action override. Since the override could favor a female or black for a promotion over her or his white male counterpart who had more seniority, the union, which prioritized seniority above all else, didn't like it. As a result, the two parties' negotiations, held in the evenings to avoid conflict with Kilberg's daytime job, began on a slightly contentious note. At the first meeting, the diminutive Leifer sat between his two muscular NET colleagues, who wore T-shirts on a cool night; a tattoo could be seen on one of their arms. Sitting across the room from them, Kilberg looked less like an equal opponent than a royal subject answering a summons from the king and his two bodyguards.

At one point that night, Kilberg made a statement, the substance of which he has now forgotten, that obviously irritated Leifer and his colleagues. In addition, Kilberg thinks they were put off by having to "come to Washington, D.C., to meet with . . . a kid in his mid-twenties who is talking about transforming the phone company."[10] In response, one of Leifer's colleagues spoke up brusquely. *If you say that again, I'm coming across this table.*

Kilberg couldn't be sure if he was serious, but he wasn't taking any chances. *If you come across this table,* he said, *I'm going behind that couch,* pointing to the green leather sofa sitting conveniently behind his chair.

After a moment's pause, everyone laughed. Kilberg had played the right card and defused the tension, which led to cordial discussions from then on, even though the IBEW reps weren't getting what they wanted. And they never did. In their two additional chats with Kilberg in late December, Leifer and his colleagues negotiated only one consent decree provision at all beneficial to them: if it wanted, the union could seek alternate ways to meet its prescribed goals and timetables outside what the decree dictated. In practice, this meant nothing. The union would never find a method, other than the affirmative action override, to meet the law's requirements.

By a week before Christmas, 1972, the individuals who had been locked up in the solicitor of labor's office for the past two months felt almost ready to send their fledgling agreement out into the world for its hoped-for final approval. The four parties of negotiators had themselves agreed, in principle, to the agreement's specifics, and they now had input, even if minimal, from the only union interested in adding its voice.

In addition, the AT&T team had already received blessings on the negotiators' product from several of its own constituents. The Kingsbury/Liebers hearings team had signed off, and Redick, through his ongoing conversations with Mark Garlinghouse and his original boss, labor lawyer Charlie Ryan, had guaranteed the legal buy-in. Concurrently Easlick, who had already made one speech to the BOC presidents about the potential for this type of settlement back in August, met with them again to share the basic points of the agreement as it now stood. Although he was sure he wasn't the most popular guy in the room, he sensed the executives would give their support when pushed. He had also taken his three negotiators, primarily to recognize them for their efforts, and pitched the settlement to John deButts, Bob Lilley, and their colleagues on the twenty-sixth floor. After visiting the hallowed AT&T board room a day ahead of time just to feel the chairs and "get comfortable,"[11] the members of the Easlick team watched as their boss "review[ed] the whole [agreement], particularly the cost, the legal protection for the company if we went ahead, the known outstanding problems and liabilities, would the company and its employees be better off and, most importantly, were we slipping into a quota system." [12] Once deButts was again reassured that the agreement called for goals and timetables only, not quotas, Easlick got the green light he needed.

Now set to send the document to all parties for formal approval, the negotiators faced an unwanted surprise. At what everyone hoped would be the last negotiating session, David Copus announced, *I'm not going to support this,* which shocked both his corporate and government colleagues, who had all believed he was on board. But, devoted to his cause and wanting the absolute maximum penalty applied to his opponent, Copus wasn't yet ready to make the compromise that would have to come.

With Copus's buy-in essential, for political, if not legal, reasons, and facing a room full of frustrated and tired colleagues, Charlie Wilson took control. To buy some time, he invoked the boss's name, saying, *We'll take it back to Bill. It's in our house now—we'll get back to you.* When the meeting broke up, Wilson asked Copus if he would walk the few blocks back to the EEOC building with him instead of taking a ride. The exact conversation they had has faded with memories, but the result was clear. When Copus and Wilson arrived in Bill Brown's office less than a half hour later, both of them recommended the agreement be accepted as it had been written. Copus remembers Wilson always trying to "get me to mellow out, cool my jets, see common sense." [13] On that day, Wilson succeeded admirably.

By the next day, the welcome news of Copus's change of heart had reached all the negotiators. Nevertheless, they still had much more to accomplish. The language in the agreement had to be finalized; opinion letters from the Department of Labor and the EEOC, which, as Clark Redick describes today, "would insulate a company from future liability if the law took a turn in the other direction," [14] had to be developed and agreed upon; and, most important, AT&T had to get the presidents of the twenty-three BOCs and the Long Lines division to formally sign off on the agreement, the most challenging assignment of all. Although the BOCs' top executives reported to the twenty-sixth floor in New York, each was in full charge of his own company, with authority at least to denounce an AT&T corporate decision, if not unilaterally reject it. Since a unified front had always been the Bell System way, deButts and Lilley were committed to getting each individual company president to sign off on the document, enthusiastically or not.

The difficulty of this task surfaced after the final document had been distributed to all the BOC presidents. When phone messages started piling up on the desks of Easlick and Garlinghouse, from BOC presidents complaining that they resented government outsiders telling them how to run their businesses, the two called their negotiating team in Washington, suggesting the deal would have to be called off. Redick, Satterfield, and Davis, exhausted and understandably upset, went through their sales pitch one more time, emphasizing that this was the best deal that they believed they could ever get. After the New York executives considered the team's comments, Garlinghouse called back and told Redick, *I think we probably should proceed.*

At that moment, Easlick's team didn't know if its bosses had convinced the BOCs to acquiesce or if Garlinghouse had walked out on a very shaky limb on the team's behalf. It took little time for the answer to surface. Bill Brown had given Bob Lilley a final deadline of just a day or two later, and the company had already scheduled a corporate jet to fly the participants to an appropriate U.S. district court for the agreement's legal filing. On that last day in early January, Lee Satterfield made a desperate call to Bill Brown. *Bob Lilley is concerned,* he said. *All twenty-three Bell Operating Company presidents have called him in the last couple of days, raising hell about rolling over and playing dead for the EEOC,* according to Brown's memory. *Lilley wants to know if today's deadline is hard and fast. Can we move it by even one day?*

With an agreement in hand and his time limit almost up, Bill Brown knew what to do. *If the agreement isn't signed,* he responded, *I won't move the deadline by one hour.*

Satterfield, happy to play the dutiful messenger in this case, called Lilley right back. *Brown is adamant,* he said. *If you don't sign, it won't go forward,* which produced the result Brown, and Lilley, wanted. Lilley applied the necessary pressure to his BOC executives, and they all capitulated.

Still, this was not the final crisis. Late Wednesday night, January 17, 1973, with the joint press conference and court appearance confirmed for the next day, Jack Pemberton, one of the EEOC's negotiators, who had already bowed out as acting general counsel, walked out of discussions over the opinion letter AT&T was demanding to insulate the company from future discrimination lawsuits. Not about to let a last-minute emotional moment threaten the government's entire agreement, Kilberg found Pemberton quickly, calmed him down, and got his signature, meeting the agreement's very last requirement.

With a final settlement at last reached, Bill Brown was ready to claim the credit the EEOC deserved. David Copus had had the original idea and had worked the hardest to enact it, while Brown himself had provided the resources and political cover Copus had needed. At the eleventh hour, the

Department of Labor had stepped in to enable a settlement, but there would have been nothing to settle, no historic agreement, without the EEOC. Not that Kilberg begrudged the EEOC's demands. He understood the professional and personal investment both Brown and Copus had made in the case, he had realized his own goal of achieving a settlement sure to gain national headlines, and, mindful of the future relationship he and his OFCC colleagues would have with GSA, he didn't want to do "too much crowing" of his own.[15] Like the political operatives behind Robert Redford in the movie *The Candidate,* Kilberg was happy to make a big contribution and let someone else get the glory.

As a result, in a break with standard procedures, the EEOC's name came first on the list of plaintiffs on the case's official complaint filed in federal court, preceding both the Department of Labor and the "United States of America." In addition, the joint press conference scheduled for late on January 18 would be held at the EEOC and would prominently feature Bill Brown and his staff. Without Kilberg's knowledge, Brown managed to grab even more of the spotlight by releasing a statement about the case's resolution on EEOC letterhead on the morning of the eighteenth, prior to the joint conference later in the day. By getting a jump start on the news coverage, Brown was ensuring that his agency would get the recognition it had earned.

However, Brown himself wouldn't appear at the crucial event of that January Thursday. For the decree to hold the force of law, the official complaint had to be filed, and the consent decree approved, in a U.S. district court in which employee complaints against the company were being processed. Both parties had easily agreed on the U.S. Eastern District Court of Pennsylvania in Philadelphia, which was close by and presided over by Leon Higginbotham, a well-known and respected jurist whom Bell's outside counsel had recommended and with whom Brown had worked during his Philadelphia lawyer days. A bear-sized African American with a distinguished judicial record, Higginbotham offered the parties two essential qualities: credibility in the civil rights community and legal acuity. With his approval, the decree would carry an unquestioned moral authority.

In the early afternoon, a handful of government and Bell System lawyers boarded the AT&T corporate jet for the short flight from Washington, D.C., to Philadelphia. Although the idea of flying on the company's private plane sounded glamorous, Larry Gartner remembers feeling jammed into one of its eight or ten seats. "I didn't feel like I was a big CEO," he says today. "I felt like I was going to crash and die."[16] David Rose from the Justice Department's Civil Rights Division was a last-minute addition to the flight. Since AT&T was trying to get every government agency possible to sign off on the settlement to minimize its risk of future legal battles and the parties needed Justice Department participation to file a complaint in district court, Rose was a very late but essential participant. Although he had had barely enough time to review the agreement before he climbed aboard, he gave it his nod because it included "the kinds of things . . . [the Justice Department] had supported and had asked for [them]selves" in the past.[17]

When the group arrived an hour and a half later in Higginbotham's courtroom, the discussion must have felt anticlimactic. The representatives of the negotiating teams present were essentially bystanders in the proceedings— the EEOC's William Carey, the agency's new general counsel; the Labor Department's Carin Clauss, representing Kilberg, who would be in Washington, D.C., at the joint press conference; and AT&T's outside counsel, Kimber Vought of Pennsylvania, and Tom Powers. Moreover, despite Higginbotham's commanding reputation, there was no debate or incisive questioning, just a bit of whining from a local lawyer with a pending class action suit on an employment discrimination issue against Bell of Pennsylvania that he didn't want to disappear. Higginbotham, swamped with other cases, had had time only to speed-read the decree in the previous couple of days, and on that afternoon he allowed each party to speak but had few questions of his own. As he remembers, "some responsible people thought there could be an alternate dispute resolution where one would not spend endless time talking about who was wrong, where the greater culpability was," so he was happy to let that resolution stand.[18] He saved his own most substantive remarks for the end. "I commend Chairman William H. Brown III, and all of his associates and those other persons of the public sector as well as the parties in the private sector for any efforts which they have made here and will make elsewhere to see that the lofty dreams of equal opportunities for all become an immediate reality."[19] Just a little more than a half an hour after the parties had arrived in his courtroom, Higginbotham signed their paperwork and dismissed them. The settlement was final.

While these EEOC and AT&T lawyers were gaining Higginbotham's official stamp of approval, the joint government press briefing had started back at the EEOC's Washington office. Easlick, one of its scheduled stars, almost missed it. He didn't leave the AT&T office until 2:45 P.M., when the hundreds of copies of the decree he needed were finally ready, and his driver encountered a huge traffic jam, requiring him to drive on the curb to reach the EEOC by the 3 P.M. conference start time. Easlick joined Bill Brown and the Labor Department's leader, Dick Schubert, along with several of their underlings on the podium to announce the historic affirmative action agreement.

As planned, Brown and Copus played the primary roles, with Brown calling the settlement "a major step by the Bell System in improving its employment record with regards to women and minorities" and Copus suggesting its significance for companies beyond AT&T "who won't have any trouble reading between the lines" to figure out what the EEOC would be after from now on.[20] After brief speeches by Easlick, Schubert, and Kilberg, a photographer took a picture of the key parties, which has become the de facto record of the case. Easlick, Brown, and Schubert sit at a table, pen in hand, with Satterfield, Kilberg, and Karl Heckman from the Labor Department standing behind them. Many people involved with the case remember the picture differently though, certain that David Copus was in it. Today Copus doesn't remember how he missed being included. Perhaps he had slipped out of the room at just the wrong moment, or maybe he left purposely, not wanting to give his imprimatur to an agreement he hadn't been certain of. Yet it's appropriate that he's remembered in the photo. It wouldn't have been a case without him.

The final and binding consent decree contained eight primary sections: (1) a commitment to affirmative action and upgrade and transfer plans; (2) goals and timetables for hiring women and minorities for traditionally white male jobs and men for traditionally female jobs for each company job classification; (3) provisions to ensure that women and minorities had a fair chance to transfer into better jobs including the affirmative action override; (4) an employee information program in which managers would review the decree with all union members; (5) preemployment testing left in place; (6) the opportunity for any female college graduate hired into a management job since 1965 to attend a management assessment center that would evaluate her potential to join the fast track to Bell System top management; (7) a pay plan to ensure that newly promoted nonmanagement employees would start their new positions at appropriate pay; and (8) back pay for any female or minority employee promoted into a craft job between June 30, 1971, and July 1, 1974, and paid an inappropriately low rate. A separate provision addressed the plight of the female Michigan Bell switchroom helpers whose salary was brought up to the level of their counterparts, the framemen, in other Bell companies.

The decree also addressed (1) reporting: the Bell System would provide statistics on its progress toward its goals at least annually; (2) the effect of the decree: anyone who accepted its benefits could make no other claim against the company; (3) compliance procedures: the government would oversee AT&T's compliance; and (4) duration: six years. It also emphasized

the importance of the opinion letters signed by the EEOC and the Department of Labor's general counsels.

On paper, with its eight succinct requirements documented on its twenty-
six pages, the consent decree seemed a minimalist summary of the thousands of hours of labor of dozens of very smart young people as well as a
few older ones. It had met the requirements of the negotiators and their
bosses and prompted the EEOC to formally request a dismissal of the FCC
hearings the day before. As such, it stood as a document powerful enough
to finally resolve the entire case.

On January 18, 1973, the AT&T corporate jet flew back to Washington early
in the evening filled with a group of exhausted lawyers. Those who had
attended the press conference felt just as fatigued. With no plans for a government celebration, Brown and Kilberg remember just going home to get
some sleep. For its part, AT&T threw an impromptu celebration in the company suite at the Watergate Hotel, which would be occupied the next day
by John deButts and Bob Lilley, who were flying in to attend President
Nixon's second inauguration. Easlick led the festivities with his three "heroes"—Redick, Satterfield, and Davis—all making an appearance along with
a few other company employees. Congratulating one another and breathing
a sigh of relief, they drank champagne and miscellaneous other libations.
After a few revelers dug into the fruit arrangement left a day ahead of time
for the company's top executives, Easlick gleefully replaced the apples and
pears with a note: *Welcome to Washington, John and Bob.* With the help of
a terrific staff, Easlick had responded to the demands of his bosses and
achieved a reasonable agreement with the government. Now they could all
get back to what they did best—running the country's telephone company.

Copus himself can't remember what he did the night the consent decree
was signed. Honestly, it felt anticlimactic to him. The agreement AT&T was
celebrating had been reached weeks before, and Copus was already thinking about what came next for the EEOC—the commission had to address
the issues the negotiators had deferred, ensure that AT&T complied with the
decree's components, start pursuing the next large-scale alleged discrimina-
tor, and continue the ongoing battle against employment discrimination.
Perhaps he also had already realized that his idyllic experience in government had come to an end. As he says today, "The AT&T case spoiled me."[21]
He had been empowered by a daring and results-oriented boss to take a
good idea and run with it, devoid of the bureaucratic drag government often provides. And in the end, with a lot of help, he had achieved a significant

result. He didn't need to celebrate that night; he would celebrate his success for the rest of his life.

Employees of AT&T and the U.S. government had given, in some cases, more than two years of their lives to a single discrimination case, fighting to do what they thought was best for the female and minority employees of AT&T. They were proud of their efforts but didn't know yet what they had achieved. Some hoped the agreement would be quickly assimilated into Bell System policies and forgotten; others hoped it would be historic. In a sense, both would be satisfied. The Bell System quickly made the changes the consent decree demanded, changes that became simply part of the company's fabric. At the same time, the settlement the parties had agreed upon would prove historic, providing a catalyst for women to enter the 1970s workforce and changing Americans' perceptions of the roles men and women can fill. The participants' pride was more than justified.

13

The Benefit

By mid-1972, Peggy Falterman was sick of traveling. She still enjoyed the company car, nice hotels, and meals out that came with her South Central Bell clerk's job, but she now had a boyfriend back in New Orleans and wanted to be home. As a result, she found another clerical position stationed permanently in the city. She was never that stimulated by her new assignment—designating cable pairs for the guys who installed telephone equipment—but at least she was back in New Orleans, and within a few months, she used it as a stepping-stone to the job she had been longing for. Soon after she started her new clerk's position, a co-worker she commuted with told her that the frame job she had been anxious to try was suddenly open to women. Wanting both more satisfying work and a bigger paycheck, Falterman decided to find out if the frame supervisor might consider hiring her.

Since this was 1972, still a year before the BOCs would be forced to implement Dan Davis's upgrade and transfer plan, the Bell System's rules for promotion were loose at best. Although many Bell companies maintained a job posting and bidding system that rated seniority as the primary qualification for advancement, supervisors would often make their own, perhaps arbitrary, decisions as to who got what job, with the union's only recourse a grievance after the fact. This laxity worked in Falterman's favor that year when she jumped the queue ahead of several older women and became one of the first female framemen in Southern Bell. She was a beneficiary of the company's newly egalitarian employment policies, inspired by the EEOC's assault, even if her new supervisor hired her only after hearing she was young, tall, thin, and very nice. Bell System policies might be requiring the company's managers to hire women for jobs that demanded more brain-power, but appearance also was a factor.

Unfortunately, Falterman's new job didn't start well. On the first day, her boss assigned her to work side by side with a male Jehovah's Witness who fervently believed in God's supremacy and women's subservience, certain they shouldn't be filling "men's" jobs. For a year and half, he did his best to make Falterman's life miserable, alternating his daily lectures between evangelical Bible lessons and diatribes about women's proper place in society. One time, she got so upset she ran to the bathroom to cry, feeling, "I can't take this much longer if he's going to act like this." [1]

Not that all the men in the office mistreated her. The switchmen, whose job fixing switching equipment troubles put them at a higher level than Falterman on the craft scale, were very friendly. But since she wasn't threatening their jobs, their kindness came easier. Her supervisor even sympathized when she complained about her preaching colleague, telling her, *Don't worry about it. You're doing a fine job, just ignore him,* but he took no action. Falterman worked closely beside her difficult co-worker for a year and a half until, convinced Armageddon was imminent, he finally quit himself.

Before his departure, in the spring of 1973, with no forewarning that she remembers, Falterman received an official letter from South Central Bell announcing that she was a beneficiary of the consent decree AT&T had just approved. If she signed the attached form, relinquishing her right to sue the company for past or present employment discrimination, she would be eligible for a one-time payment of $300 and a raise to the standard male craft rate, nearly $200 a week. With no awareness of this impending settlement and little understanding of its significance, Falterman focused on the one thing she found important: the money. She would have quickly signed.

But before she could, another woman, recently promoted into a frame-man job and at least thirty years older than Falterman, called to ask her not to sign the form.

Why not? Falterman asked.

If you do, you're signing away your rights, she responded. *We could get a lot of back pay, more than this. A lot of us aren't going to sign it.*

Falterman agreed to consider the woman's request because she had some sympathy for her perspective. That woman had twenty-five years or more of Bell System service, as did several other women who had just been promoted into craft jobs. If the phone company was forced to compute back pay appropriately, to make up for all the years these older women had been denied higher paying jobs, the dollar figure on the face of their checks would be much, much higher. The total it would cost AT&T, across all the

BOCs, might even add up to the $175 million Copus and his EEOC colleagues had originally demanded to settle the case.

But Falterman, with only six and a half years of service, had little sense of solidarity for women she didn't know and had little in common with. She quickly returned to her first reaction. She could make up her own mind, she wanted the money, it was to her advantage, she was going to sign the form. And she did.

The check came within a couple of weeks—*oh, boy, extra money*—and she spent it immediately, although she can't remember on what. She doesn't even remember telling her family about what happened, since the lawsuit "was no big deal to me." Certainly she was happy to be earning the salary she had deserved since her first day as a frameman. And although she had no desire to become a first-level supervisor, seeing it as the worst job in the company because you "were trapped in the middle and had to deal with craft and with those above you telling you what to do," she was pleased with how her career was turning out.[2] She had always worked to better herself in each new job. The consent decree was giving her that chance.

In 1971, two years into her job as station assigner in NET's Roxbury central office, Gwen Thomas was also feeling pleased. She outright loved her work. Feeling challenged as she faced something new every day, she got excited just walking into the office each morning. She felt like she was in a race with herself to see how much she could produce well, how fast.

Although her bosses were thrilled with this strategy, it did nothing to improve Thomas's relationship with her union colleagues. Her mere promotion into the station assigner's job two years earlier, making her one of the company's first black female semiskilled craft workers, had angered them, and now, through all her hard work, done quickly, she was showing them up in the responsibilities they had held for far longer than she. Their reaction was "Slow down!"—which frustrated her, driving her to stick more and more pencils through the bun of hair piled on her head. But, as she says today, "I wasn't going to allow myself to be compromised—if they didn't like it, tough."[3] Management rewarded her attitude, loaning her to other offices and promoting her again in 1971, when AT&T was just beginning to feel the EEOC's influence, to a full craft position of estimate assigner.

These were not tranquil days in an inner-city Boston office. Martin Luther King Jr. had been assassinated only three years earlier, and although busing itself wouldn't rock the city's streets for another three years, the conflict that produced it was already simmering throughout Boston's neighborhoods. Despite the passage of the statewide Racial Imbalance Act in 1965, which prohibited de facto segregation in Massachusetts, Boston's schools were becoming more and more racially segregated. In 1971, accusing the city school board of encouraging racial isolation, the state board of education froze $200 million in school construction projects and withheld $14 million of state aid to Boston while, concurrently, local parents teamed up with the NAACP to file a lawsuit demanding that the city provide access to quality schools for all African American children. Everyone was mad: blacks because their kids were getting a lousy education, whites because their own children might soon have to be bused across town to those same lousy schools.

Thomas understood the issue firsthand. As her Roxbury neighborhood migrated from a multiracial mix into an almost all-black community in the early 1960s, she had watched her own junior high deteriorate from a fun place to learn into a school where teachers, both white and black, kept liquor bottles in their desk drawers and allowed disruptive students to take over their classrooms. Her mother had been so distressed with the environment, she'd achieved a feat thought impossible—she implemented her own personal busing plan and got Thomas transferred to lily-white Dorchester High a few miles away. But she couldn't save Thomas or her other kids from the poisonous cloud the desegregation issue had put in the city's air. While previously Thomas had feared being called a "nigger" when traveling into downtown Boston to shop at Filene's Basement, now she worried someone might beat her up. As she describes today, "A line had been drawn. Never before had I felt I don't belong, now they had made me feel separate and different."[4]

Since it was impossible to leave this racial turmoil outside Thomas's office at NET, she herself was careful to do "nothing to promote the conflict" with her white peers in her job every day.[5] She came in, said *Good morning,* did her job, and tried to ignore the raised voices or curt words she sometimes heard when she asked a white male peer a simple question. But sometimes the tension did explode. On "an awful day in the history of our office," a black woman and colleague of Thomas's slapped one of their older white colleagues across the face, finally sick of being called *You Spade,* even if everyone knew it was meant as a joke. And it was hard not to resent the white supervisors who staged their own muggings, leaving the office with an exposed twenty-dollar bill in a pocket and returning with a ripped shirt, a claim of no money, and a demand to be transferred out of the Roxbury central office, which was invariably granted.

The treatment Thomas and her African American peers faced in that central office was certainly racist and probably sexist, too. But Thomas, for the most part, let it go, primarily because she knew she and the other blacks working there had their own power. With all the racial unrest swirling around their world outside the office walls, "there was a lot of concern on the part of white folks because they weren't sure what the black folks would do," as Thomas points out today. The two groups were locked into their opposing seesaw seats, maintaining an uneasy equilibrium.

When Thomas received a letter from the union in the spring of 1973, she was concerned that the request it made could upset that delicate balance. The letter explained the consent decree AT&T had recently signed with the federal government and asked Thomas to document how her work responsibilities as an estimate assigner, the skilled craft job she had now held for two years, overlapped or differed from those of her white male peers. Although the request probably originated within the local union, with any response to be seen only by the office's union steward, it still made her uncomfortable. She knew she could easily justify the content and quality of her work, but, in an office that had struggled to achieve its wobbly truce, she was loath to squeal on her less energetic colleagues.

Yet when she heard those same co-workers grousing about the impending payments for women and minorities, her attitude changed. The men claimed their jobs were harder, that women hadn't endured worse treatment, statements Thomas knew were false. As a result, she buckled down and completed the union paperwork plus the forms the company had sent. Within a few weeks, she received a 40 percent raise and her lump-sum back-pay check, which she proudly announced to her family. She remembers looking at her passbook and smiling when she saw the large total after the dollar sign on its bottom line.

Despite her pride, at first she felt guilty about her windfall. After all, she was still quite young, unmarried, and without children, while her male peers were older and had families to support. As she says today, "You walk around a little uneasy, almost that battered-wife kind of syndrome." But after a week or two, as she again observed her colleagues' casual approach to their work, that feeling disappeared. She realized she was "being rewarded for the good job I was doing." The consent decree had finally allowed her hard work to be recognized for what it was truly worth.

By 1979, Margaret Hoppe had been rewarded, more than once, for her good work at Seton Hall University. After spending three years running the women's residence hall as assistant dean of students, she was promoted to assistant to the vice president of student affairs and then, three years later, in 1977, into the vice president's job itself. A casual observer might have assumed she would have a challenging career at Seton Hall for years to come. She had developed a reputation for hard work and creative thinking as the only woman and youngest on the university's executive team. At the time, the school was facing an identity crisis: with enrollment down and its notoriety for enrolling immigrants and winning basketball games in its past, its leadership needed to find something new to attract students, a project seemingly tailor-made for Hoppe's skills. But Seton Hall's leadership wasn't quite moving at her speed. One evening in the fall of 1979, a member of the college's board of trustees took her to dinner and suggested she might want to move her talents elsewhere, to the corporate world. *You have very creative business ideas,* he said gently, *but Seton Hall isn't ready for this. You'll get frustrated and before you know it, you'll have eaten up a lot of your career here.*

Hoppe's reaction probably wasn't what he expected. Instead of being upset, she welcomed the suggestion. "I could see that a long career in the public sector, especially not being an academician, might be frustrating on a lot of levels," she recalls today.[6] In addition, she had recently been feeling bored with her night classes in the combined M.B.A. and Doctorate in Education program she was attending. She wasn't learning anything new and was beginning to find the business courses far more compelling than those in education, her supposed career field. Open minded, ambitious, and fully aware that the Seton Hall board members represented some of New Jersey's largest companies and therefore could open corporate America's doors for her, Hoppe started to interview for a corporate job. She also turned to her husband, the college sweetheart she had married in 1973, who was a marketing manager at AT&T Long Lines. He recommended the company's management training program, called MDP, which was open to individuals, particularly women, with advanced degrees and work experience.

Since 1973, when AT&T signed the consent decree, its executives had been steadily working to achieve the required goals for hiring women and minorities at each company location into specific job classifications, including the first three levels of management. The numbers would be met both by promoting existing employees and by hiring women and minorities into each Bell company's training program and assigning them second-level management jobs—the next step up from the supervisory level Peggy Falterman was avoiding. In the first few years of the decree, management recruiters looked for candidates straight from college, preferably with an engineering degree. The company's motivation was simple: by hiring college graduates with no other work experience, salaries could be kept low and Bell System managers could mold their future leaders into the image they chose. At the same time, achieving a technical degree suggested efficient thinking and the capacity to manage an engineering-driven business like the phone company.

But in the waning years of the six-year consent decree, the company was trying something new. The 1968 Carterphone decision, which allowed other equipment to be attached to AT&T's network, and the 1970 formation of MCI were slowly putting competitive pressures on the monolithic AT&T, an influence felt in the company's personnel department by the mid-1970s. As a result, the search for MDP candidates shifted from engineering undergrads to experienced managers with advanced degrees, preferably from top business schools, who could immediately make a measurable contribution to the company's operation.

Hoppe was a solid candidate under the Bell System's new approach— she held a master's degree, eight years of impressive work experience, and status as a woman. Plus, she fit the company mold with her emphasis on results and her conservative dress, including a navy blue suit, red ribbon tie, and sensible pumps. As a result, she moved quickly through AT&T's recruiting process after sending in her résumé in early November 1979. With her interviews complete in just a couple of weeks, the company offered her a job in early December and asked her to start by the middle of the month, which she promptly told them was impossible. *I have a senior management position at Seton Hall,* she said. *I have to give at least a month's notice. The earliest I can start is January.*

When the AT&T recruiter wouldn't relent, Hoppe started to worry "there was some issue with the work [in the new job] that had to be done," but that assumption would have been wrong.[7] The company needed her on the payroll by the end of 1979 solely for affirmative action purposes. The original six-year consent decree between AT&T and the U.S. government would expire in just a few weeks, and the recruiter wanted to make sure Hoppe counted as one of its very last beneficiaries. Since Hoppe stood by her responsibility to her present employer, the recruiter finally devised a simple, if slightly disingenuous, solution. He assigned her "Bell System net credited service date" as December 26, 1979, and she actually started work in the middle of January 1980, allowing her to keep her commitment to Seton Hall and giving the company credit for another white female second-level manager on its consent decree compliance form for 1979.

Although Hoppe was thrilled to have made the transition from higher education to corporate America, she was disappointed with her first corporate assignment. Of all the places the MDP recruiter could have sent her—from the Sales Department to supervise account executives or Operations (equivalent to Plant in the BOCs) to oversee craft workers or anywhere else within Long Lines—he had placed her in the Personnel Department with responsibility for recruiting candidates, just like her, for MDP. Hoppe knew she wouldn't be there that long, since an employee on the MDP fast track typically stayed in her job for only a year or two as she headed for third-level management within four to six years. But even so, Hoppe felt she had been shoehorned, from the start, into "a woman's job" that was outside the mainstream of the business. Even in the public sector world of Seton Hall, she had figured out she needed to be part of any organization's moneymaking apparatus, whether a professor in a university or an operations or sales manager in a corporation, to advance.

But the recruiter was adamant, and despite Hoppe's initial misgivings, she came to appreciate his insistence. With Hoppe's management experience at Seton Hall and her knowledge of college recruiting, she "was able to contribute right away" to AT&T's bottom line. She immediately started developing a recruiting program at the top five M.B.A. programs in the United States, which was easy for her because she knew the ins and outs of the college recruiting business from the college's side and essential to the company because of its increasing need to be competitive in the telecommunications marketplace. And she benefited, too, building her own confidence. The consent decree had finally ignited the high-powered career she'd spent her life preparing for.

14

The Impact

Once AT&T and the U.S. government signed the consent decree on January 18, 1973, a series of celebrations, speeches, and written accounts naturally followed. AT&T had a bigger entertainment budget: Dave Easlick took his three star negotiators and their wives out for dinner at New York City's Waldorf-Astoria, Don Liebers threw a party at Windows on the World for the FCC hearings team, and AT&T's chairman, John deButts, hosted a luncheon in honor of his employees' hard work. The EEOC's party, where Copus received an Academy Award for his amazing achievement, took place in an EEOC friend's Washington, D.C. home. On the more substantive side, Bill Brown initiated a series of speeches that promoted the agreement's contents and importance, and Dan Davis's and Bill Kilberg's comments appeared, respectively, in the *Daily Labor Report* and *Equal Employment* magazine. In addition, the *New York Times Magazine, Fortune,* and *Ms.* all featured stories about the case soon after the decree was signed. No one could begrudge the parties for wallowing a bit in their joint accomplishment.

In the meantime, however, there was still work to be done. AT&T was the busiest—computing and awarding back-pay checks to the 13,000 female and 2,000 minority male beneficiaries; reviewing the specifics of the agreement with every employee; figuring out the intermediate targets for women in traditionally male jobs, men in traditionally female jobs, and minorities in traditionally white jobs for each Bell location; and, most important, aggressively promoting and hiring women and minorities to meet those goals on the correct timetable.

The federal government participants, on the other hand, should have had little left to do, since their remaining job, to monitor AT&T's compliance with the decree, wouldn't even start for several months. But other issues dragged them back into the case's action. First, the unions, recognizing the impact of the decree, were angry and had to be appeased. The IBEW, which had achieved nothing substantive in its negotiations with Bill Kilberg, had now joined the CWA in demanding that the decree be overturned, a request Judge Leon Higginbotham never granted during the following several months of debate. Still, the intervention of the two unions meant that the EEOC lawyers and AT&T personnel executives had to invest hours of time writing affidavits to defend their work. In addition, lawyers from both the government and the company, many of whom had worked on the original decree, negotiated a second consent decree to address the issue of inequality between AT&T's female and male management salaries; the opposing parties signed this new agreement on May 30, 1974.

Bill Brown was happy to have escaped from the AT&T case with a significant settlement for the company's aggrieved female and minority employees and the credit for achieving it, so happy that he decided to try to replicate his success. In the spring of 1973, he formed a new group within the EEOC called the National Programs Division, modeled on the Copus-led AT&T Task Force, which he empowered to go after major companies for their widespread discrimination. Frustrated by the EEOC's historical "bottoms-up" approach, whereby individual complaints of discrimination were investigated one at a time by the agency's field investigators, Brown was implementing a "top-down" strategy whereby an EEOC commissioner's charge of nationwide discrimination would be issued and investigated against companies as a whole. He assigned Copus to lead the division; named a half dozen lawyers and a couple of dozen investigators to support him; chose General Electric, General Motors, Sears, Ford, and three automobile and electrical workers' unions to be the first targets; and set the team to work.

Those first four targeted corporations, not to mention the 496 other Fortune 500 firms, weren't just waiting for the EEOC to come after them. Top executives read the newspapers and socialized with Bob Lilley and Dave Easlick and their colleagues throughout the Bell System. Each understood that his company could be the government's next prey. Some corporate managers reacted in anger, like the Sears executives who nearly heckled Dave Easlick out of one of their meetings, but others used a more proactive strategy. Several approached Bill Brown with one simple question: "What can we do to avoid that kind of thing?"[1] At least one, a General Motors executive, turned to AT&T for help, requesting a copy of the consent decree from Clark Redick. Many also consulted professional experts who had recently opened firms specializing in equal employment opportunity as they prepared for a potential EEOC or Justice Department assault. They got advice on where to find female and minority candidates and how to enhance the skills of those already on staff, two efforts to help them avoid lawsuits. If those endeavors failed, they then welcomed assistance in defending themselves against the charges filed against them and negotiating fair settlements.

This heightened corporate awareness, courtesy of the AT&T settlement, combined with the strength of America's civil rights laws and the EEOC's year-old power to take companies to court, produced real results. In the four years following AT&T's 1973 consent decree, nearly a dozen suits were settled between the federal government and some of the country's highest-profile companies, including Delta Air Lines, Merrill Lynch, Prudential Insurance, and NBC, with the agreements guaranteeing women and minorities millions of dollars in back pay and thousands of jobs newly available to them. In arguably the most significant settlement modeled on the AT&T agreement, the EEOC and the departments of Labor and Justice settled a nearly $31 million discrimination case against the country's eight largest steel companies and largest steelworkers' union in the spring of 1974. Directly echoing the phone company's agreement, forty thousand employees would receive back pay, and goals and timetables would be established for hiring women and minorities into craft and supervisory jobs.

Because AT&T's workforce was more than half female and the beneficiaries of its settlement were almost 90 percent women, the consent decree served particularly to highlight the plight of women in corporate America and remind American companies that the country's civil rights laws weren't reserved solely for black men. As a result, high-profile suits benefiting women only followed, including the 1977 *New York Times* settlement, whose plaintiffs included Eileen Shanahan, the reporter on the AT&T case, and which benefited the paper's 550 female employees; the $2 million NBC agreement the same year that was shared by nearly 3,000 women; and the 1979 $1.375 million settlement by Bechtel, the nation's largest construction company, which resolved two class action lawsuits.

At the same time, success at advancing women became a statistic important unto itself. Since the passage of the 1964 Civil Rights Act, many companies' annual reports featured a detailed description of their minority employment, with companies like Philip Morris, McDonnell Douglas, and General Motors reporting on their efforts to hire more blacks, establish additional franchises under black ownership, and purchase more services from black-owned companies. But by the mid-1970s, more companies, including Sears, Hewlett Packard, and Polaroid, began to report on their success at hiring women into high-level and technical jobs, too. Companies also began to change their documentation of new members of their board of directors, now proudly announcing women who had joined along with the African Americans they had trumpeted in the past.

The EEOC's large-scale efforts to aid female and minority workers, through Bill Brown's National Programs Division, met significant success in three of its four corporate cases. GE settled with the government in 1979 for $29.4 million, Ford in 1980 for $23 million, and GM, along with the United Auto Workers union, in 1984 for $42.4 million. Unfortunately, the agency never achieved equivalent success with Sears. The parties couldn't reach an agreement themselves, and the trial and appeals courts reviewing the case rejected the EEOC's claim that Sears discriminated against its female workers, citing the agency's unimpressive statistical evidence and witness testimony. Long before that failure, however, the National Programs Division had declined in importance within the EEOC. When Eleanor Holmes Norton became EEOC chair in 1977, she emphasized reducing the backlog of individual cases, now totaling 100,000 or more, instead of pursuing major corporate discriminators. David Copus, who ran the National Programs Division until he left the EEOC in 1977, also attributes the division's decline to a power shift from the EEOC to the companies it was chasing. Corporate executives, armed with the awareness the AT&T case had provided, had now prepared themselves to fight discrimination charges, and the EEOC couldn't afford the required high-level resources, equivalent to what Brown had assigned to the AT&T case, to battle multiple companies simultaneously. The gangbusters strategy just wouldn't work any more.

By the end of 1973, Bill Brown himself had left the EEOC. Despite his significant success in achieving fairness in the workplace for women and minorities, President Nixon chose not to reappoint him. Press reports at the time suggested that Nixon had made that decision because Brown had subverted the original expectation, borne of his status as a low-profile black Republican, that he was "coming in to keep the lid on."[2] He had instead proved extremely effective in his job, particularly with the AT&T case, an outcome that made his reappointment unattractive to the conservative Nixon administration, according to the *Washington Post*'s Jack Anderson and several other reporters. Today Brown minimizes this suggestion and strongly disagrees with the rumors that AT&T executives lobbied for his ouster. Other knowledgeable observers within the EEOC and beyond remember little political pressure from Pennsylvania Avenue during Brown's tenure and therefore question that explanation for Brown's early departure. In any case, the reason Brown left isn't particularly important. By early 1974, John Powell, an African American lawyer with experience in corporate law and Republican politics, had moved into the EEOC chair's office, and Bill Brown had headed back to Philadelphia. Brown's activist reign at the EEOC was over.

Today AT&T is virtually a shadow of its former self. With technology advancements driving a competitive telecommunications industry outside the Bell System, on January 1, 1984, the U.S. government forced AT&T to spin off its local telephone exchange services into seven units known as the regional Bell operating companies. Over the past twenty years, these seven "Baby Bells" reorganized into just four, still massive, corporations—Verizon, BellSouth, Qwest, and SBC—that offer local, long-distance, and equipment services, making them similar in many respects to their former parent.

That parent company, AT&T, has undergone a much more radical transformation. Western Electric, its subsidiary that manufactured telephone equipment, was spun off into two stand-alone entities—Lucent, which makes equipment for phone companies, and Avaya, which produces phone systems for private businesses—while the AT&T name remains associated with long distance. The company has also expanded into cable television, Internet access, and cellular phone technology. Today it employs only about 75,000 employees and counting down, compared with the three-quarters of a million it had in the consent decree era.

Despite the Bell System's mutated structure, the decree's impact can still be seen in the remains of the companies whose executives approved it three decades ago. Symbolically at least, the woman sitting in the president's seat at AT&T today, Betsy Bernard, proves the decree's importance. AT&T Long Lines hired Bernard in 1977 as one of the "white women" who filled its consent decree–driven goal for second-level managers that year, and twenty-five years later, with a brief hiatus from Ma Bell to work for another telecommunications firm, she ascended to take the seat Bob Lilley once held.

Demonstrating the decree's influence through employment statistics is a bit more challenging, since the company's structure today looks so different than it did thirty years ago. With former Bell companies having been reconfigured several times, a direct comparison between statistics from 1970 and those of today is impossible. However, because more than three-quarters of the employees reflected in the EEOC's annual employment summary of the telephone communications industry work for AT&T and its former components, using these figures we can do a relevant analysis. First, the good news: women have made tremendous progress in semiskilled craft jobs, filling 49.2 percent of them in 2001 versus less than 2 percent in 1970, and some progress in skilled craft jobs, filling 16.1 percent now versus just over 1 percent thirty years ago.[3] For men, the changes have been substantial, if less dramatic—men held 23.7 percent of office and clerical positions in 2001, up from the minuscule 3.1 percent they filled in 1970 but still far less than half. (Disappointingly, telephone operators, now nearly an extinct position, are lumped in with clerical jobs, so we can't empirically evaluate the movement men have made into those positions or the steps women have taken out of them.)

Over these three decades, women's strides can also be seen in professional jobs, management-level staff positions typically requiring a college education, where women once held 20.5 percent but in 2001 held more than 40 percent, and professional sales positions, where women have increased from 26.2 percent to just over 50 percent. Unfortunately, women's success in management can't be fully evaluated through these figures because the levels of management aren't delineated in EEO-1 reports. The percentage of women in all management jobs remains the same in 2001 as it was thirty years ago, still approximately 41 percent, which seems discouraging. However, statistics from 1982 tell us that the number of women at the third level of management and above quintupled by the decree's expiration in 1979.[4] In addition, because of the success of Betsy Bernard and many other females in executive jobs within the former Bell companies, we know women are no longer pinned down into the bottom two levels of management like they were in 1970. Based on all this data and what we have observed, in what remains of Ma Bell, the consent decree has produced real change for its female, and male, employees.

Many of the women who directly benefited from this change—those who got a back-pay check and promotion to craft—are now near the end of their careers or have already retired. Peggy Falterman (now Plakotos) is still employed by the phone company—BellSouth today—with thirty-six years of service and retirement on the not-too-distant horizon. She now works on a computer as a "switchman," monitoring BellSouth's circuits, a step up from her old frameman position, which is now obsolete. In her more than twenty years in the switchman's job, her responsibilities have changed as technology has advanced, and she is now earning an annual salary of approximately fifty thousand dollars, an amount she had perhaps never dreamed of but today believes is fair. She hasn't encouraged her only child, a daughter on the brink of college graduation, to emulate her corporate career, however. Instead she tells her to follow her dream of working with kids because work "has got to make you happy every day [even if it] may not pay the most."[5] Although the Bell System never gave Falterman the drawing or architecture career she had imagined, she is happy with her career there. The consent decree righted a wrong she was facing, allowing her to take a "man's" job and earn more money. As a result, she was able to fulfill both of her lifelong goals—she has traveled throughout the United States and to Europe, and, as her craft job has changed based on each new technology, she has improved her skills and bettered herself.

Gwen Thomas (now Hickman) is also still earning a salary from the company that was once NET—Verizon—although she took an extremely short lived retirement in 1996. After an initial reticence to move into supervisory jobs, she rose to second-level management by 1980, running a repair service bureau of sixty technical employees who served two million customers and later working directly with a vice president setting corporate policy. When offered an attractive early retirement package in 1996, she signed the paperwork fifteen minutes before the deadline. Though she still loved her work and its related salary and benefits, her corporate mentors had already left the company, and she wasn't sure if another equivalent package would be available any time soon. Therefore, she made the difficult decision to take this one. She was gone only the month she needed to enjoy her son's college graduation, however, returning on a contract basis as a first-level supervisor and becoming full-time again in 2000 once she had confirmed that her original pension wouldn't be jeopardized. For Thomas, the consent decree opened up access to higher-level, more challenging jobs and guaranteed her equal pay, benefits she still takes advantage of today. She finds her present project management work serving Verizon's largest customers fulfilling, and the equal and higher pay she earns now allows her to indulge her taste for Coach bags, new cars, and trips to Paris. She knows her late mother, always her biggest booster, would have been ecstatic about what she has achieved in her career, which is the very highest praise.

Of those hired into management because of the consent decree's goals, a few, like Betsy Bernard, climbed to the executive levels of one of the former Bell companies, many settled into AT&T careers after reaching responsible jobs in middle management, and still others, like Margaret Hoppe (now Barrett), used their Bell System experience as a launching pad to other companies' corporate ladders. Hoppe achieved fifth-level management in AT&T Long Lines but left in 1995 when GE Capital recruited her to establish its new Consumer Direct division. At the time, Hoppe's motivation was less a desire to leave AT&T and more the excitement of moving to GE Capital, a company that was decisive and took risks. Later she took top jobs at the Bank of Montreal and in a joint venture between Merrill Lynch and HSBC Bank in London, achieving an annual salary and bonus package of more than a million dollars in her most recent position. Today, as an admittedly regulatory-phobic person, she reflects back positively on the consent decree. Because of AT&T's commitment to that agreement, Hoppe, a woman with only public sector experience, got an opportunity to enter "the private sector in an industry that was just getting exciting."[6] At the same time, her ensuing career offers an excellent example of what women can accomplish once they are given the chance they have always deserved.

Beyond AT&T, women have also made tremendous progress in the American workplace over the past thirty years. Women filled 49.8 percent of management and professional jobs in the United States in 2000, compared with 40.2 percent in 1970, and 20.4 percent of engineering and technician positions now, versus only 11 percent back then. In addition, over these three decades, they have gone from representing 92 percent to 79 percent of the clerical workforce.[7] Women have also made financial gains. American women workers' average salary has increased nearly tenfold over these three decades,[8] at the same time that median house prices, as a proxy for the cost of living growth, increased just six times.[9] Although none of these statistics prove that American working women have achieved equality with their male counterparts, they do show what has been accomplished in thirty years. Filling more jobs and making more money, women have become an integral part of the American workforce in good-paying jobs, a territory historically reserved for men.

Of course, many factors produced these improved statistics, not solely the U.S. government/AT&T consent decree. One of the twentieth century's deepest recessions began soon after the consent decree was signed, driving many women into the workplace alongside their husbands, simply to earn adequate income to feed their children. In addition, the women's movement was exploding in America in that time period. From the late 1960s through the mid-1970s, mainstream women, the soccer moms of that day, joined consciousness-raising groups to discuss their frustrations and become empowered. In addition, a group of feminists founded *Ms.* magazine in 1971, Congress passed the Equal Rights Amendment in 1972, and the first woman governor unattached to a late husband's coattails was elected in 1975. Women were coming to see themselves as capable individuals, a fact the average American accepted. As a result, women looked for jobs, and companies hired them.

Just as the EEOC's effort made only some of the difference for America's working women, its lawyers were only partially correct about those women's ambitions. AT&T's experts had been right that not all women were anxious to claim the highest-paying craft or supervisory job they could find. The company was able to meet its goals for male telephone operators more easily than for female craft workers, having particular difficulties filling the outside plant positions it had so aggressively advertised to the opposite sex. Even two of the Bellwomen beneficiaries profiled in this book initially resisted promotions beyond the craft assignments they first took. Peggy Falterman never changed her mind, staying in an inside craft job for her entire career.

AT&T's experts may have been right on the facts; however, they were wrong on the reasons. As Gwen Thomas exhibited when she overcame her aversion to promotion and achieved a successful management career, a woman's disinterest in advancing typically relates more to her upbringing than her innate beliefs. Thomas, as a black female, had been raised to believe she could become a successful telephone operator or clerk, not a line manager with more than fifty employees, a job she eventually handled well. Likewise, as Margaret Hoppe prepared to start college in the late 1960s, she imagined she could become a nurse or teacher when she graduated but not a vet, and certainly not the corporate executive she became. The women who came to work at AT&T had been socialized—by their parents, teachers, ministers, and bosses—to see themselves in certain roles, a contributing factor to the company's sex-segregated and unequally compensated workforce.

This issue of sex segregation in jobs extended far beyond AT&T. A late 1960s/early 1970s study by sociologists William Bielby and James Baron reveals the tremendous numbers of sex-segregated jobs in 290 California workplaces. In that era, more than 75 percent of all occupations studied and more than 95 percent of all job titles were limited to one gender.[10] The study doesn't analyze whether socialization, corporate intent, or both produced these divisions, although understanding their genesis may be less important than simply eliminating them. By forcing one of America's most well respected companies, AT&T, to hire women for jobs men traditionally held and vice versa, the consent decree produced a new set of role models for American workers and, in so doing, helped create a more just workplace.

When the individuals who implemented the AT&T case are asked about its impact, most emphasize this same point. They talk little about the increased numbers of women and minorities in good jobs today. Instead they focus on the consent decree's success in upending the institutional discrimination the company had perpetrated and its influence on American culture. David Copus remembers that when a top ten list of significant changes was prepared for American POWs returning from North Vietnam in the mid-

1970s, male telephone operators made the cut. And Bill Brown reflects to-day that "we came out of [the agreement] changing the whole structure, not only of AT&T. We really changed it for most corporations."[11] Women could now become telephone installers, assembly-line foremen, and top executives; men could become operators, secretaries, and nurses. The agreement signed that January Thursday ensured that American girls and boys would have nearly any job to choose from when they started their careers.

When we glance at the historic timeline of the United States during the first few weeks of 1973, we are jolted back into the momentous events we endured. On January 22, the Supreme Court decided *Roe v. Wade*, which guaranteed every American woman the right to abortion. Five days later, President Nixon announced a cease-fire with North Vietnam, and on February 7, the Senate established the Select Committee on Presidential Campaign Activities to investigate the Watergate break-in. Though the signing of an affirmative action agreement lacked the drama of abortion, war, and presidential scandal, it too signaled a momentous change in our country's history. On January 18, 1973, AT&T and the U.S. government signed a consent decree that opened the doors of the corporate workplace to minorities and particularly women, altering our view of men's and women's capabilities. The world of work would never be the same.

Epilogue

Today, the case's key Bell System participants no longer work for AT&T or the four redesigned companies once under Ma Bell's umbrella. John Kingsbury and Hal Levy both died while still employed at the company, and all the others retired by the early 1990s. In their post–Bell System lives, Clark Redick, Don Liebers, and Lee Satterfield each pursued other professional ventures in business and law, and George Ashley taught at his alma mater, the University of Missouri Law School at Columbia; Dan Davis puts his free time into volunteer work, and Dave Easlick spends his on the golf course.

For some, the AT&T settlement proved a career booster. Easlick became the president of Michigan Bell soon after the case was settled, finally escaping his two-hour rural New Jersey–to–Manhattan commute, while George Ashley moved first to become general counsel of New York Telephone and then back to AT&T as the associate general counsel for the entire company. Others, however, felt their careers stunted. Neither Dan Davis nor Don Liebers received another promotion during their nearly twenty additional years of AT&T employment. Despite frequent accolades for the job they had accomplished, they had been out of the mainstream of the business, focused on an issue distasteful to many company managers. Alvin von Auw, Davis's mentor and an AT&T executive vice president, once told him he'd "never known anyone to get promoted by going down to Washington."[1] The company executives had wanted the job done but then didn't want to think about it again.

On the other hand, the government lawyers are all still working, having taken one of two paths after the case, divided, in a somewhat ironic twist, by gender. All the leading male lawyers—David Copus, Bill Brown, Larry Gartner, and Bill Kilberg—left their government jobs by 1977 to practice in private firms, specializing in employment law, just on the other side of the fence. None of these men, who work in law offices from Washington, D.C., to Los Angeles and earn several hundred dollars an hour, sees his switch as a betrayal of the fight for civil rights within the government. Bill Brown has kept his finger in public service by chairing the MOVE Commission, which investigated the disastrous 1985 police bombing of a residential Philadelphia neighborhood, and serving on the board of the NAACP Legal Defense Fund. In any case, as Copus says today, his clients "are definitely good guys [who] invariably want to do the right thing." [2] In the twenty-first century, with employment discrimination laws well known and society more accepting of female and black professionals, the government lawyers who forced AT&T to capitulate now help its peers fight the legitimate equal employment battles they face and settle the others as quickly and fairly as possible.

Even Randy Speck and Bill Wallace, the nonlawyers in the government crowd, couldn't buck the legal trend. Driven by the intellectual challenge of learning something new and the desire to overcome their frustration at being bystanders without legal degrees during the case, they both graduated from law school by 1977. Today Speck also practices in a private firm, while Wallace, true to his bohemian roots, eventually retired to the Seattle area as a stay-at-home dad.

The government's women took the other path, to teaching careers. Judy Potter, who left the EEOC before the case had been settled for a job at the University of Maine Law School in Portland, still teaches there and also ran their Legal Aid Clinic for sixteen years. Susan Ross joined the Georgetown University Law School faculty in 1983 after several years in an all-female law firm she started with friends. She teaches employment and sex discrimination law, heads the school's International Women's Human Rights Clinic, and was one of Anita Hill's legal advisers during the 1991 Clarence Thomas hearings. After succeeding Bill Kilberg as solicitor of labor for four years, Carin Clauss took a job teaching at the University of Wisconsin Law School at Madison. She has negotiated labor standards for the NAFTA agreement and volunteered locally on health care, ACLU, and school workers projects. Today Potter attributes the women's drift away from high-paying, high-powered corporate legal jobs to the sexism that still reigned twenty years ago despite the AT&T case and others like it. Perhaps more important, the content of their work seems more important to the women. Ross has committed her career to fighting for women's rights, and Potter says maintaining a civil rights focus has always been personally important to her: "It wasn't just a cause for us."[3]

Affirmative action itself has had a history far beyond this case. Although its programs have achieved many successes over the past thirty years, today it is mired in controversy. In the late 1990s, both California and Washington outlawed the use of affirmative action in public hiring or school admissions decisions, while the most recent related Supreme Court ruling, on June 23, 2003, agreed that the University of Michigan could take race into account in admitting students only on an individual case basis, not in a "mechanical way."

If that had been the law in 1973, the fate of the AT&T/U.S. government consent decree might have been much more tenuous. Although the recent University of Michigan ruling directly addressed only institutions of higher education, the decision exhibited the Supreme Court's distaste for mechanical strategies to advance disadvantaged groups. As a result, Dan Davis's affirmative action override, the clever consent decree technique used to ensure that AT&T had enough qualified women and minorities to fill targeted jobs, would seem a risky approach at best.

Today affirmative action generates more questions than solutions. Do we use it to remedy wrongs done to certain groups in our population or to promote diversity to prepare young Americans for our increasingly multicultural society? Or, put another way, are we trying to ensure nondiscrimination, as the Labor Department's Revised Order #4 requires, or to increase minority and female education and employment via preferential treatment? The program's appropriateness seems less clear in the twenty-first century, but we should be grateful for its use thirty years ago. By basing a legal action on the preferential treatment affirmative action allowed, the EEOC drove one company to change, and American roles in the workplace followed suit. We are a better country for it.

The importance of this project to the individual men and women who made it happen is unmistakable. Randy Speck calls it "the most significant thing I ever worked on," David Copus exclaims it "was the thrill of my life," and Don Liebers has stated his pride in his role because "[I always wanted] to do something that went on after I left the job."[4] In settling this case, all the participants have left a permanent mark on corporate America.

Acknowledgments

From the moment she received an unpolished book proposal about the landmark 1973 AT&T sex discrimination case many years ago, Emilie Jacobson believed in the project and helped steward it through the mercurial publishing world. Gail Pool was continuously enthusiastic about the idea, even after seeing endless drafts of the book's early chapters as she took on the challenge of teaching me how to write. Gwen Baker gave me time away from my job at the YWCA of the U.S.A. to pursue the required research and supported my efforts throughout. Marlie Wasserman of Rutgers University Press expressed exuberance when she first read the book proposal. The faith of these four women in a project some saw as esoteric sustained my own.

Many people helped me produce *The Bellwomen*, although I take full responsibility for any errors in the text. I constructed the narrative largely from interviews, and dozens of people obliged my requests. I am particularly grateful to Bill Brown, Dan Davis, Larry Gartner, Bill Kilberg, Don Liebers, Judy Potter, Clark Redick, and Randy Speck, who gave hours of their time to educate me about this case in all its dimensions. Special thanks go to David Copus, without whom this book wouldn't exist and whose infectious enthusiasm inspired me as I researched and wrote it, just as it inspired his EEOC Task Force thirty years ago. In addition, I am appreciative of the willingness of Peggy Plakotos, Gwen Hickman, and Margaret Barrett to tell their stories about how the consent decree affected their lives.

Research was also a huge part of this endeavor. Thanks to Alyssa Gagnon and Amy Robidas, who spent hours in the University of Southern Maine library digging up dozens of newspaper articles and needed facts that inform the manuscript. I myself sat for days in several libraries, including the Schlesinger Library at the Radcliffe Institute for Advanced Study, Harvard University, Cambridge, Massachusetts (where Sarah Hutcheon was particularly helpful); the AT&T Archives in Warren, New Jersey (where Sheldon Hochheiser, AT&T corporate historian, was very helpful), the U.S. District Court for Eastern Pennsylvania Archives in Philadelphia; the Columbia University Rare Book and Manuscript Library in New York City; the Portland (Maine) Public Library; and, most important, the National Archives in College Park, Maryland. Thanks to those individuals who helped me find what I needed from each set of stacks. Friends from my corporate days and since took time to remind me of and educate me about the world of AT&T. Thanks to Dave Carey, Maureen Gorman, Carol Mather, Dennis Scanlan, Judy Simonson, Curt Sweet, and Don Tompkins. Thanks also to my brother Dan Stockford, who helped me translate the legalese I encountered.

Armed with degrees in engineering and business, I was grateful for help as I learned how to tell a compelling story on paper. Thanks to the women and couple of men in the Radcliffe Seminars' Writing for Publication class in the mid-1990s who taught me to get to the point. I'm also indebted to Wynelle Evans, Beth Nichols, Marilyn Schmidt, and David Shactman, who invested many hours commenting on chapter drafts. In addition, many thanks to the Rutgers University Press team, including Marilyn Campbell, Michele Gisbert, Alison Hack, and Grace Buonocore, who helped me turn my typed pages into a professional-looking book.

I am fortunate to have a cadre of close friends who have offered a place to stay, a shoulder to cry on, a glass of wine to relax with, and/or a piece of crucial advice, all produced at exactly the right moment. Thanks so much to Sandy Coyle, Lynn D'Ambrose, Wynelle Evans, Mary Ellen Forster, Lorrie Foster, Lydia Lazar, and Mary Murphy. And thanks to Amy Arenstein, whose help with child care enabled me to finish the book on time.

During the time period in which I was writing *The Bellwomen,* the Stockford family faced two concurrent health crises, the likes of which, as many friends noted, have torn other families apart. I am proud and relieved to say that the glue holding us together strengthened as we faced our fears and grief, and I am grateful for the support each family member gave me. Love and thanks to my siblings, Lynn, Nancy, and Dan, and their own families; my mother, Joan; and David Witzel, Claudia Williams, and Susan Barry. And joyous love and thanks to my daughter, Kanha, who arrived late in the production of this book, just in time to remind me who I was writing it for and how much wonderful and rewarding life there is outside of writing books.

Finally, I must thank the two Chips in my life: my late and beloved father, Chip Stockford, whose fundamental belief in the equality of all human beings is a major inspiration to my work and who provided a key catalyst for me to write this book; and my partner, Chip Crothers, who, through all the ups and downs of cohabitation, child rearing, and book writing, has been my steadfast friend and supporter. I am lucky to love them both.

Notes

Introduction

1. U.S. Department of Labor, Bureau of Labor Statistics, *Labor Force Statistics for the Current Population Survey, Series ID: LFS1601702,* http://146.142.4.24/cgi-bin/surveymost, accessed on January 31, 2000.
2. U.S. Bureau of the Census, *Characteristics of Business Owners,* 1992 Economic Census,Table A: Business Ownership Group: 1992, p. 7, accessed via the U.S. Bureau of the Census Web site http://www.census.gov/prod/3/97pubs/cbo-9201.pdf on June 26, 2003.
3. U.S. Bureau of the Census, *Statistical Abstract of the United States: 2001* (Washington, D.C., 2001), Table 621, Full-Time Wage and Salary Workers—Number and Earnings: 1985–2000, p. 403.
4. *CEOGO,* CEO Facts, Demographics, http://www.ceogo.com/CEOFACTS/DEMOGRAPHICS/, accessed on June 26, 2003, originally reported in the *New York Times,* January 13, 2002.

Beneficiary Profile: Peggy Falterman

The information in this profile originates from interviews with Peggy Plakotos (née Falterman).

1. Direct quotations in this profile from Peggy Plakotos, telephone interview with author, April 24, 2003.

1: The Idea

Information in this chapter originates primarily from interviews with Bill Brown, David Copus, Al Golub, Bill Oldaker, George Sape, Randy Speck, and Bill Wallace; FCC Docket #19143 files, National Archives, College Park, Md. (hereafter cited as National Archives); the EEOC's thirty-fifth anniversary Web site, http://www.eeoc.gov/35th; the FCC Web site, http://www.fcc.gov; U.S. District Court, District of Columbia, *PEPCO and EUEU v. Public Service Commission of DC,* Civil Action Nos. 2382-70 and 2384-70, February 23, 1971; and Sonny Kleinfield, *The Biggest Company on Earth: A Profile of AT&T* (New York: Holt, Rinehart and Winston, 1981).

1. David Copus, telephone interview with author, October 7, 2002.
2. David Copus, telephone interview with author, October 30, 2002.
3. David Copus, interview with author, August 23, 1993, Washington, D.C.
4. Ibid.
5. David Copus, telephone interview with author, October 15, 2002.
6. Copus interview, August 23, 1993.
7. Ibid.

8. U.S. Bureau of the Census, *Statistical Abstract of the United States, 1972* (Washington, D.C., 1972), Table 2312, Earned Degrees Conferred, by Level of Degree: 1940 to 1970, p. 134

9. Copus interview, August 23, 1993.

10. David Copus, telephone interview with author, March 19, 2003.

11. Adele Hast, ed., *International Directory of Company Histories* (Detroit: St. James Press, 1992), 5:259.

12. Mary Beth Norton, David M. Katzman, Paul D. Escott, Howard P. Chudacoff, Thomas G. Paterson, and William M. Tuttle Jr., eds., *A People and a Nation: A History of the United States,* 4th ed. (Boston: Houghton Mifflin, 1994), 2:999.

13. Bill Brown, telephone interview with author, October 10, 2002.

14. U.S. Bureau of the Census, *Statistical Abstract of the United States, 1972,* Table 792, Bell Telephone Companies—Summary: 1950–1971, p. 492.

15. Copus interview, August 23, 1993.

16. Bill Brown, interview with author, June 30, 1993, Philadelphia.

2: The Petition

Information in this chapter originates primarily from interviews with Bill Brown, David Copus, Larry Gartner, Jim Juntilla, Don Liebers, Chuck Reischel, Susan Ross, and George Sape; FCC Docket #19143 files, National Archives, including the Petition for Intervention, December 10, 1970, vol. 1, and other related materials filed in this docket; Facts on File Yearbook 1971, The Index of World Events, vol. 31, 1972; and the EEOC thirty-fifth anniversary Web site, http://www.eeoc.gov/35th.

1. "AT&T Seeks Higher Long Distance Rates," *Washington Post,* November 18, 1970, D1.

2. Susan Ross, telephone interview with author, January 10, 1995.

3. Ibid.

4. Aileen Hernandez to Bill Brown, January 4, 1971, Ann Scott Papers, Folder 59, Schlesinger Library, Radcliffe Institute for Advanced Study, Harvard University, Cambridge, Mass. (hereafter cited as Schlesinger Library).

5. Ann Scott to Merrillee Dolan, undated memo, Ann Scott Papers, Folder 60, Schlesinger Library.

6. Direct quotations in this and the next 2 paragraphs from Bill Brown, telephone interview with author, October 10, 2002.

7. Paul S. Boyer, Clifford E. Clark Jr., Joseph F. Kett, Neal Salisbury, Harvard Sitkoff, and Nancy Woloch, eds., *The Enduring Vision: A History of the American People,* vol. 2: *From 1865* (Lexington, Mass.: D. C. Heath and Co., 1993), 1041.

8. Sonny Kleinfield, *The Biggest Company on Earth: A Profile of AT&T* (New York: Holt, Rinehart and Winston, 1981), 135–136.

9. EEOC Sixth Annual Report, 1970/1971, U.S. Equal Employment Opportunity Commission, Washington, D.C.

10. Petition for Intervention, December 10, 1970, FCC Docket #19143, vol. 1, National Archives.

11. Ibid.

12. Ibid.

13. Ibid.
14. Jim Juntilla, telephone interview with author, December 15, 1994.

3: The Reaction

Information in this chapter originates primarily from interviews and e-mail exchanges with and written responses to author questions from George Ashley, Doug Bray, Bill Brown, David Copus, Dan Davis, Joe Kruse, Don Liebers, William Mercer, Clark Redick, and George Sape; FCC Docket #19143 files, including the Opposition to Petition for Intervention by EEOC, December 18, 1970, vol. 1, and other related materials filed in this docket; Sonny Kleinfield, *The Biggest Company on Earth: A Profile of AT&T* (New York: Holt, Rinehart and Winston, 1981); and John Brooks, *Telephone, the First Hundred Years: The Wondrous Invention That Changed a World and Spawned a Corporate Giant* (New York: Harper and Row, 1976).

1. Don Liebers, interview with author, May 2, 2003, Dennis, Mass.
2. Don Liebers, interview with author, November 7, 1994, Morristown, N.J.
3. Ibid.
4. Sonny Kleinfield, *The Biggest Company on Earth: A Profile of AT&T* (New York: Holt, Rinehart and Winston, 1981), 8.
5. Frank Hobbs and Nicole Stoops, U.S. Census Bureau, Census 2000 Special Reports, Series CENSR-4, *Demographic Trends in the Twentieth Century* (Washington, D.C.: U.S. Government Printing Office, 2002), figs. 3-3, Distribution of Total Population by Race: 1900 to 2000, and 3-4, Percent Races Other Than White or Black by Race: 1900 to 2000, p. 77, accessed via Web site http://www.census.gov/prod/2002pubs/censr-4.pdf on October 15, 2003.
6. U.S. Bureau of the Census, *Statistical Abstract of the United States, 1972* (Washington, D.C., 1972), Table 341, Labor Force and Participation Rates, 1960 to 1971, and Projections to 1985, by Race, Sex and Age, p. 217.
7. Statement by H. I. Romnes, Chairman, AT&T Company, December 11, 1970, EEOC Record Group 403, box 102, National Archives.
8. Kleinfield, *Biggest Company on Earth*, 4.
9. George Ashley, telephone interview with author, October 22, 2002.
10. Ibid.
11. Statement by Romnes, December 11, 1970 (cited in note 7 above).
12. William E. Farrell, "AT&T Head Denies Job Bias; Terms Utility Leader in Equality," *New York Times*, December 12, 1970, 16.
13. "Federal Bias Suit Assails U.S. Steel" and "AT&T Head Denies Job Bias; Terms Utility Leader in Equality," *New York Times*, December 12, 1970, 1, 16.
14. Quotations in this paragraph from William Mercer, interview with author, January 31, 1995, Wellesley, Mass.
15. First quotation: John Brooks, *Telephone, the First Hundred Years: The Wondrous Invention That Changed a World and Spawned a Corporate Giant* (New York: Harper and Row, 1976), 29; second: Kleinfield, *Biggest Company on Earth*, 202.
16. Opposition to Petition for Intervention by EEOC, December 18, 1970, FCC Docket #19143, vol. 1, National Archives.
17. Quotations in this and the next paragraph from ibid.
18. Mercer interview, January 31, 1995.

4: The Beginning

Information in this chapter originates primarily from interviews with and written responses to author questions from George Ashley, Bill Brown, David Copus, Larry Gartner, Jim Juntilla, William Mercer, Bill Oldaker, Judy Potter, Clark Redick, Susan Ross, George Sape, Randy Speck, and Bill Wallace; the February 22, March 5, and April 8 transcripts of FCC Docket #19143, vol. 1, National Archives, and other related materials filed in this docket; the EEOC Web site, http://www.eeoc.gov; and AT&T Management Reports.

1. George Sape, interview with author, March 22, 1995, New York City.
2. David Copus, interview with author, August 23, 1993, Washington, D.C.
3. Bill Brown, telephone interview with author, October 10, 2002.
4. Copus interview, August 23, 1993.
5. Randy Speck, interview with author, November 3, 1994, Washington, D.C.
6. George Ashley, telephone interview with author, October 22, 2002.
7. Ibid.
8. Bill Brown, telephone interview with author, October 10, 2002.
9. Discovery Requests, FCC Docket #19143, vol. 19, National Archives.
10. David Copus to Frederick Denniston, February 12, 1971, FCC Docket #19143, vol. 1, National Archives.
11. Quotations in this and the next several paragraphs from February 22, 1971, Transcript, FCC Docket #19143, vol. 1, National Archives.
12. David Copus, telephone interview with author, March 19, 2003.
13. Ibid
14. Bill Wallace, interview with author, March 10, 1995, Maple Valley, Wash.
15. Speck interview, November 3, 1994.
16. April 8, 1971, Transcript, FCC Docket #19143, vol. 1, National Archives.
17. Ibid.
18. March 5, 1971, Transcript, FCC Docket #19143, vol. 1, National Archives.
19. Ibid.
20. Comments of AT&T Company and the Associated Bell System Companies on "Pre-Hearing Memorandum of the EEOC on the Law of Employment Discrimination," EEOC Record Group 403, box 1, National Archives.

Beneficiary Profile: Gwen Thomas

The information in this profile originates from interviews and e-mail exchanges with Gwen Hickman (née Thomas) and Carol Mather.

1. Gwen Hickman, telephone interview with author, April 10, 2003.
2. Ibid.
3. Gwen Hickman, telephone interview with author, April 15, 2003.
4. Hickman telephone interview, April 10, 2003.
5. Hickman telephone interview, April 15, 2003.
6. Ibid.

5: The Paper

Information in this chapter originates primarily from interviews and e-mail exchanges with George Ashley, Bill Brown, David Copus, Jim Crain, Dan Davis, Al Golub, Elihu

Leifer, Don Liebers, Katherine Mazzaferri, William Mercer, Brigid O'Farrell, Bill Oldaker, Jack Pemberton, Judy Potter, Susan Ross, Lee Satterfield, Randy Speck, and Bill Wallace; the March 5, 1971, and January 21, 1972, transcripts of FCC Docket #19143, vols. 1 and 2, and other related materials filed in this docket; former National Organization for Women (NOW) Papers at Schlesinger Library, including those of Wilma Scott Heide, Ann Scott, and Sally Hacker; personal files of Dan Davis; and affidavits filed in Civil Action 73-149, U.S. District Court for Eastern District of Pennsylvania.

1. William Mercer, interview with author, January 31, 1995, Wellesley, Mass.
2. Dan Davis, telephone interview with author, June 13, 2003.
3. Al Golub, interview with author, November 2, 1994, Washington, D.C.
4. Katherine Mazzaferri, interview with author, November 1, 1994, Washington, D.C.
5. Ibid.
6. Bill Wallace, interview with author, March 10, 1995, Maple Valley, Wash.
7. Randy Speck, interview with author, November 3, 1994, Washington, D.C.
8. David Copus, telephone interview with author, October 30, 2002.
9. Ibid.
10. Don Liebers, interview with author, May 2, 2003, Dennis, Mass.
11. Bill Brown, interview with author, June 30, 1993, Philadelphia.
12. Jim Crain, interview with author, February 28, 1995, Marco Island, Fla.
13. Ibid.
14. Quotations in this paragraph from David Copus, telephone interview with author, September 30, 2002.
15. Quotations in this and the next two paragraphs from Dan Davis, interview with author, May 10, 1995, Staten Island, N.Y.
16. Draft memo from Dan Davis–led task force to FCC Steering Committee, March 15, 1971, from Davis's personal files.
17. Draft letter from Dan Davis–led task force to Robert Lilley, February 26, 1971, from Davis's personal files.
18. Ibid.
19. January 21, 1972, Transcript, FCC Docket #19143, vol. 2, National Archives.
20. Bill Brown, telephone interview with author, October 10, 2002.
21. Ibid.
22. David Copus, telephone interview with author, November 4, 2002.
23. Speck interview, November 3, 1994.
24. David Copus, telephone interview with author, October 7, 2002.

6: The Case

Information in this chapter originates primarily from interviews and e-mail exchanges with and written responses to author questions from Whitney Adams, George Ashley, Doug Bray, Bill Brown, David Copus, Dan Davis, Dave Easlick, Larry Gartner, Jane Lang, Don Liebers, Bill Oldaker, Judy Potter, Clark Redick, Chuck Reischel, Susan Ross, George Sape, Randy Speck, Nancy Stanley, and Bill Wallace; FCC Docket #19143 files, National Archives, including the January 21 and 31, 1972, Hearings Transcripts, the EEOC report *A Unique Competence: A Study of Equal Employment Opportunity in the Bell System,* the EEOC testimony Findings of Fact and various internal Bell System memos, letters, and other related materials filed in this Docket; *Congressional Record,* February 15, 1972; National Organization for Women (NOW) Papers, Schlesinger Library, including those of Wilma Scott Heide; and affidavits filed in Civil Action 73-149, U.S. District Court for Eastern District of Pennsylvania.

1. September 8, 1971, Transcript, FCC Docket #19143, vol. 1, National Archives.
2. David Copus, telephone interview with author, March 19, 2003.
3. David Copus, telephone interview with author, October 7, 2002.
4. Bill Brown, telephone interview with author, October 10, 2002.
5. Randy Speck, interview with author, November 3, 1994, Washington, D.C.
6. *A Unique Competence: A Study of Equal Employment Opportunity in the Bell System,* December 1, 1971, p. ii, Testimony in FCC Docket #19143, National Archives.
7. December 1, 1971, Transcript, FCC Docket #19143, vol. 2, National Archives.
8. *Unique Competence,* chaps. 2, 5, 10.
9. Quotation in *Unique Competence,* chap. 6.
10. Speck interview, November 3, 1994.
11. *Unique Competence,* chap. 3.
12. Christopher Lydon, "Job Bias at Bell Charged by Panel," *New York Times,* December 2, 1971, 1.
13. Joseph A. Beirne to Robert D. Lilley, December 14, 1971, U.S. District Court of Eastern Pennsylvania, Civil Action 73-149, Rex Reed Affidavit.
14. Speck interview, November 3, 1994.
15. Brown telephone interview, October 10, 2002.
16. January 21, 1972, Transcript, FCC Docket #19143, vol. 2, National Archives.
17. Judy Potter, interview with author, October 16, 1994, Cape Elizabeth, Maine.
18. W. R. Carter to South Central Bell Vice President (Louisiana), Vice President and General Managers, and President's Staff, memo, May 20, 1970, FCC Docket #19143, vol. 2, National Archives.
19. David Copus, interview with author, August 23, 1993, Washington, D.C.
20. David Copus, telephone interview with author, October 30, 2002.
21. David Copus, telephone interview with author, November 4, 2002.
22. First quotation: George Sape, interview with author, March 22, 1995, New York City; second: Chuck Reischel, telephone interview with author, February 22, 1995; third: Clark Redick, interview with author, June 26, 1995, Fort Myers, Fla.; fourth: Don Liebers, interview with author, November 7, 1994, Morristown, N.J.
23. Dave Easlick, interview with author, February 28, 1995, Naples, Fla.
24. January 21, 1972, Transcript, FCC Docket #19143, vol. 2, National Archives.

7: The Testimony

Information in this chapter originates primarily from interviews with George Ashley, Daryl Bem, Bill Brown, David Copus, Larry Gartner, Don Liebers, Katherine Mazzaferri, William Mercer, Jack Pemberton, Judy Potter, Randy Speck, and Bill Wallace; FCC Docket #19143, National Archives, including the January 31, February 1, 2, 4, 7–9, 14, 16, 23–25, and 29, and March 1, 2, 6, and 22–24, 1972, Hearings Transcripts, written testimony of all EEOC witnesses, particularly Daryl and Sandra Bem, Helen Roig, and Lorena Weeks, and other related materials filed in this docket; and National Organization for Women (NOW) Papers at Schlesinger Library, including those of Sally Hacker.

1. David Copus, telephone interview with author, June 10, 2003.
2. Randy Speck, interview with author, November 3, 1994, Washington, D.C.
3. Testimony in this and the next several paragraphs from January 31, 1972, Transcript, FCC Docket #19143, vol. 2, National Archives.
4. Bill Wallace, interview with author, March 10, 1995, Maple Valley, Wash.
5. This quotation and those in the next two paragraphs from January 31, 1972, Transcript, FCC Docket #19143, vol. 2, National Archives.
6. Testimony in this and the next several paragraphs from February 1, 1972, Transcript, FCC Docket #19143, vol. 2, National Archives.
7. Bill Brown, telephone interview with author, October 10, 2002.
8. First quotation: George Ashley, telephone interview with author, June 2, 2003; second: William Mercer, interview with author, January 31, 1995, Wellesley, Mass.; third: Don Liebers, interview with author, November 7, 1994, Morristown, N.J.
9. Copus telephone interview, June 10, 2003.
10. Testimony in this and the next several paragraphs from February 4, 1972, Transcript, FCC Docket #19143, vol. 3, National Archives.
11. Daryl Bem, telephone interview with author, October 3, 2002.
12. Testimony in this and the next several paragraphs from February 4, 1972, Transcript, FCC Docket #19143, vol. 3, National Archives.
13. This and the following three quotations from February 7, 1972, Transcript, FCC Docket #19143, vol. 3, National Archives.
14. This and the following quotation from February 23, 1972, Transcript, FCC Docket #19143, vol. 4, National Archives.
15. Quotations in this and the following two paragraphs from March 6, 1972, Transcript, FCC Docket #19143, vol. 5, National Archives.
16. Quotations in this and the following paragraph from February 14, 1972, Transcript, FCC Docket #19143, vol. 4, National Archives.
17. February 7, 1972, Transcript, FCC Docket #19143, vol. 3, National Archives.
18. Quotations in this and the following several paragraphs from February 8, 1972, Transcript, FCC Docket #19143, vol. 3, National Archives.
19. Testimony in this and subsequent paragraphs from February 9, 1972, Transcript, FCC Docket #19143, vol. 3, National Archives.

8: The Field

Information in this chapter originates primarily from interviews with Whitney Adams, George Ashley, David Copus, Don Liebers, Judy Potter, Gay Semel, and Randy Speck; FCC Docket #19143, National Archives, including the March 22–24, April 7, and 17–20, May 8–12 and 31, and June 5 and 8–9, 1972, Hearings Transcripts and letters, telegrams, memos, petitions, motions, responses, orders, opinions, decisions, and other related materials filed in this docket; National Organization for Women (NOW) Papers at Schlesinger Library, including those of Wilma Scott Heide, Ann Scott, and Sally Hacker; Paul S. Boyer, Clifford E. Clark Jr., Joseph F. Kett, Neal Salisbury, Harvard Sitkoff, and Nancy Woloch, eds., *The Enduring Vision: A History of the American People,* vol. 2: *From 1865* (Lexington, Mass.: D. C. Heath and Co., 1993), 996–

1063; and the U.S. Federal Communications Commission Web site, http://www
.fcc.gov.

1. George Ashley, telephone interview with author, October 22, 2002.
2. David Copus, telephone interview with author, October 7, 2002.
3. Judy Potter, interview with author, October 16, 1994, Cape Elizabeth, Maine.
4. Testimony in this and the next several paragraphs from April 20, 1972, Transcript, FCC Docket #19143, vol. 8, National Archives.
5. Copus telephone interview, October 7, 2002.
6. Letter and petition from Mary Pinotti to FCC Common Carrier Bureau, February 10, 1972, FCC Docket #19143, vol. 3, National Archives.
7. FCC Order by Frederick Denniston, April 5, 1972, FCC Docket #19143, vol. 6, National Archives.
8. May 8, 1972, Transcript, FCC Docket #19143, vol. 9, National Archives.
9. Don Liebers, interview with author, November 7, 1994, Morristown, N.J.
10. Testimony in this and the next several paragraphs from May 8, 1972, Transcript, FCC Docket #19143, vol. 9, National Archives.
11. Gay Semel, telephone interview with author, January 9, 2003.
12. Ibid.
13. Quotations in this and the following two paragraphs from May 8, 1972, Transcript, FCC Docket #19143, vol. 9, National Archives.
14. Testimony in this and the next two paragraphs from May 9, 1972, Transcript, FCC Docket #19143, vol. 9, National Archives.
15. May 11, 1972, Transcript, FCC Docket #19143, vol. 10, National Archives.
16. Ibid.
17. Ibid.
18. May 12, 1972, Transcript, FCC Docket #19143, vol. 10, National Archives.
19. Ibid.
20. Sally Hacker to Dave Easlick, June 6, 1972, Sally Hacker Papers, NOW/AT&T Newsletters Folder, Schlesinger Library.
21. Copus telephone interview, October 7, 2002.
22. Ibid.
23. David Copus, interview with author, August 23, 1993, Washington, D.C.

Beneficiary Profile: Margaret Hoppe

The information in this profile originates from interviews and e-mail exchanges with Margaret Barrett (formerly Hoppe).

1. Direct quotations in this and the next paragraph from Margaret Barrett, interview with author, February 1, 1994, Short Hills, N.J.
2. Margaret Barrett, e-mail message to author, May 28, 2003.

9: The First Agreement

Information in this chapter originates primarily from interviews and e-mail exchanges with and written responses to author questions from George Ashley, Doug Bray, Bill Brown, David Copus, Dan Davis, Dave Easlick, Bill Kilberg, Jane Lang, Don Liebers, Judy Potter, Clark Redick, Lee Satterfield, and Randy Speck; FCC Docket #19143 files, National Archives, including the April 7 and 18 and November 28, 1972, Hearings

Transcripts and motions and other related materials filed in this docket; National Organization for Women (NOW) Papers at Schlesinger Library, including those of Sally Hacker; EEOC Record Group 403 files, National Archives, including letters, handwritten notes, and other related materials; documentation on civil rights laws from the EEOC thirty-fifth anniversary Web site (http://www.eeoc.gov/35th/), *In Motion Magazine* Web site (http://www.inmotionmagazine.com/aahist.html), and Americans for a Fair Chance Web site (http://www.fairchance.civilrights.org/the_facts/chronology/); personal papers of Dan Davis; and affidavits from Civil Action 73-149 from the U.S. District Court of Eastern Pennsylvania.

1. George Ashley, telephone interview with author, June 2, 2003.
2. Clark Redick, interview with author, June 26, 995, Fort Myers, Fla.
3. Bell System Objection to General Admissibility of Appendix C of EEOC Exhibit 1, February 4, 1972, FCC Docket #19143, vol. 3, National Archives.
4. Jane Lang, telephone interview with author, November 18, 2002.
5. Ibid.
6. Randy Speck, telephone interview with author, March 20, 2003.
7. "A statement on equal opportunity by Chairman deButts," *AT&T Management Report,* no. 21, May 4, 1972, 1.
8. David Copus to Orley Ashenfelter, May 23, 1972, EEOC Record Group 403, box 102, National Archives.
9. EEOC thirty-fifth anniversary Web site, Executive Order 10925, March 6, 1961, http://www.eeoc.gov/35th/thelaw/eo-10925.html, accessed on June 26, 2003.
10. Americans for a Fair Chance Web site, History of Affirmative Action Policies, http://www.fairchance.org/about/history.htm, accessed on May 20, 2003.
11. "System companies unveiling new equal opportunity programs," *AT&T Management Report,* no. 21, May 4, 1972, 4.
12. David Copus, telephone interview with author, October 15, 2002.
13. Bill Brown, telephone interview with author, October 10, 2002.
14. Bill Brown to Ed Mitchell, March 30, 1972, EEOC Record Group 403, Chronological File, National Archives.
15. Dan Davis, e-mail message to author, April 27, 2003.
16. Dan Davis, e-mail message to author, September 30, 2002.
17. Ibid.
18. Dave Easlick, interview with author, February 28, 1995, Naples, Fla.
19. "An Agreement between GSA and AT&T by Arthur F. Sampson, Acting Administrator of General Services," GSA Press Conference, September 20, 1972, Washington, D.C.

10: The Explosion

Information in this chapter originates primarily from interviews and e-mail exchanges with and written responses to author questions from Bill Brown, David Copus, Dan Davis, Dave Easlick, Bill Kilberg, Don Liebers, Elihu Leifer, Jack Pemberton, Clark Redick, David Rose, and Lee Satterfield; FCC Docket #19143 files, National Archives, including NOW and NAACP press releases and other related materials filed in this docket; EEOC Record Group 403 files, National Archives, including letters and other related materials; William Kilberg, "Progress and Problems in Equal

Employment Opportunity," *Equal Opportunity* 24, no. 10 (October 1973); affidavits from Civil Action 73-149 from the U.S. District Court of Eastern Pennsylvania; and Phyllis Wallace, ed., *Equal Employment Opportunity and the AT&T Case* (Cambridge: MIT Press, 1976).

1. Bill Brown, telephone interview with author, October 10, 2002.
2. Ibid.
3. David Copus, telephone interview with author, October 15, 2002.
4. R. G. Keim to NWB Public Relations Department Heads, telegram, September 20, 1972, Sally Hacker Papers, carton 2, folder NOW AT&T 1972, Schlesinger Library.
5. Lee Satterfield, interview with author, November 2, 1994, Washington, D.C.
6. Clark Redick, interview with author, June 26, 1995, Fort Myers, Fla.
7. Dan Davis, e-mail message to author, September 30, 2002.
8. Dan Davis, interview with author, May 10, 1995, Staten Island, N.Y.
9. Brown telephone interview, October 10, 2002.
10. Bill Kilberg, interview with author, May 15, 1995, Washington, D.C.
11. Bill Kilberg, telephone interview with author, October 3, 2002.
12. Kilberg interview, May 15, 1995.
13. Bill Kilberg, interview with author, May 17, 1995, Washington, D.C.
14. Ibid.
15. David Copus, telephone interview with author, June 10, 2003.
16. Kilberg interview, May 17, 1995.
17. Kilberg telephone interview, October 3, 2002.
18. David Copus, telephone interview with author, October 30, 2002.
19. Ibid.
20. Brown, telephone interview, October 10, 2002.
21. Ibid.
22. Davis e-mail message, September 30, 2002.

11: The Defense

Information in this chapter originates primarily from interviews with Doug Bray, David Copus, Larry Gartner, Ann Howard, Jane Lang, Don Liebers, Judy Potter, and Randy Speck; FCC Docket #19143 files, National Archives, including the August 1, 1972, Bell System written case, the October 30–31, November 1–2, 8–9, 13, 15–17, and 28, and December 1, 5–7, 12, and 15, 1972, Hearings Transcripts, and letters, memos, motions, responses, orders, and other related materials filed in this docket; *The Statistical Abstract of the United States, 1973;* and EEOC files related to this case.

1. "Bias Charges in Hiring: AT&T Fights Back," *U.S. News and World Report,* August 14, 1972, 66.
2. Ibid.
3. Eileen Shanahan, "AT&T Contends Government Exaggerates Job Discrimination Charges," *New York Times,* August 2, 1972, 13.
4. David Copus to Bernard Anderson, October 2, 1972, EEOC Record Group 403, box 102, National Archives.
5. October 30, 1972, Transcript, FCC Docket #19143, vol. 12, National Archives.
6. Ibid.

7. All quotations in this and the next three paragraphs from David Copus, telephone interview with author, November 4, 2002.

8. Testimony in this and the next several paragraphs from October 30, 1972, Transcript, FCC Docket #19143, vol. 12, National Archives.

9. Testimony in this and the next several paragraphs from October 31, 1972, Transcript, FCC Docket #19143, vol. 13, National Archives.

10. David Copus, telephone interview with author, September 30, 2002.

11. November 13, 1972, Transcript, FCC Hearing Docket #19143, vol. 14, National Archives.

12. David Copus, telephone interview with author, June 10, 2003.

13. Testimony in this and the next several paragraphs from November 16, 1972, Transcript, FCC Docket #19143, vol. 14, National Archives.

14. Testimony in this and the next several paragraphs from November 13, 1972, Transcript, FCC Docket #19143, vol. 14, National Archives.

15. David Copus, interview with author, August 23, 1993, Washington, D.C.

12: The Settlement

Information in this chapter originates primarily from interviews and e-mail exchanges with and written responses to author questions from George Ashley, Bill Brown, David Copus, Dan Davis, Dave Easlick, Larry Gartner, Leon Higginbotham, Bill Kilberg, Elihu Leifer, Bill Oldaker, Clark Redick, David Rose, and Lee Satterfield; *Consent Decree: Equal Employment Opportunity Commission, James D. Hodgson, Secretary of Labor, United States Department of Labor, and United States of America v. American Telephone and Telegraph, et al.,* January 18, 1973, in the U.S. District Court for the Eastern District of Pennsylvania, Civil Action 73-149 and related affidavits from this action; and Facts on File 1972.

1. Clark Redick to author, April 25, 2003.

2. Clark Redick to author, September 20, 2002.

3. Bill Kilberg, interview with author, May 17, 1995, Washington, D.C.

4. Dan Davis, interview with author, May 10, 1995, Staten Island, N.Y.

5. Bill Kilberg, telephone interview with author, October 7, 2002.

6. Elihu Leifer, telephone interview with author, November 26, 2002.

7. Ibid.

8. Ibid.

9. National Labor Relations Act of 1935, Section 8 (d), 29 US Code SS 151 to 166, viewed on Our Documents Web site, http://www.ourdocuments.gov/content .php?page=transcript&doc=67, accessed on June 27, 2003.

10. Kilberg telephone interview, October 7, 2002.

11. Clark Redick, interview with author, June 26, 1995, Fort Myers, Fla.

12. Redick to author, September 20, 2002.

13. David Copus, telephone interview with author, November 4, 2002.

14. Redick interview, June 26, 1995.

15. Bill Kilberg, telephone interview with author, June 9, 2003.

16. Larry Gartner, telephone interview with author, March 20, 2003.

17. David Rose, telephone interview with author, October 7, 2002.

18. Leon Higginbotham, interview with author, January 4, 1995, Cambridge, Mass.

19. Transcript, January 18, 1973, Civil Action 73-149, U.S. Eastern District Court, Philadelphia.
20. Brown quotation: "Major EEO Agreement Reached by Government and Bell Telephone Companies," press release, Equal Employment Opportunity Commission, January 18, 1973; Copus quotation: "AT&T to Grant 15,000 Back Pay in Job Inequities," *New York Times,* January 19, 1973, 1
21. David Copus, interview with author, August 23, 1993, Washington, D.C.

13: The Benefit

Information in this chapter originates primarily from interviews and e-mail exchanges with Margaret Barrett, Gwen Hickman, and Peggy Plakotos.

1. Peggy Plakotos, telephone interview with author, April 24, 2003.
2. Ibid.
3. Gwen Hickman, telephone interview with author, April 15, 2003.
4. Gwen Hickman, telephone interview with author, April 10, 2003.
5. Quotations in this and the next several paragraphs from Hickman telephone interview, April 15, 2003.
6. Margaret Barrett, e-mail message to author, May 28, 2003.
7. Quotations in this and the next two paragraphs from Margaret Barrett, interview with author, February 1, 1994, Short Hills, N.J.

14: The Impact

Information in this chapter originates primarily from interviews and e-mail exchanges with and written responses to author questions from Bill Brown, David Copus, Dan Davis, Dave Easlick, Bill Kilberg, Elihu Leifer, Don Liebers, Clark Redick, Randy Speck, and Bill Wallace, and Margaret Barrett, Gwen Hickman, and Peggy Plakotos; FCC Docket #19143 files, National Archives, including speeches, articles, and other related materials filed in this docket; affidavits from Civil Action 73-149 from the U.S. District Court of Eastern Pennsylvania; *Consent Decree: Peter J. Brennan, Secretary of Labor, United States Department of Labor, Equal Employment Opportunity Commission, and United States of America v. American Telephone and Telegraph, et al.,* May 30, 1974, in the U.S. District Court for the Eastern District of Pennsylvania, Civil Action 74-1342; Business & Society Review, *Company Performance Roundup,* Spring 1972 to Winter 1977–78, published by EBSCO; *New York Times* and *Wall Street Journal* articles related to equal employment opportunity between 1973 and 1978; the U.S. Equal Employment Opportunity Commission thirty-fifth anniversary Web site, http://www.eeoc.gov/35th/history/index.html; Peter Temin, with Louis Galambos, *The Fall of the Bell System* (Cambridge: Cambridge University Press, 1987); and EEOC Record Group 403 files, National Archives.

1. "4 to 6 Giant Companies Being Picked as Federal Target on Discrimination," *New York Times,* July 30, 1973, 17.
2. Bill Brown, interview with author, June 30, 1993, Philadelphia.
3. Statistics in this and the following paragraph from EEO-1 Aggregate Report for Telephone Communication, SIC 481: Telephone Communication, *The U.S. Equal Employment Opportunity Commission,* accessed on the EEOC Web site, http://www.eeoc.gov/stats/jobpat/2001/sic3/481.html, on June 20, 2003; and

A Unique Competence: A Study of Equal Employment Opportunity in the Bell System, December 1, 1971, p. ii, Testimony in FCC Docket #19143, National Archives.

4. Ellen Sweet, "Is What's Good for AT&T Good For Women?," *Ms.,* April 1982, 63.

5. Peggy Plakotos, telephone interview with author, April 24, 2003.

6. Margaret Barrett, telephone interview with author, June 15, 2003.

7. U.S. Bureau of the Census, *Statistical Abstract of the United States: 2001* (Washington, D.C., 2001), Table 593, Employed Civilians by Occupation, Sex, Race and Hispanic Origin: 1983 and 2000, p. 381; and U.S. Bureau of the Census, *Statistical Abstract of the United States, 1977* (Washington, D.C., 1977), Table 662, Experienced Civilian Labor Force, by Sex and Occupation, 1960 and 1970, and by Selected Characteristics, 1970, pp. 408–410.

8. U.S. Bureau of the Census, *Statistical Abstract of the United States, 1972* (Washington, D.C., 1972), Table 379, Median Earnings of Civilians, by Sex and by Occupation of Longest Job: 1958–1970, p. 237; and U.S. Bureau of the Census, *Statistical Abstract of the United States: 2001,* Table 621, Full-Time Wage and Salary Workers—Number and Earnings: 1985–2000, p. 403.

9. U.S. Bureau of the Census, *Statistical Abstract of the United States: 2001,* Table 942, Existing One-Family House Sold and Price by Region: 1970–2000, p. 599.

10. William Bielby and James Baron, "Men and Women at Work: Sex Segregation and Statistical Discrimination," *American Journal of Sociology* 91 (January 1986): 759–799.

11. Brown interview, June 30, 1993.

Epilogue

1. Dan Davis, interview with author, May 10, 1995, Staten Island, N.Y.

2. David Copus, e-mail message to author, June 11, 2003.

3. Judy Potter, interview with author, March 25, 2003, Portland, Maine.

4. Randy Speck, interview with author, November 3, 1994, Washington, D.C.; David Copus, interview with author, August 23, 1993, Washington, D.C.; Don Liebers, interview with author, May 2, 2003, Dennis, Mass.

Interview Dates

Whitney Adams:	November 1, 1994 (by phone)
George Ashley:	October 22, 2002, and June 2 and 30, 2003 (by phone)
Margaret Barrett:	February 1, 1994 (Short Hills, N.J.); May 28, 2003 (e-mail response); June 15, 2003 (by phone)
Daryl Bem:	October 3, 2002 (by phone)
Barbara Bergmann:	November 3, 1994 (Washington, D.C.)
Doug Bray and Ann Howard:	May 13, 1995 (Tenafly, N.J.)
Bill Brown:	June 30, 1993 (Philadelphia); October 10, 2002 (by phone)
David Cashdan:	April 28, 1995 (by phone); May 15, 1995 (Washington, D.C.)
David Copus:	August 23, 1993 (Washington, D.C.); December 7, 1994, September 30, October 7, 15, and 30, November 4, 2002, March 19 and 20, 2003, June 10, 2003 (by phone)
Jim Crain:	February 28, 1995 (Marco Island, Fla.)
Dan Davis:	April 18, 1995 (by phone); May 10, 1995 (Staten Island, N.Y.); September 30 and October 29, 2002, and April 27, 2003 (by e-mail); June 13, 2003 (by phone)
Dave Easlick:	February 28, 1995 (Naples, Fla.)
Catherine East:	February 21, 1995 (by phone)
Larry Gartner:	March 14, 1995 (Los Angeles); March 20, 2003 (by phone)
Al Golub:	November 2, 1994 (Washington, D.C.); December 13, 1994 (by phone)
Gwen Hickman:	April 10 and 15 and June 17, 2003 (by phone)
Leon Higginbotham:	January 4, 1995 (Cambridge, Mass.)
Jim Juntilla:	December 15, 1994 (by phone)
Bill Kilberg:	May 15 and 17, 1995 (Washington, D.C.); October 3 and 7, 2002 and June 9, 2003 (by phone)
Patricia King:	October 27, 1994 (by phone)
Joe Kruse:	March 21 and 26, 2003 (e-mail exchange)
Jane Lang:	November 18, 2002 (by phone)
Elihu Leifer:	November 26, 2002 (by phone)
Don Liebers:	November 7, 1994 (Morristown, N.J.); May 2, 2003 (Dennis, Mass.)
Carol Mather:	February 16, 1995 (Boston); June 5, 2003 (by phone)

Katherine Mazzaferri:	November 1, 1994 (Washington, D.C.)
William Mercer:	January 31, 1995 (Wellesley, Mass.)
Brigid O'Farrell	October 26, 1994 (by phone); November 1, 1994 (Washington, D.C.)
Bill Oldaker:	February 21, 1995 (by phone)
Jack Pemberton:	March 13, 1995 (San Francisco)
Peggy Plakotos:	April 24 and June 13 and 16, 2003 (by phone)
Judy Potter:	October 16, 1994 (Cape Elizabeth, Maine); March 25, 2003 (Portland, Maine)
Clark Redick:	June 26, 1995 (Fort Myers, Fla.); September 20, 2002, and April 25, 2003 (written response to questions)
Chuck Reischel:	February 22, 1995 (by phone)
David Rose:	October 7, 2002 (by phone)
Susan Ross:	January 10, 1995 (by phone); June 2, 2003 (by e-mail)
George Sape:	March 22 and May 11, 1995 (New York City)
Lee Satterfield:	November 2, 1994 (Washington, D.C.)
Gay Semel:	January 9, 2003 (by phone)
Randy Speck:	November 3, 1994 (Washington, D.C.); March 20, 2003 (by phone)
Nancy Stanley:	October 26, 1994 (by phone)
Burke Stinson:	October 1994 (by phone); November 8, 1994 (Basking Ridge, N.J.)
Bill Wallace:	March 10, 1995 (Maple Valley, Wash.)

Index

About the Author

Marjorie A. Stockford is a writer and consultant who was a beneficiary of AT&T's 1973 landmark employment discrimination settlement with the U.S. government. Formerly an executive with the YWCA of the U.S.A., she holds degrees in engineering, business, and public administration, the last from Harvard University's Kennedy School of Government. She lives in Portland, Maine.

11/04	DATE DUE	
APR 2 5 2005		